# A Cornishman Reflects on Cruising

*Looking back on two decades of Cruising*

By George Williams

Copyright © 2023 George Williams

All rights reserved.

ISBN: 9798870896267

# Contents

Contents

Introduction

Early memories of the sea

A Bit of History about the Cruise Industry

Could Cruising Really Be That Good?

New Destinations on that 'Summer Spectacular' Cruise

2002 – The 'Grand Mediterranean' Cruise

Updating the P&O Story

'Grand Voyage to Venice' (with a balcony)

History 2002 - 2006

'Captivating Canaries' Cruise - 2004

2005 – 'Renaissance and Rivieras'

2006 - The Azores & the Canaries

New Ship and New Destination

2007 – Venetian Affair

2008 – Two More Cruises

How has booking a cruise changed?

10th Year of Cruising

Becoming Cruisers

Changes to the P&O Fleet (2008 to 2016)

2010 - Going North, and Going Big

2011 - Our Lives were Changing

2011 Summer Cruise

Final Preparations for the World Cruise and Retirement

Around the World Without Wings

The Remainder of 2012

Baltic Cruise on Aurora – August 2012

Time in the hands of the NHS

2013 – A New home, and another Cruise

2014 - A Busy and Varied Year

Fluid Pricing, and Our First Visit to Ireland

2016 – Fred Olsen Cruises

Life is not all about holidays

Back on Aurora

Oriana

2017 Searching for New Sunrises

Adonia Returns to the Fleet

2018 - Four Cruises Again!

Our Final Great Seafaring Adventure

Farewell to Oriana

Moving House Again

Our Last Cruise on Oceana

2020 – Boxes Ticked

Covid

Spring 2021

The Modern Saga Cruises Company

Our 2021 Saga Cruise Experience

A Cruise for 2022

Flavours of the Mediterranean

Medical Matters

Pre-Hip Cruise

Cruising Twenty-Three Years on

The Modern Cruise Experience

Welcome to your cruise

Prices of a Cruise

Saga Cruises

Last Thoughts

Other books in 'The Cornishman Goes Cruising' series

# Introduction

A quick glance up to the top shelf of a travel agent display led to discovering a new style of holiday, that changed the second half of my life.

There, amongst the glossy brochures of exclusive island resorts, was one advertising P&O Cruises. I took it off the shelf with little more than curiosity, but over two decades later, that moment was the beginning of something that could almost be described as an addiction. Ocean cruising was supposedly just a *'one off'* thrill of a lifetime for me and my wife Deb, but it turned out to be the solution to our holiday dreams.

It has to be pointed out here that I'm one of those people who is so terrified with the thought of flying, that I break out into a sweat at the tiniest suggestion of entombing myself in a steel cigar tube. But before anyone scoffs at my words, let me make it clear that I **have** actually flown, and my psychological misgivings were proved correct. As a part of my job, I was forced to fly to and from San Francisco, and I hated every claustrophobic minute of those 11-hour flights. I vowed never to repeat the experience, and while in San Francisco I even considered the idea of emigrating to the USA to avoid the homeward flight. Fortunately, my wife and son were a powerful enough reason to come home.

Anyway, the outcome of my air-travel phobia, was that our family holidays were restricted to visits to see relations, plus going to holiday camps around Britain and the near continent which could be reached by a ferry. My wife (Deb) did take our children on flights for breaks away from Britain, but I was more than relieved to stay at home.

Of course, my phobia meant that I had to give up any thoughts of experiencing distant lands, and hundreds of amazing sights around the world were nothing more to me than pictures in books, or verbal descriptions, that merely tantalised my senses.

That was until the year 2000 when Deb and I were seeking a way of celebrating our 25th wedding anniversary, and we eventually decided to look at that brochure, and chose our very first cruise which would be taking us to the Mediterranean.

Before we were half way through those 17 days and nights of feeling the sun's warmth on our backs; seeing amazing new sights; experiencing the history and architecture of Greece and Turkey; seduced by the magic solitude of long lazy days at sea, and lapping up the luxury of the ship, we were hooked. Deb and I knew it was never going to be that *'one off'* treat.

Since then we have cruised at least once every year and have now been on 40 ocean adventures. We have sailed on a dozen different ships from three companies. Our adventures have visited every continent except the Antarctic, and we have circumnavigated the globe twice. Amazingly we have been at sea for over 500 days, and sailed seriously more than 100,000 miles.

*… and yes, we have seen a lot of changes*

Two decades on, and hundreds of those tantalising photographs and verbal descriptions of distant places have come to life, and like a visual drug we want to see even more.

Our friends and family think we are slightly mad spending so much time (and money) sailing away our lives, but we don't apologise for our perceived mania. We simply smile and sigh at our memories and look at the brochures for new destinations and ideas to tempt us into another cruise.

The only regret is that we hadn't discovered it earlier, and possibly given our children a chance to experience cruising while we had the money to pay for them to accompany us. Maybe they would have also fallen in love with cruising, and realised what our addiction was all about.

# Early memories of the sea

From the book's title, you may have probably realised I am Cornish. My hometown was Helston which is the most southerly town in mainland Britain, and situated less than three miles from the sea. In this county the sea is never very far away, and everyone knows about its beauty, the power, and yes, the dangers of the sea. Strangely, although as a child I enjoyed relaxing on the beaches, I wasn't that excited to get overly up close and personal with the water. Yes, I could float, and could make floundering progress through the water, but swimming wasn't something I wanted to master. Neither had I much experience of boats. In fact, apart from rowing small boats on the town's lake, I had only once ventured out onto the sea with a school friend on his father's speedboat to go fishing.

I quickly discovered that even a flat calm sea made me feel quite nauseous.

Well, that just about covered my maritime adventures until the early 1970s when I took a girlfriend (Lucille) on a trip to St Mary's on the Isles of Scilly. This was on board the Scillonian that was a virtually flat-bottomed ferry sailing to the islands from the port of Penzance. For those of us with weak stomachs, this rather ***active*** boat was far from pleasant. Fortunately, the sea was calm that day and I maintained my dignity.

The island of St Mary's is just a little over 30 miles from the south western tip of mainland Britain, and it is a beautiful place with a micro-climate of its own. We only had two or three hours there that day, and I have to admit I have never been back.

Three years later I had long forgotten Lucille, and was married to Deb. We set up home in the fishing village of Porthleven with a sea-view from our bedroom window. Over the next twenty years we became a family of four and my career allowed us to have quite good holidays - as long as they didn't involve air travel. We began with regular trips to see Deb's parents in Oxfordshire, before venturing to various Pontin's Holiday Camps around England. Only as the children grew old enough to appreciate adventures further afield did we first take the ferry to the Isle of Wight, and eventually to the coastal resorts in France and Belgium.

These were never overly adventurous holidays, but I was very fortunate to have a wife who understood my phobia, and children who naively never knew any better.

In the year 2000 things had to change.

It was our silver wedding anniversary and we promised ourselves something special. This led me to reach for that P&O brochure, which accompanied us home from the local Lunn Poly travel agents.

The rest, as they say, is history.

In September of that year, we spent 17 days on a P&O Cruise Ship called Oriana, that took us to the eastern extremity of the Mediterranean Sea. Our lives instantly changed, and there was no chance of returning to Holiday Camps as our main summer options.

Over the following ten years while we continued to cruise, I began to chronicle that first adventure as a book. The book was never meant to be anything other than a personal challenge, but when it was finally completed and published, it began a hobby that I have continued with ever since.

That short book was called '**A Cornishman Goes Cruising**' and has stayed popular with the cruising fraternity for ten years. Although its sales have now dwindled to just an occasional purchase, I still enjoy reading it every now and then to remind me of the excitement, the surprises, and the magic that enveloped me and Deb during that cruise.

# A Bit of History about the Cruise Industry

There was a historian on one of our recent cruises giving talks about the *Golden Days of Ocean Liners*. He described it as being during the early decades of the 20$^{th}$ Century. I can see his point with the glamourous vessels of the British P&O and Cunard fleets alongside the flagships of France and the USA, ploughing back and forth across the Atlantic Ocean. The magical names of the 'Queen Mary', 'Queen Elizabeth', plus 'SS Normandie' and the 'SS United States' will survive forever in the history of cruising.

To be more accurate, *'cruising'* was not a term in common use during that time. Those iconic ships were making scheduled trips between Europe and the USA, and so travelled back and forth on a line across the Atlantic Ocean.

Hence these ships were referred to as *'Liners'*.

As well as the glamourous passengers in their posh suits and dresses, many thousands of people sailed to America on these ships to begin new lives. These emigrants seeking a new life were generally travelling in the lower-class accommodation, and rarely saw or experienced the luxurious areas of the ships. That guest speaker did briefly mention these people, but his talk concentrated on the more palatable luxury enjoyed by lords, and ladies, film stars and royalty who could afford the superb service in the very best cabins, that history prefers to remember.

I think the historian was correct when he looked upon this era as a *'Golden Age'*, but my personal view is that another golden age began in the mid-1960s. This was when the industry had to find an alternative way of filling cabin space, when the rich and famous deserted ships for the faster travel solutions provided by aeroplanes.

*The P&O Story*

As Deb and I dipped our toes in the world of cruising, I soon became curious about the cruising business, and more especially about P&O. I have no intention of swamping you with nearly two centuries of facts and figures, but I want to share just a little of the history of a very British company.

The 'Peninsular Steam Navigation Company' came into existence in 1837, when it won a government contract to carry mail to and from the peninsular area of Spain and Portugal, plus the Mediterranean Sea. The first delivery of that contract was initiated when the *'Don Juan'* left Falmouth on the 4$^{th}$ September 1837 towards Gibraltar. This little ship was a wooden paddle steamer less than 150 feet in length with a small engine capable of pushing her along at seven knots. Although it successfully dropped off its mail at Gibraltar, the Don Juan became lost in fog on the return journey and sank just off Tarifa Point on the southern tip of Spain.

Perhaps not the best of starts, but this small beginning was the birth of a company that now sails all over the world making thousands of people smile each year as they enjoy a cruise holiday.

The connections that the owners (Arthur Anderson and Brodie McGhie Willcox) had in the Peninsular Region won many favours in Spain and Portugal, allowing their ships to fly the red and yellow colours of the Spanish Bourbons as well as the blue and white of the Portuguese House of Braganza. A combination of these four colours remains to this day as the P&O pennant.

As well as carrying mail, the ships attracted a growing number of paying passengers and the venture became a success. In fact, it was so successful that the company quickly sought out ways of expanding, and this began by merging with the 'Transatlantic Steam Navigation Company'. They also won a mail contract with Egypt allowing them to open routes into the Indian Ocean. This was achieved by incorporating an overland route across Egypt to access the Indian Ocean, where more of the company's ships carried the mail to India, before pushing onwards to the Orient. In 1840 the name changed to become the 'Peninsular and Oriental Steam Navigation Company' from which the more familiar 'P&O' name originated.

By 1845 they were taking mail to and from as far as Hong Kong, and by 1850 they had 23 ships in their fleet. In 1852 there was another major moment when the *'Chusan'* became the first of their ships to arrive in Australia after an 84-day voyage from England. This began a regular service from Britain to Australia.

Of course, there were some less than happy days for P&O, and one of the most serious moments came with the completion of the Suez Canal in 1869. It brought easier access for European ships going to and from the Indian Ocean and hence greater numbers of competitors coming into the market. P&O survived and eventually prospered with their mail and passenger lines plus pure freight ships as well. The major competition came from the 'Orient Steam Navigation Company' based in Australia, and alongside P&O they dominated the market in this area of the world.

In 1904 an unused P&O mail ship (called the *'Rome'*) was refitted as a dedicated passenger ship and renamed *'Vectis'*. This was their first ship that offered luxury cruise holidays. It would be a few years before this became a profitable venture, but the P&O that we know today was being shaped during those early years of the 20th Century.

Two World Wars seriously affected P&O's passenger trade. The Second World War was especially damaging when within days of its commencement, the government requisitioned all the available passenger ships from every cruise line. There was a heavy loss of all types of shipping and when peace returned the P&O fleet was decimated, meaning a major programme of rebuilding was necessary. This led to some very famous passenger ships coming into service during the late 1940s and early 1950s with names such as *'Orcades'*, *'Oronsay'*, and *'Himalaya'*, plus one bearing the familiar name of *'Arcadia'*.

*Some names have been used several times over.*

P&O and the Australian Orient lines were working less like competitors and more like partners by now and they both built brand new passenger superliners. The Orient ship launched in 1959 was named *'Oriana'*, and P&O launched brought their very famous vessel *'Canberra'* in 1960. These two ships sailed the world's oceans for many years. In 1960 the Peninsular and Orient line finally gained the controlling stake in Australia's Orient line, and the P&O Company was truly born. Canberra and Oriana were the last of the P&O fleet to be regarded as 'liners' as the market was now demanding 'cruises' rather than point to point journeys.

Another ship that was launched around the turn of the decade was the *SS Uganda* which spent some time in the P&O fleet. She was known to me because I was offered a chance to have a school trip on her in the late 1960s. There was no way that my family could afford money for that sort of luxury, and it was over 30 years later before I finally took my first cruise.

A further significant landmark in the cruise business occurred in 1967 when Cunard launched the QE2. This was a magnificent ship bringing new levels of style and luxury to cruising. Initially the QE2 was designed to allow high speed crossings of the major oceans, and travelling at over 30 knots she was certainly the fastest vessel of its type. The QE2 could take in excess of 1700 passengers and was the first ship to successfully cross the gap from Liner to Cruise ship. She offered differing levels and standards of accommodation from an inside cabin through to superb suites, and even some with balconies if your wallet bulged sufficiently.

The QE2 continued to make regular crossings of the Atlantic, but also took passengers to the sunshine of the Mediterranean for a holiday that began and ended in Southampton.

The cruise industry had truly begun.

Over the next decade there was another shift of emphasis as more and more people wanted the shorter cruise holiday to the sunshine. Ships were catering for a wider range of passenger, and the British market was growing. Competition was also growing with different companies attracting British holidaymakers, so something had to be done by P&O to maintain their popularity.

By the beginning of the 1970s the vast P&O organisation consisted of a sprawling number of different companies working in the seafaring and transport industry. It was time to change the shape of the organisation, so it was split into separate divisions with their own specific identities. Whilst ferries and cruise ships had been operating as a single company, they now separated and the P&O Cruises brand was launched. In the middle of that decade P&O Cruises expanded again by taking over another company called Princess Cruises. They remained separate but would share vessels to match market demand.

Canberra and Oriana remained the main P&O ships but they were getting older.

In the early 1980s Lord Sterling became the executive chairman of P&O Cruises and he came along at a difficult time. His aging fleet was nearing the moment to be replaced, and the direction of the company had to be decided. He also had to deal with a major crisis in April 1982 with the Falklands conflict. A number of passenger ships were handed over to the MOD including the QE2, Uganda, and Canberra. Uganda was used as a hospital ship while Canberra (known as the great white whale) became a troop ship and sailed into some of the major war zones. When she returned to Portsmouth in July, Canberra looked less than glamourous but was greeted by a tumultuous welcome with waving flags and bands on the quayside. It took a while to refit her back as a passenger liner before returning to service with an even greater popularity.

Lord Stirling now began the job of modernising the P&O cruise ship company, and many regard his tenure in the job as the moment that the modern British cruise market was created. He decided to build new ships and commissioned vessels that were specifically for cruising, and styled to attract British passengers.

Meanwhile Canberra continued but the Australian ship Oriana was taken out of service in 1986. This very popular vessel became a hotel in Japan, before being moved to China. Here the ship partially sank during a storm in 2004, resulting in her being scrapped.

Another ship with quite a history appeared in Australia around this time. She was launched in 1965 with the name of *Kungsholm* but moved to the Princess Line with a new name of *Sea Princess*. In the early 1990s her name was changed again as she moved her home port to Southampton. Now flying the P&O colours this little ship was named *Victoria*.

In 1995 the first of Lord Stirling's new ships was launched. She took the name *Oriana* and became the lead ship of the fleet. Oriana was one of the biggest cruise ships afloat at that time, and designed specifically for the British market. She was 'classless' meaning that all guests were allowed to go everywhere, without rooms or areas being reserved for First Class passengers.

Oriana featured delightful wooden finishes everywhere with artwork and sculptures to thrill the eye while sitting in the sumptuous chairs. There were superb restaurants, delightful bars to suit different tastes, plus show lounges to entertain its 1800 passengers. It even had what was described as the first ever theatre at sea. This beautiful ship provided a wonderful choice of food with attentive service, and generally looked after the passengers in a way never seen before. Oriana had cabins that gave real comfort to suit different passenger budgets, while it provided thrilling adventures and sunshine filled holidays.

Initially Oriana was very much perceived as just another ship offering luxury for the wealthy, but that image was changing by the year 2000 when we discovered her. Cruising was becoming affordable to a wider range of people, and although Deb and I initially felt as if we were perhaps invading the holiday world reserved for the rich, we lapped up the superb quality of service and the sensational atmosphere that the ship offered us.

In 1997 it was time to bid farewell to Canberra. She was replaced by a ship that started life in 1988 as the *'Fair Majesty'* for the Sitmar cruise company. P&O bought out the Sitmar company and in 1989, Fair Majesty moved to the Australian Princess Cruises and renamed as the *Star Princess*. The ship was moved to Britain to begin a new life sailing for the P&O fleet with the name *Arcadia*.

... she was the third P&O ship to sail under that name

Meanwhile Canberra had completed her farewell season, and the final voyage was to the Gadani shipyard in Pakistan, where she was scrapped.

Moving forward to 2000, and as well as being when Deb and I took our first cruise, P&O launched another new ship called *Aurora*. She was a sister ship to Oriana and increased the company's passenger numbers by almost a further 2000 people.

There was no looking back, and the cruise industry that we see today grew and grew. As more cabins became available, more passengers appeared to fill them. Ships grew in size, and they also included new features to satisfy the demands of those new passengers.

## Could Cruising Really Be That Good?

By the time we had returned from our first cruise, our holiday lives had changed. Our heads were full of memories of the sunshine filled days, different architecture and different cultures. We told everybody about how good it had been, and how we really hoped to be doing it again.

So, to be sure our first experience of cruising really was that special, we were on the road to Southampton docks again less than a year later on Saturday 21st July 2001.

The adventure was for more Mediterranean sunshine, but this time on a different P&O ship called Arcadia. She may have been a few years older than Oriana, and slightly smaller, but as far as we were concerned (and most passengers) Arcadia was just as bright and glitzy.

Cruise ships are all very similar internally with multiple decks of passenger cabins plus at least a couple of decks assigned as public areas with restaurants, bars, and entertainment venues. Yes, different ships have their own particular style of décor, and Arcadia was more about glass and shiny finishes compared to our first experience on Oriana.

Perhaps designed to suit the American passenger market, Arcadia featured a large and quite spectacular Atrium area that welcomed passengers as they boarded on Deck 5. It had a grand staircase leading up to the shop level, and hanging from above, there was a strange metal sculpture with two arms that revolved in opposite ways. As well as the reception desk, Deck

5 level had a coffee shop that also sold alcohol, plus a relaxing lounge area around a small but popular dance floor.

It is a long time ago now, and many details of Arcadia have been forgotten, but a few of her venues have stuck in my mind.

Arcadia's theatre (The Palladium) was more of a show lounge than the theatre style we experienced on Oriana, but the entertainment was just the same. At that time P&O had a song and dance troupe on their ships known as the *'Stadium Theatre Company'*. They were truly professional, and we always adored their shows in the main entertainment venue.

In addition to the Palladium Theatre, there was a smaller venue called the Festival Theatre where they had talks in the daytime from the tours team or visiting speakers. In the evening it had classical concerts, and it was also the cinema.

Turning to food, and the large Pacific Dining Room was the only main eating venue, but there was also the Conservatory buffet that was our preferred venue for breakfast. We ate most evenings in the Pacific restaurant where we shared a table for 10 people. It had a wonderful position next to a wall with a huge tribal canoe set into it. We usually had our lunch in the buffet, but there was also a Pizzeria out on the open deck as an alternative for snacks.

There were plenty of places to have a drink both inside and out on the open decks, but one that we used a lot was high up on deck 13. It was called the 'Horizon Lounge' where we enjoyed quieter daytime drinks as we watched the world sail by. In the evenings there was usually some form of musical entertainment, as well as strict tempo or disco on the small dance floor. The Horizon had a bit of a quirk, as when the sea was lumpy, the ceiling spotlights rattled.

… strange how you remember small things like this.

Another bar where we spent a lot of time was the pub style lounge known as 'The Oval' which was as close to a pub at sea that we have ever seen. It had dark wooden seating with several mirror partitions etched with drink names. It felt like a local, and had regular evening entertainment coming from a resident husband and wife keyboard and vocal duo.

Our cabin was an outside one, just as we had on Oriana, but it was slightly larger, and the bed was against a wall, rather than under the window. It was perfectly adequate for us, especially as at that time we had very little to compare it to. It was our home for 14 nights, but we didn't spend too long in the cabin except to sleep. We still wanted to experience the atmosphere of ship life, and the draw of sunshine and warmth kept us on deck during sea days, and in the entertainment venues in the evenings.

At that point in our maritime adventures, all the cruises had names to describe them, and that first one on Oriana had been titled *'Greek and Turkish Delights'*. As the name suggests it had focussed on the ancient countries of Greece and Turkey, and it really was delightful. Our Arcadia cruise was called *'A Summer Spectacular'* and we visited several ports in the western bowl of the Mediterranean, discovering some amazing sun-drenched cities in Italy, France and Spain.

A cruise ship Sail-away has always been a special moment, and the start of this second cruise from Southampton was just as special as the first. At that time there was no air-bridge to block our view of the quayside at the Mayflower terminal, where a brass band called the South-West Trains Woodfall Band, played to entertain us while we sipped champagne and watched the final departure activities. As excitement rose, Captain Hamish Reid made his announcement that everything was ready for us to leave, and soon the ropes were dropped and the horn roared out a farewell to the people watching from the gallery above the departure lounge.

We threw our streamers up and away from the ship and the coloured tangled paper web brought smiles to everyone's faces. Like the other hundreds of passengers watching the scene, we waved to total strangers on shore who waved and whistled their choruses of *"cheerio!"* at us. Soon Arcadia was gliding down the Solent to the open sea, and the crowds on deck watching the passing ferries and yachts began to disperse as dinner beckoned.

In the early 2000s there was no Freedom Dining, and those who didn't want the waiter service simply used the buffet. For all of our cruises to date, given a choice we have always opted to have the early sitting for dinner in the main dining room. We quickly fell in love with the atmosphere, especially on Formal Evenings, and it was a thrill to have the courses brought to our table by smiling waiters who always seemed to enjoy looking after us. Once the plate with its meat had been put in front of us, the vegetables were brought and served to suit each individual's choice. It was as close to having silver service as I have ever experienced. The waiters had time to talk with us, and quickly sensed if someone had a problem. They would ask if we wanted more, or something different. They learnt our names immediately and welcomed everyone as if we were their personal friends.

The menu had a different cover each night, and inside there was always a thought for the day and recommended wines. Each different starter, main course or pudding was described with a little bit of flair rather than simply stating its content, and choosing dishes often became a discussion around the table. Deb and I sank into the atmosphere of what we perceived to be fine dining with unbelievable service.

With dinner over we would regularly make our way to the main entertainment venue, but on first nights we rarely did much. This was especially true in those early years when we drove to Southampton on the morning of our cruise, and tiredness quickly set in. The gentle movement of the ship gathering speed also increased our weariness as it made its way down the Channel. So, after a leisurely drink we usually had an early night.

Back in 2001, even being on the ship for just a few hours, we had already confirmed that cruising really was exactly what we wanted.

# New Destinations on that 'Summer Spectacular' Cruise

As we woke on the first morning of our 2001 Arcadia cruise, the cabin steward knocked on the door at the requested time to bring our tea with a packet of biscuits each to dull any hunger before we went to breakfast. He did this without question every morning, and although it had been a surprise on Oriana, we now knew what to expect. It would soon be time to explore what this ship had to offer in the daytime as we sailed across the infamous Bay of Biscay.

The maritime professionals describe this as 'The Transit of Biscay', but some of the modern captains are trying to change the way that passengers think of what can be a traumatic 24 hours. Most of us refer to it as *'Crossing the Bay of Biscay'* but it seems we are all wrong. In reality we are crossing a patch of water that is at the entrance of the bay, so technically we do not enter it. I think this is being a bit pedantic and a little patronising by some maritime experts. I suspect most of us will ignore our error and continue to cross the Bay of Biscay.

On this Sunday morning the ship had come to life properly. There were introduction sessions for the energetic in the gym, and instructions on how to play the deck games of 'Shuffleboard' and 'Deck Quoits' for the competitive. As the first round of the deck games began, other passengers took part in dancing lessons that were ballroom style for many, but line dancing (Yee Hah!) for others. Elsewhere there was a golf chipping competition, or Bridge for the card players, plus

'Guess the distance travelled since yesterday', and even Clay Figure sculpting. Of course, the majority of the passengers settled for a lounger around the swimming pool.

We went to the Port Talk for our first stop in Gibraltar.

In the afternoon there was a repeat of the morning activities before it was time to get dressed up for the 'Welcome on Board' cocktail party, hosted by the captain and his officers. That was followed by our second dinner where we strengthened a friendship with our table mates.

The evening had dancing from a band called 'Kool Blue' that are still playing on the ships to this day, but I doubt all the musicians are the same. The Stadium Theatre Company performed their first of many shows, and the night was rounded off with the Syndicate Quiz for those still awake.

This would be the pattern for the sea days to come, and the typical evening entertainment during the fortnight. We did what took our fancy, experimented with a few new activities, sampled all the bars and lounges, and generally had a good time.

After Sunday and Monday at sea, our first stop was Gibraltar. We had been slightly bored on our first visit here when we just walked down Main Street looking for bargains. This time we took a tour that included a visit to the St. Michael's Caves that were absolutely fascinating. Then it was outside to see some views down over the town to where Arcadia sparkled in the sunshine. We also got up close and personal with the Apes, or more accurately the Barbary Macaques.

We managed to come away unscathed.

Late in the afternoon we were off again across the Mediterranean, and the weather was delicious with plenty of sunshine during the coming days, and beautiful sunsets at night. We even had our first ever loyalty party as members of the POSH club. After our first cruise on Oriana, we weren't sure if we should pay the small fee to become members, but it turned out to be a very good idea. We received quite special little presents on each cruise, and gained loyalty points for each night on the ships. Luckily those points were eventually moved to the future loyalty variants of the Portunas, and then Peninsular Clubs.

*Palau – Sardinia*

After a couple of sunny days sailing east across the Mediterranean Sea, we arrived at the island of Sardinia.

Sardinia is the second largest of the Italian islands, in fact it is the second largest Mediterranean island. Its nearest neighbour is the French island of Corsica just over 7 miles to the north, with the Italian mainland some 120 miles to the east. The island is a crude rectangular shape, about 150 miles north to south and some 50 miles west to east, and has a population of around 1.6 million.

Although the island is quite large, its ports are small, so Arcadia was anchored a little way offshore, close to Palau on the northern most tip of Sardinia. This was to be a Tender Port where some of the ship's lifeboats would be used to ferry passengers between the ship and the town of Palau.

Various tours were available, and we decided on the simple option of a tender to Palau and a short ferry ride from there to a smaller island called La Maddalena. It was a beautiful trip across to the island on the ferry-come-pleasure boat, where we sat up on the top deck to get some superb views. One special treat was being able to photograph Arcadia from the water as a wonderful memory of this ship.

La Maddalena is one of a number of small islands making up the archipelago of the same name. As we made our way to the port on the biggest island we passed smaller islands, such as San Stefano, Caprera, and a tiny pimple on the sea called Chiesa. The port and town of La Maddalena is a sleepy one with pastel-coloured buildings and palm trees all over the place. We had looked in the guide books to see what the island offered, and decided that nothing really stood out as somewhere to visit, so this was a morning to have a stroll and stretch our legs. This cruise was a busy one with several major ports, and today was a day to top up our batteries.

There are many days on a cruise when we have no urge to explore a port beyond a gentle walk and just getting a feeling for a place. That day we didn't even go beyond the Piazza Umberto which is a paved square dotted with palm trees.

There are shops and cafés nearby, and after looking in a few shop windows we chose a café to sit and have a wonderful cappuccino. The town seemed almost deserted, so perhaps it hadn't been identified as a holiday resort at the time we were there. By now it could be a noisy and overcrowded resort, and totally commercialised like so many of the beautiful islands and seaside towns around the Mediterranean.

Anyway, after our coffee we were quite satisfied with our morning out and made our way back to the harbour for the return to Palau. The journey back was just as good as the outward one, with gentle seas that we could hear slapping against the hull over the noise of the engines. To one side of us there was a little flotilla of tiny yachts, presumably a training school for the youngsters, and looking the other way we could see our beautiful white floating home.

Less than three hours from when we left Arcadia after breakfast, we were back on board. It had been a very nice morning, but we had seen and done enough. For lunch we sat at a table out on the deck at the stern of the ship with a salad from the buffet. There was hardly a cloud in the sky and the sun was shining down on the calm deep blue sea as we chatted and glanced around us at some sensational views of Palau and La Maddalena. This was just one of so many magical moments that can be experienced on a cruise. In the afternoon we took part in serious sun-worship until it became too hot and we retreated to the shaded side on the Promenade deck.

*... what a life!!*

*Naples, and Pompeii*

After yet more blue skies and hot sunshine we turned slightly south and arrived at one of the highlight ports of the cruise. It was the Italian city of Naples and it was my 50th birthday.

What a present this day turned out to be.

Deb and I took a tour which began with a panoramic coach trip along the stunning Amalfi coastline overlooking the Bay of Naples. There was a stop to look down from the cliffs at the Bay and a beach scene below us where hundreds of people were enjoying the warmth and sparkling clear water. Onwards again and we arrived at the beautiful city of Sorrento for a guided wander through the streets, where oranges and lemons grew on the trees lining the pavements. To round off the morning the tour ended with lunch in this delightful city.

As we returned towards Naples we stopped at the historic city of Pompeii.

This was absolutely fascinating, amazing, and thought provoking. On 24th August AD 79 this city was busy with merchants going about their trades, women shopping for their family's food, and children were playing in the streets. Perhaps over the previous days a few people had looked up and commented that Mount Vesuvius was grumbling a bit, but with no prior knowledge of volcanoes, they weren't aware that these would be some of their final conversations.

Suddenly the volcano erupted and instantly propelled steam dust and ash into the air. That volcanic detritus shot 20 miles into the sky at a rate of 100,000 tonnes per second, and what goes up has to come down. With no escape possible the ash and rocks rained down on the city burying houses, shops, temples and brothels. The people hadn't time to do anything but stare upwards in horror.

In the mid-18th century, the buried city was discovered, and for the next 200 years it was slowly uncovered to reveal the amazing scene of a city that simply stopped in an instant and disappeared.

Now almost 2000 years after it was swallowed up by the eruption, we were walking down its cobbled streets passing water troughs, remains of shops, houses, public baths, temples, the amphitheatre, and yes, those brothels. Walls still had painting and metal hooks, the gardens had mosaic pathways around them with urns and water features, and the shops still had remains of their counters, pottery, and even some of the items that had been on sale.

This wasn't simply a chance to see history, it was a moment where you were actually taken back to a distant time, and with the superb descriptions from our guide, the city was brought back to life.

The stop at Pompeii was only for about 45 minutes, and nowhere near long enough to appreciate just how much has been recovered and can be viewed. We promised ourselves we would return to Pompeii one day, and spend more time looking around this amazing place, where history became real.

*The Island of Elba*

Early on Saturday 28th July Arcadia was anchored in a sheltered bay just off the island of Elba. By 7:30 am our breakfast was over and the lifeboats-come-tenders were already in the water waiting to take passengers ashore.

So where is Elba?

It is about 30 miles east of the French island of Corsica and perhaps seven or eight miles west of the mainland Italian port of Piombino. Although quite small, Elba is actually the third largest Italian island after Sicily and Sardinia. It is about 12 miles long from west to east and not much more than a couple of miles from north to south. It has a population of about 30,000 people, with most of them living in the capital town of Portoferraio.

The island has a few hills and small mountains that allow spectacular views down to the bays and coastal villages. These views are important, as the main industry is tourism, although many decades ago the island was a major iron ore producer.

We had a tour booked to show us around the island, and once ashore in Portoferraio, our friendly guide rounded up her party and we boarded a coach. We set off across the island and listened to her commentary, giving us a basic introduction to Elba. We learnt about its most famous inhabitant, Napoleon

Bonaparte, who was exiled there in 1814. As we drove towards the more mountainous western side our guide became quite poetic with her descriptions, but perhaps talking in English was proving to be a little complicated. At one point she was talking about Elba's historical industry and having told us that the iron mines were long closed, she started to tell us what the island did now, but the sentence tailed off, and we never found out. A few minutes later she asked us to look at a particular mountain. It was just an unremarkable mountain, but she appeared dreamily carried away by it.

For a moment the guide became silent as she stared at the view, and then said:

**"Pretty - yes?"**

Anyway, we had a brief stop at a little fishing harbour called Marciana Marina to explore and buy souvenirs. The guide told us to look out for *Drunken Cake* as a speciality of the island. I am not sure if it is still the case but apparently in 2001, Elba had just one cow whose primary function was to teach the children about them. Hence there were little or no dairy products on the island and so the famous cake uses alcohol for moisture.

It proved to be rather pleasant.

From Marciana we made our way back across the island, and had another stop to view the remains of a Roman Villa at a place called Punta delle Grotte. Now at this moment in my life archaeology did not sit highly on my list of interests, and this site was little more than an occasional section of knee-high walls amongst a number of piles of stones. Our visit to this Roman relic came just a couple of days after visiting Pompeii, and unfortunately the archaeological remains we saw then were truly spectacular, so what we were seeing now paled in comparison.

There was one positive aspect to the site however. The hilltop location had a wonderful view out across Portoferraio Bay with our ship at anchor, looking absolutely beautiful.

Back on the coach we completed our return drive to the port and finished our time on Elba by looking around the shops near the harbour. Soon we jumped on a tender boat and we were back on-board Arcadia in time for a late lunch.

Elba was a lovely island with beautiful views of mountains and coastal villages. I would certainly recommend it to people considering a visit there, but with a warning that we hadn't seen a lot of tourist attractions back in 2001. By now the island could well have geared itself up to attract visitors and tempt them to open their purses and wallets.

In hindsight I actually think I liked it because it was so *untouristy,* and somewhat unprepared for cruise ship passengers' demands.

In Britain we are used to having easy access to so many different examples of Nature. Within an hour's drive you can move from miles of golden sandy beaches, to green hills of forest or crops, and then rugged hills and vast lakes that are probably as big as the island of Elba. We take our good fortune for granted. There is space to grow vast amounts of food, or to be grazed by cows and sheep to supply our Sunday roasts or dairy treats.

On an island, things are different. Yes, there were beautiful sleepy fishing coves, and Nature had created hills and mountains to capture the rain to provide drinking water. To the islanders those hills and mountains were a daily sight that they recognised as home. They had to leave the island for a holiday if they wanted to see a different vista, but our guide showed that most of the population were happy with what they had.

Elba had very limited areas for crops, and there was certainly no spare land to have cows, so milk had to be imported, but not for the locals, it was to make the coffee that tourists demanded.

When our guide was about to talk about the island's current industry, she would have talked about us, the tourists. The island almost certainly depends on cruise ships and ferries to bring holidaymakers with their credit cards and their enthusiasm to sample a little of a quieter way of life. So, when I scoffed at the sight of the mountain, I wasn't considering how our guide thrilled daily as she pointed out the mountain to her latest group of tourists who were providing her salary.

Yes, that mountain was pretty, but our eyes couldn't see it.

*Santa Margherita and Portofino*

In the north-western area of Italy, less than 50 miles from the border with France, is the little port of Santa Margherita. On Sunday 29th July 2001 we made our first of three visits to this peaceful town, but it is little more than a fishing harbour, and not large enough for Arcadia to dock. So Captain Reid dropped the ship's anchors a little way offshore before 8:00 in the morning, and lowered some of the lifeboats into the calm waters to tender passengers ashore.

We had a tour booked, but there was plenty of time before that to simply stand on the promenade deck and look at the scene before we had to get ready. Santa Margherita is built at the foot of a hill with lush vegetation and the occasional villa for the better off residents. One or two church towers and steeples rose above the houses, and a fortress at one side of the harbour was the only reminder that this was another Mediterranean region, that had been fought over by the various armies for several hundreds of years.

With breakfast over we collected our tour stickers and queued for the short tender ride to shore on this lovely sunny morning. Once at the dockside, we left the tender and stared around at this beautiful little town, but there was no time to explore. Almost immediately, the numerous tour guides gathered their particular groups together, and soon a young Italian lady called for all of us on tour D to follow her towards a local pleasure boat. We were going for a scenic trip around the coast to the stunning little fishing village of Portofino.

Our boat ride was a wonderful and relaxed 30 minutes as we purred passed a delightful coastline, but as the boat turned into a bay, we saw a magical sight of the tiny port of Portofino. There were houses covered in flowering shrubs seemingly clinging to a cliff, then harbourside buildings that were so colourful with pastel shades of yellows, pinks, and oranges that made us all smile. It is a place that can make visitors quietly sigh with pleasure.

Portofino is a magnet for the beautiful and powerful that have serious bank balances. They come here to enjoy the stunning atmosphere, but also to be seen as they look at the designer label boutiques and sip coffee on the waterfront, while looking at the harbour full of millionaire yachts. As we left our pleasure craft I felt as if I was stepping into a fairy tale village.

Assembled on the tiny pebbled beach, our guide explained what we would be doing, and asked that anyone wishing to do their own thing, should be sure to get back at that spot at the agreed time. Deb and I had no immediate plans to desert her and soon we followed her to explore.

The first stop was the church of St George, yes the same as our own patron saint. To one side of the church was a flagpole with the cross of St George fluttering in the gentle breeze. It was Sunday and we couldn't go in, but the architecture, and especially a beautifully carved door kept our cameras busy as the guide explained a little of its history.

From there we had a lazy walk along a cliff path, with views down to the clear Mediterranean Sea, as we passed by several stunning villas. Our group had a mixed age profile, and Deb and I struggled with the slow walking pace, so after a few minutes of frustration we broke away and made our own way down the lane to enjoy the scenery.

Eventually back at the harbour, we walked up a side road to look at the shops. This was the first time we realised just how expensive this little Italian town is. The clothes were really special and the designer labels were way beyond our budget, so we restricted ourselves to looking in the souvenir outlets for a memory to take home. Even the ice-cream was expensive but its taste was sensational and refreshing on a very hot morning.

At midday most of us were back on the beach with carrier bags of goodies and tired cameras. To round off the morning we had an impromptu musical show from the bells of a little church near the harbour. It had been a lovely morning and as we sat on our boat returning to Santa Margherita, the majority of us had semi-permanent smiles while we looked at the cliffs again, and sipped a cool drink supplied by the guide.

Back in Santa Margherita there was an opportunity to look around the town, but the majority quickly joined the queue for the tender boats back to Arcadia. It had been several hours since we last ate and stomachs were demanding food. Perhaps we should have come back after lunch and explored the town, but I think we had satisfied our needs for the day and simply enjoyed the afternoon on a lounger by the swimming pool.

*Marseille*

Overnight Arcadia made the short journey into French waters, and on Monday 30th July we arrived at the busy port of Marseille. It is the second largest city in France (after Paris) and has a population of around 850,000 people. It is the largest French port and important for its commercial container business, as well as fishing. The city itself has the usual mix of architectural styles resulting from a history of occupation by different armies and peoples over the centuries.

Deb and I had an early tour, and were quickly sitting in the Palladium Theatre to get our little stickers to identify the group we were with. Called *'The City of Marseille'* our tour began with a coach trip into the old town before starting a walk to look at some of the city's history. I remember very little about the coach ride except for the guide pointing out a poster on a wall showing Zinedine Zadine who had been born in Marseille. He was a very popular French footballer at that time, but was to become rather infamous for head-butting an opponent in the 2006 World Cup Final.

It wasn't long before we left the air-conditioned coach to begin our walk taking us through the Old Town down towards the harbour. The busy city seemed eerily quiet as most of our route was spent in narrow lanes with tall buildings on either side, but at least we were in the shade, and away from the heat. We made our way down several flights of steps, and the guide was doing a good job at keeping us moving, while giving us information about the buildings around us.

One sprawling cluster of buildings and courtyards in the Old Panier Quarter of the city attracted my attention. This was La Vielle Charité which started out as a hospital for the destitute but eventually became a museum. It featured a rather beautiful three-storey building with a galleried walkway around a central courtyard, and a superb ovoid shaped dome on a chapel roof.

When we arrived at the waterfront again the coach driver took pity on our aching feet, and we had a ride towards the city's Neo-Byzantine Cathedral, known as the Basilica de Notre Dame de la Garde. It is up on the highest point of Marseille and as well as being visible from miles away, it is a rather special building. Externally it has a huge dome and also a square bell tower with a belfry, that supports a 30-feet high statue of the Madonna and Child which is covered in gold leaf. Inside, the cathedral is a mix of gold leaf and stonework that appears to be red and white stripes.

Being a non-believer, I don't spend much time in religious buildings. Yes I find them totally beautiful and architecturally wonderful, but I feel uncomfortable as I clumsily invade a place that is special to so many people. I am much happier just looking at the outside views and leaving the inside to those with faith.

The last stop on the tour was the Palais Longchamp. As a building it now houses a museum, but the impressive bit is the monument in front of it which is a huge fountain surrounded by statues and arches. It is a water feature to thrill a visitor and

I spent ages taking photographs of the water as it spouted and trickled and flowed.

*We returned to Marseille on two further cruises, but my only major memory was from 2010 when we were leaving the port. Our departure was late due to the Mistral winds that had become quite strong during the afternoon, and were making the sea conditions rough. We had had sunshine all day, but late in the afternoon the wind was creating high waves that were running across the harbour exit. Captain Ian Walters delayed departure because the conditions were making it tricky to get out of the harbour without being smashed against the walls.*

*We were actually having dinner when the ship finally left Marseille, and the captain warned us that it might be a bit bumpy as we rounded the breakwater. The ship was actually travelling quite quickly by the time we went through the harbour exit and then we were pushed sideways by the wind. The violent movement made many of the diners utter an obvious gasp. But any disturbance being suffered by the unusual movement was just temporary and everyone quickly returned to their food.*

*Barcelona*

It was 31$^{st}$ July 2001, and this morning we arrived in the Spanish city of Barcelona for the first of several enjoyable visits here over the years.

Barcelona is the second biggest city in Spain (only Madrid is bigger) with a population of some 1.6 million people. It is the capital city of the region of Catalonia and has a very busy cruise ship terminal often hosting three or more large vessels in port at the same time. Barcelona is one of the popular ports to join a fly-cruise, with many major cruise lines using it regularly throughout the summer months.

Deb and I rarely go crazy and get off a ship as soon as the gangplank is open, but today we had a tour during the afternoon, and wanted to have a morning walk around the city. So, after an early breakfast, we were some of the first to board a shuttle bus to the city centre. Our bus took us over a large bridge that crosses the dock area before reaching the main road system of the city. We were taken to a designated coach stop that was about 100 metres from the end of the famous avenue called La Rambla, with a tall statue of Christopher Columbus directly in front of us.

For those who have never been to La Rambla, it is a road about 200m long that has a pedestrian central tree lined avenue about 20 metres wide. There are numerous permanent shops and cafes, but more interesting are the stalls and street theatre, that make it both a crowded market and tourist attraction. Even quite early in the morning, it was already packed with tourists from all over the world, alongside local people out shopping. There were all the usual stalls selling fruit and vegetables as well as flowers, newspapers, souvenirs and even pets. Several artists drew sketches of anyone willing to pay, and others produced watercolour paintings of Barcelona landmarks.

On either side of this boulevard were busy roads and then shops, but one very special place about half way along is a permanent covered market known as La Boqueria. If the area outside was busy, inside it was absolutely packed with shoppers. The market is divided into areas selling different products, and as you move around the smell in the air changes from fruit to sweets to flowers or cheese or sausages or fish, and everything looks gloriously fresh and tempting.

We had been warned to be careful while walking along La Rambla as there are a lot of pick-pockets, and several gangs of conmen tempting unsuspecting strangers to try and win at dodgy card games. Over the years this crowded avenue has created thousands of insurance claims, but there seems to be no effort to stop the crimes other than a few police officers walking up and down. I don't ever remember seeing a CCTV camera anywhere, and if they are hidden away, they do not provide any deterrent.

The morning flew by with the buzz of La Rambla, and we had a late lunch back on the ship, plus a short rest before we joined a coach for our panoramic tour of the city.

It was a tour specifically for members of P&O's POSH loyalty club, and offered a chance to see some of the major sights with very little walking. It began with a drive along the waterfront to see the yachting marina and the modernised buildings. This was just a taster of the new city, as soon we turned into La Rambla again and drove by the stalls and into the older parts of Barcelona. The knowledgeable guide pointed out a strange building that looked like an apartment block carved out of a cliff. This was our first sighting of the buildings designed by Antoni Gaudi that confuse and amaze so many visitors.

Already thrilled with what we had seen, we arrived at another Gaudi fantasy called La Sagrada Familia. This will eventually be a cathedral and is a gigantic construction project which began in 1892, with various estimated completion dates between now and 2040. We got off the coach here and had a few minutes to take a closer look at this amazing building, along with an interesting introduction by our guide.

When I described it as a fantasy I was not exaggerating. There is hardly a wall or feature that is the same as any other. It looks like a skeleton of a construction whose base level is once more like a rock, with openings to create doors, windows. Other sections have areas with figures depicting various religious themes or stories. I apologise for not being able to describe it in depth because there is nothing quite like it, and I can only suggest going to see it, or at least find some photos of it to see my problem.

... but it is fantastic!

From La Sagrada Familia we began a ride on the coach to the area of Monjuic, passing much of the Olympic complex from 1992. It might be interesting to the sports fanatics to know that the stadium used was actually built for the 1936 Olympic Games. Unfortunately, the Spanish Civil War meant the Games were transferred to Berlin, and it took Barcelona half a century to win the Games again. As we drove close to the main Olympic Stadium, our guide was quite happy to simply describe it, but many of us pleaded with her to allow us to see more. She reluctantly gave in to our demands and we stopped for ten minutes to take a peek inside.

... sensational!

Minutes later our coach set off again with a steep climb to the gardens at the top of the hill known as Monjuic. This stunning high point is a park with lots of attractions including the Spanish Village and Magic Fountain. We quickly explored the series of areas with grassy patches, marble mosaics, majestic steps, statues and most importantly views down over the city. We could see our ship in one direction, and in the other La Sagrada Familia standing out of the heat haze that covered the city.

By the time we left this sensational park I felt totally gobsmacked by the experience of Barcelona. This had been a wonderful day from the moment we arrived at La Rambla, until we eventually made it back on Arcadia late in the afternoon.

The afternoon tour had been a wonderful way of getting to know a little about this city, and like so many places we discovered on our cruises, Barcelona was somewhere we would look forward to visiting again.

Just like on Oriana the previous year, my head was spinning with the thrills of visiting sensational destinations that had been denied me because of my flying phobia. I was hooked on the experience of cruising.

*Homeward Bound*

That was the end of our stops on the 2001 cruise, so we settled down to the final few sea days before arriving home on 4$^{th}$ August.

As well as the regular Stadium Theatre shows, our entertainment included cabaret acts from two separate comedians called Olly Day and Tony Wallace, various vocalists such as Petrina Johnson and Danny Walten, plus classical concerts from the duo of Anthony Goldstone and Caroline Clemmow. Strangely, I have no recollection of ever seeing these acts again on the many ships we have been on.

Alongside the Kool Blue group I mentioned earlier, there was our favourite duo in The Oval called 'Rebound'. They were there most evenings and Deb and I often sat at the front listening to their humorous chatter between some favourite songs. They looked after their regular followers, and one evening amazed me. The bar was unusually full of crew and we struggled to find a table, but the singer saw our plight and immediately stopped singing. She pushed her way through the crowded bar, found a table and two chairs which she dragged to the front and told us to come and sit down.

Embarrassing maybe, but a wonderful moment, which showed the care they had for their audience. I might say that such a gesture would be unheard of now.

On another evening I was spotted singing along under my breath and the lovely lady came over and stuck the microphone close to my mouth. My singing was never as good as hers, but again a memorable unsolicited moment. My singing was less than audibly pleasant and I was shocked to see her microphone was plastered with her lipstick, so I never got too close to it.

Our days and evenings involved a lot of time with the ship's own entertainment team led by Cruise Director Nigel Travis, with his ever-smiling group of girls and boys. They fronted sports competitions, quizzes, Karaoke sessions and generally kept us happy for the fortnight. Some of these youngsters are still with the fleet but it is hard work, and many have fallen by the wayside.

It was a fantastic cruise full of sunshine plus a chance to sample amazing places that tickled our senses with history, ancient and modern architecture, the slow pace of dreamy islands and the cultural excitement of bustling cities. We had enjoyed the comfort and service of the ship, savoured wonderful food, and smiled through superb evenings of entertainment.

This really was the way we wanted to spend our holidays, and we had hardly been home for more than a few days before we began making plans for another adventure at sea.

While Deb and I had enjoyed just two cruises for a total of 31 days, we had already visited six different countries, wandered around numerous busy bustling towns and cities (of which two were capitals) and melted in to the tranquillity of several quiet sleepy islands.

We had soaked up the wonderful sunshine, been thrilled by different cultures, and thoroughly loved seeing new places. On top of that were the wonderful ships, with sensational service, ate superb quality food, made new friends, and smiled and laughed every day at the new experiences on offer.

Life at sea was for us, and we repeated the cruising holidays with at least one per year until the present day.

It changed our lives, and we feel so honoured to have had the opportunity that cruising has given us.

*What happened to Arcadia?*

Our adventure that year was the only experience of that particular Arcadia ship. In 2003 she left the P&O fleet and went to Australia where she became the 'Ocean Village'. This was an experimental style of cruising with little or no formality, which suited the Ozzie holiday preference.

That experiment came to an end in 2010, and the ship joined the P&O Australia Fleet sailing under the name of the Pacific Pearl. At sea for almost 30 years, her life in Australian waters ended in 2017 when she was sold to a company called Cruise & Maritime Voyages (CMV) and sailed with the new name of 'Colombus'.

The Covid Pandemic resulted in the CMV company ceasing trading during 2020, and the Colombus was sold on, but with no serious interest, she was scrapped.

## 2002 – The 'Grand Mediterranean' Cruise

Our third cruise was back on Oriana, and it was returning us to the western Mediterranean Sea fir yet more new destinations, including another capital city.

By now we were already hooked on cruising, but still like a pair of children in a sweet shop, we boarded Oriana on the 18th August with huge wide-open eyes and shivers of excitement.

*Oriana*

Built at the Meyer Werft shipyard in Papenburg Germany, Oriana began service with P&O Cruises in 1995. She was designed specifically for the British cruise market, and at that time was one of the biggest cruise ships afloat.

Oriana was named by Queen Elizabeth II and set off on her maiden voyage on Sunday 9th April 1995, to the Canary Islands and the Iberian Peninsula. She had a capacity of around 1800 passengers and became the flagship of the fleet.

In 2000 we had our first cruise on her, and over the years we had seven further wonderful holidays on this very special ship. Our last trip on her was in 2019 that was to become her farewell season. The ship was sold to the Astro Ocean company and was renamed as 'Piano Land'. Oriana was very much our favourite ship over the 20 years of cruising, and like many hundreds of the P&O faithful, it was a sad moment when she left the fleet.

Our first impression as we entered her was the magnificence of the atrium on deck 5 with a waterfall behind the ornate stairs. Those stairs wound their way up to deck 8 where a beautiful Tiffany style ceiling completed a magical sight.

There were two main dining rooms called the Oriental and the Peninsular, plus a buffet on deck 12 called the Conservatory. To the side of one of her three swimming pools there was also the Al Fresco pizza restaurant for the peckish sun lovers.

The entertainment venues included the fantastic Theatre Royal at the front end of the ship on Promenade Deck (deck 7). At the stern end of that same deck was the Pacific Lounge that featured various cabaret acts. Deck 7 offered a third venue called Harlequins which was slightly smaller but still had one of the biggest dance floors at sea. Promenade Deck was the main public area and also had two major bars with the lively pub style Lords Tavern, and the quieter club like Andersons to have more peaceful moments.

Going up to deck 8 there was the peaceful Curzon room adjacent to the Tiffany Court coffee area. The Curzon room was somewhere to enjoy classical concerts, or relax and read a book, although many people preferred to fall asleep there. Although quite popular, this room was never very busy, and eventually became the Sindhu restaurant. A little further along the corridor was the library that sat next to Crichtons where people played cards, or board games. To finish the list of entertainment venues, there was the Chaplin's cinema with a small statue of the little film star outside its doors.

There were numerous bars out on the open decks, but the main one that we enjoyed was on the highest deck (deck 13) and called the Crow's Nest. Here we could sit and have a coffee in the daytime while staring out of the large windows that allowed a 270° view of the seas and oceans she sailed through. In the evening there would be music while passengers chatted over their cocktails.

This ship managed to fit in a lot of entertainment venues, and compares favourably with the ships that followed her. Admittedly the modern giant floating towns that now masquerade as cruise ships, do have unbelievable choices for passengers, but they have sacrificed the quiet rooms where you can read, chat quietly, or doze, and that was all part of the traditional cruise experience.

Oriana was a beautiful ship, and had a huge loyal band of passengers that would go back on her time after time. Being built while the cruise market was just beginning to grow, her cabins were mainly inside and outside ones, with just a few balcony cabins, and rare suites. By the time her sister ship (Aurora) joined her in the fleet in 2000, ship designers had spotted the popularity of balconies.

I thank Oriana for giving us the cruising bug, she changed our holiday experiences for ever.

*Gibraltar*

Anyway, back to August 2002, and Oriana set off from Southampton for a fortnight of sunshine filled days exploring the Western Mediterranean. After a couple of days at sea, we arrived at Gibraltar.

We had no desire to wander around the town again, so booked a very special tour that took us on a boat called the 'Brixham Belle' to look for dolphins.

... It was wonderful.

After perhaps 15 minutes while the little boat got away from the shore, the first of a large pod of dolphins appeared, and they entertained us for over 30 minutes. Many of the passengers struggled to capture photographs of the amazing creatures, but I just turned my video camera on, and pointed in the general direction of the show.

I came away with some wonderful memories of getting so close to the beautiful dolphins.

*Calvi (Corsica)*

From Gibraltar Oriana sailed east across the Mediterranean for two days before arriving at a new destination for us. This was the port of Calvi on the French island of Corsica.

The almost diamond shaped island of Corsica is geographically less than 10 miles north of the Italian island of Sardinia, separated by the Strait of Bonifacia. It is split into two districts with the north being known as the Haute-Corse (Upper Island) and the south being Corse-du-Sud (Lower Island). Corsica is about 110 miles north to south, and some 50 miles west to east and has a population of around 300,000. The island's capital is Ajaccio in the south, which is famous as the birthplace of Napoleon Bonaparte.

In a small sheltered bay near the north western tip of the island is the town of Calvi. The town only has a population of a few thousand people, but is famous for being the birthplace of Christopher Columbus. There is a small harbour, but not big enough to allow Oriana to dock, so Captain Hamish Reid anchored our ship in the bay and passengers were tendered to and from the shore. Our first impressions were very positive with a vista of mountains in the distance behind the little town. From the deck we could also see a tempting Citadel built into the rock and looking like a fortress. It overlooked the harbour and faced out towards us in the bay.

We had decided that this was where we would be heading, and once the tour groups had left the ship we queued for a tender and were soon on our way towards the harbour for a couple of hours exploring.

We had a map to help our adventure, but it wasn't really necessary, and we were soon strolling up the road toward the Citadel. To our left was a rock face occasionally covered in trailing flowers while on the other side was the cliff overlooking the sea. There were some rough paths leading down the cliff where locals obviously took short cuts to beaches through a forest of giant cactus plants. These cacti all had tall spikey stems and flowers, and would have taken no prisoners. The cactus leaves were enormous and many had names carved into them showing love pacts between youngsters whose scratched names would probably survive for many years.

Deb and I walked up the winding cliff road until the rooflines of the buildings inside the fortress walls were visible. We reached the Citadel gateway and took a peek inside at the houses and occasional shops. Satisfied with our little adventure we returned down the hill past the 'man-eating' cacti and beautiful flowers. We spent a few minutes looking round the shops of the Lower Town before returning to Oriana for lunch.

In the afternoon we enjoyed the tanning warmth of the Mediterranean sunshine, before Oriana set of again for the highlight port of the cruise.

*Rome*

It is hard to imagine anyone going to Rome and not coming away with a sense of amazement at how much is packed into a single city. Our first experience began with a coach ride from the cruise terminal in the port of Civitavecchia. This busy port is some 40 miles to the west of the Italian capital city of Rome and takes around 90 minutes by coach. The traffic can be incredibly busy and that 90 minutes could be a considerable underestimate.

We arrived at an underground coach station, and when we emerged into the Italian sunshine, we discovered we were virtually at the Pope's front door in St. Peter's Square. What a way to be welcomed to Rome. This square itself is impressive enough to warrant the long coach ride, but there is so much more.

If you look at a map, the area (known as the Vatican City) resembles a keyhole with a circular area at one end and an elongated square at the other. This square area is St Peter's Square where religious pilgrims and worshippers gather in front of the various elements of the vast domed Basilica of St Peter. To one side there is the Sistine Chapel linked to the Apostolic Palace where the head of the Roman Catholic Church resides.

The circular area is known as the Piazza San Pietro and surrounded on two sides by a multi pillared colonnade, that gives a welcome shade from the intense heat that Deb and I have experienced on our visits to Rome. Directly opposite the Basilica is an opening in the circle with a long and wide straight road called the Via della Conciliazione. That is where we began our walking tour of Rome looking at a few of the city's highlights.

Our guide rounded up her group and welcomed us to the Eternal City. She outlined what we would be seeing, and then we set off initially along the busy Via della Conciliazione towards the 'Castel Sant' Angelo' (often called Hadrian's Mausoleum) but our route soon took us through the quieter backstreets.

Our first stop was a square where there was a chance to buy a delicious ice-cream from what was described as the most famous and best ice-cream shop in Italy. Our experience of the wonderful Italian sweet delight was quite limited, but it certainly was delicious, but very, very expensive.

Refreshed, we continued for the morning exploration with a stop at the Trevi Fountain where we joined hundreds of other tourists throwing coins into the water. This is supposed to guarantee you will return to the city, and yes, we did return.

We spent quite a while at a major historical area, known as the Forum, with several attractions that were within a short walking distance. The guide pointed out different buildings, and one in particular has a balcony where Mussolini used to speak to his people. We wandered through ruins of temples with enough examples of marble pillars to satisfy an archaeologist, let alone first-time visitors to the city. The guide gave a continuous history of what we were seeing to bring this ancient city to life.

After another walk in the hot sunshine, we came to the magnificent Colosseum. We didn't have time to go inside but the photo opportunity was sufficient to ensure we would come back again, when we did explore inside this amazing building.

There was quite a shock here, as it began to rain.

Suddenly the gangs of salesmen who had been tempting us with sunglasses and models of the Colosseum disappeared. They were away for no more than 10 seconds before returning with ponchos and umbrellas. We bought nothing, but just laughed at their ingenuity. Just as suddenly, the rain stopped and the hot sunshine returned ...

... plus sunglasses and models of the Colosseum of course.

We took our final photographs and enjoyed the atmosphere with numerous actors dressed as Roman gladiators or centurions.

It was time to begin the return walk to the Vatican area for the finale of the day's tour with a look around the Basilica of St Peter.

I am not a lover of churches and cathedrals but there was no way not to be amazed by this religious masterpiece. It is vast, and it echoed with the chatter of hundreds of visitors. Some were tourists like us, but many were nuns and Catholics making a pilgrimage to the centre of their beliefs.

I was busy videoing the different chapels and statues until my viewfinder caught sight of a group of nuns praying at one of the many alters. This was the moment I realised I was invading a very special religious place, and I was filming people who were not just there on holiday. The camera was put away, and I simply looked in awe at the scale and architecture, of all that was around me.

Outside in the square we had a few minutes to soak up more of the atmosphere or buy souvenirs. It was strange to realise that just a stone's throw away was the private residence of the Pope who was going about his daily business ...

... or perhaps he was resting and enjoying repeats of 'Father Ted'.

Our visit was over and we re-boarded the coach for the drive back to Civitavecchia and Oriana. It had been a long and tiring day, but we had only sampled a tiny bit of what Rome had to offer.

After a sensational day in Rome, we sailed north overnight for a second visit to the Italian port of Santa Margherita. This time we ignored Portofino, and limited our exploration to a long (and very hot) walk to the small town of Rapallo. That was sufficient to stretch our legs after the exhaustion of Rome.

*Toulon*

Oriana said goodbye to Italy and she sailed westwards overnight to the French port of Toulon.

Toulon is less than 100 miles east along the coast from Marseille and is a small city with a population in the region of 170,000 people. It's a naval base, and the port is busy with some of the larger French navy ships. Our early morning views were of a cityscape of high-rise apartment blocks with a pretty series of hills in the distance.

Tours offered by the ship didn't appeal to us, with the majority taking passengers around the surrounding Provence area to the town of Aix or the resort town of Bandol. Sadly, there were no tours of Toulon itself, which would have been our preferred option.

So, we set off on foot to explore the city.

The weather wasn't being kind to us that day, as this was one of the rare days of cruising around the Mediterranean when it was dull and drizzly. Our walk took us along the dockside and then into the back streets and market squares. One of our finds was a small square with the rather pretty Municipal Opera House fronted by a façade of balconies, towers and arches. A statue stood a few metres in front of the building, and unusually it was not of Christopher Columbus. The name on the plaque unfortunately didn't really explain his significance.

We were dressed as if it was a typical Mediterranean day and the drizzle was making us damp. Undeterred, we strolled down more of the narrow streets between three-storied and four-storied houses with shutters on their windows and an abundance of Juliet balconies.

Going around one corner we discovered a large statue with a water feature. It was called 'The Fountain of the Three Dolphins', but the carved creatures were the strangest dolphins I have seen, and we decided it might have been more accurately titled as '*The Fountain of the Three Cod*'.

I am sure the people of the city are proud of their home and have lots to offer visitors. If it had been a sunny day we might have explored further and enjoyed ourselves, but on this occasion, Toulon didn't work for us.

Damp and a little disappointed, we made our way back to the ship.

From Toulon, Oriana continued west to our final stop of the cruise at Barcelona.

This was our second visit to this delightful Spanish city, and the pair of us decided to have separate tours here. While Deb went on a cycling tour around the back streets of the city, I opted for a 'sporting themed coach tour'.

Deb had a wonderful time, but I felt rather let down when my tour concentrated on football, and more particularly, the Barcelona Nou Camp stadium. The rest of the time we spent on a coach with the guide pointing out another football stadium, and just a drive-by with little description of the Olympic stadium.

Perhaps this suggests the city has forgotten about its Olympic history, and football is all that matters.

In the evening, Captain Reed pushed hard on the accelerator, and Oriana set off towards home.

This cruise was focussed on visiting Rome, and it was oh so special.

There is a well-known saying that "Rome wasn't built in a day", and just as true is that Rome cannot be seen in a day. But we did dip our toes into the history and culture of Rome, and we absorbed just a little of a city that is one of the greatest spectacles in the world.

That is the thing about cruising, you may never get the full story of a place, but you can get a flavour. I think it is better to taste as many different flavours of life as possible, and while you might stick to what you like best, cruising at least allows your senses to be tantalised by new and varied experiences.

When we got back home, we began planning another adventure, and wondered where we could go next.

# Updating the P&O Story

## Goodbye Victoria

Victoria was the oldest of the ships and a firm favourite of the traditional P&O cruise faithful, but 2002 became its final season, and she was pensioned off by P&O.

The little ship then began various short spells with smaller cruise lines. First it was with a company called Holiday Kreuzfahrten with the new name of Mona Lisa.

In 2007 she changed name again and became Oceanic II in the Pullmantur Cruises fleet. Less than a year later sad little Victoria returned to the name of Mona Lisa with a company called Peaceboat.

It was all downhill by now, and in 2010 she ceased life as a cruise ship. Her new role was as a floating hotel in Oman called The Veronica, but in 2016 she was taken to the Indian City of Alang and scrapped.

## Welcome to Oceana

Continuing the P&O story, and as one ship left the fleet in 2002, another appeared, and it involved a vessel moving from the Princess fleet to fly the P&O pennant. Launched in 1999 as the Ocean Princess, she was transferred to P&O in 2002 and gained the new name of Oceana.

Oceana offered P&O a further 2000 passenger places, and the fleet's capacity rose to over 7000. Her style was less British than Oriana or Aurora, and one night when we were on this ship, I remember a comment from a couple passing by our cabin door:

**"Why have P&O wasted their money on this chrome plated American crap, they should have built another one like Oriana".**

This was not the view of everyone who sailed on her. Oceana became a very popular ship and sailed with P&O for nearly two decades. I must add that Deb and I had three quite delightful cruises on her.

… but we do agree that a new Oriana or Aurora would have been a better choice.

Everything appeared to be going absolutely wonderfully for P&O cruises.

The glitzier style of Arcadia and Oceana plus the more traditional British atmosphere on Oriana and Aurora, were attracting new customers. Cruising provided an alternative experience for people yearning for a touch of luxury compared to basic package holidays. The vast number of different destinations available tickled the fancy of many British holidaymakers fed up with beaches and all-day English breakfasts.

P&O's ships sailed out of Southampton, and most cruises were giving British holidaymakers the thrill of Mediterranean sunshine. But some of the cruises went north to experience the awe-inspiring Fjords or the historic magnificence of the Baltic region. Alternatively, the ships sailed southwards to Madeira and the Canary Islands.

In the following year (2003) there was another departure, when Arcadia left the fleet to become Ocean Village sailing out of Australia. This was an experiment where the ship was targeted at people who wanted less formal cruises, with casual clothing and relaxed dining arrangements. The Australians prefer this style of holiday and popular enough for a second ship (Ocean Village 2) to be added. The Ocean Village experiment lasted until 2010 and perhaps seen as a failure, but almost certainly pointed the direction that P&O Australia's fleet of ships would take.

To replace Arcadia yet another ship moved over from the Princess fleet. The Sea Princess was the same design as Oceana and the name chosen was Adonia. Her design (like Oceana) made more balcony cabins available compared to earlier ships.

The P&O (UK) fleet now had four almost new ships giving a capacity of over 7500 passengers sailing from Southampton. This is like taking everyone from a village or small town away for a holiday.

The two almost visually identical ships (Oceana and Adonia) were marketed as the White Sisters, and that marketing must have been very successful, as Deb and I booked our 2003 holiday on Adonia for yet another sensational cruise experience.

# 'Grand Voyage to Venice' (with a balcony)

On Wednesday the 18th June 2003 we were back in Southampton, and after the usual early arrival at the Mayflower Terminal we were boarding the wonderful Adonia. This was the first time we had experienced using the 'Air-Bridge' to cross from the departure lounge onto the ship, but we would get very familiar with it in the years to come.

*Adonia*

Deb and I quickly explored Adonia while it was still relatively quiet, and without doubt the atrium was an impressive starting point. As well as the usual feature staircase there were a pair of lifts with glass fronts to take passengers up and down the palm tree lined focal point of the ship. The décor and glitz demanded to be photographed, and there were numerous other places as backdrops for those special photos as well.

The main entertainment venues were on Deck 7 (Promenade Deck) and at the usual place at the front was the Limelight theatre. We enjoyed several shows from the Stadium Theatre Troupe plus cabaret acts there. Immediately outside of the theatre was the 'All That Jazz' bar with a small dance floor. Moving towards the stern there were other bars and places to relax before coming to the Starlights lounge that was the alternative entertainment venue.

There were two main dining rooms called The Traviata, and The Rigoletto, plus the Pavilion Buffet that was high up at the front of the ship. This was where we normally expected to find the Crow's Nest observation bar, but not on Adonia. To be honest, our only cruise on Adonia was a long time ago, and although we enjoyed the 16 nights exploring the venues, I remember very little about her.

Adonia was already five years old, but she looked and felt very new. The cruise was to be another wonderful and exciting holiday with five of the seven ports of call being new to us.

Our cabin was a similar size and layout to the others we had stayed in, but there was one major difference.

We had a balcony.

It was the smaller rectangular hole in the steel bulkhead type, but to us, it was absolute luxury. To be able to lean on the wooden rail and stare down at Southampton's Mayflower terminal was amazing, but sadly the air-bridge was a major obstacle to seeing the band as it bid us farewell on our fourth maritime adventure.

Not to be beaten, we went down onto Promenade Deck to maintain the tradition and watch the final moments before we set sail. Of course, that meant a glass of champagne, plus friendly chatter to total strangers standing beside us. After a few minutes watching the final shore side activities, the stevedores dropped Adonia's ropes and the booming voice of Captain Rory Smith gave us the usual announcement that we were about to set sail. The band in their bright red uniforms played the traditional farewell tune of *'We are Sailing'* and soon hundreds of paper streamers were tangling together in a coloured web.

We didn't know it at the time, but that was our last experience of the sail-away streamers. Before we began another cruise, this tradition was stopped on environmental grounds.

This was our fourth cruise, on our third cruise ship, and we had two full days and nights at sea before we would arrive at the first port.

The weather was spectacularly hot and sunny again as we made our way down past the Portuguese and Spanish coastline before entering into the Mediterranean Sea. On the Saturday morning we were enjoying the warmth on deck when a helicopter flew over us quite low, and began rather obviously circling around our ship. After a few moments of confusion, the captain made an announcement that it was there to film some publicity footage of us and Adonia's sister ship (Oceana) that was sailing close by.

In reality Oceana was on her way back to Southampton, but had temporarily turned around to sail beside us while the video footage was taken. It became the basis of a marketing video called *'The White Sisters'*. The two ships were actually a quarter of a mile apart, but it looked remarkably closer as passengers on both ships waved and shouted across the Mediterranean. It was a rather impressive 20 minutes until Captain Rory told us that Oceana was breaking away and turning for home, and we were making our final approaches to our afternoon stop in Malaga.

... and yes, when we got home, we bought the video as soon as it was available.

*Malaga*

During the preceding three years we had booked P&O tours for most of the cities we visited, but Deb and I were growing in confidence and we finally began to do more of our own thing at some ports.

Malaga was just an afternoon visit, and became an example of where we saved money and simply strolled around and explored a beautiful city. We spent quite some time in the old Alcazaba fortress. This fortress was built in the 10$^{th}$ Century by Muslims and much of the architecture dates from that period, but over the subsequent hundreds of years, the city of Malaga was invaded by various armies whose people gave the fortress continual makeovers. Hence there are examples of Arabic and Roman architecture and features as you stroll from place to place within the fortress walls.

After our look at historical culture, we walked into the shopping area of the city. Sadly, the people of the city were enjoying their middle of the day siesta period, and many of the smaller shops were shut until later in the afternoon. We had an ice-cream, as we do in most places we visit, and followed that up with a delicious cup of coffee.

I doubt we were ashore for more than a couple of hours before returning to Adonia to enjoy the cooling relief of our cabin's air conditioning.

Our lovely ship set off again in the evening to cross the Mediterranean. The voyage gave us sensational sunsets to round off the blue skies and heat of each day. The weather was absolutely amazing during the cruise, and we were beginning to think that this was how it always was in the Mediterranean.

*Eastwards towards the Adriatic*

As we sailed eastwards, we made our second visit to the Italian island of Sardinia, but this time it was at the port of Cagliari. Totally confident to do our own thing we set off with plans to climb up a hill to look at a Roman Amphitheatre. Unfortunately, it was not open to the public while they set up the site for a concert. Undeterred we did a little shopping, bought a couple of souvenirs, and sampled some more ice-cream and coffee.

From Sardinia we rounded the toe of Italy through the Straits of Messina. This narrow strip of water between the boot of Italy and the island of Sicily is a busy shipping lane, with all the maritime traffic between the eastern and western basins of the Mediterranean passing through it. At one point it is less than two miles wide, and along with larger ships there was the constant criss-cross of ferries between the island and mainland. To make matters even worse for our captain there were little boats with sometimes just a pair of fishermen seemingly oblivious to the mayhem around them.

Although we must have sailed through these Straits on our first cruise in 2000, it was the first time we had knowingly been through this patch of water, and like scores of other passengers, we enjoyed the sunshine on deck and watched the scene around us. Having safely passed through the maritime bottle-neck, Adonia gathered speed and set a north-easterly course up the eastern coast of Italy towards the Adriatic Sea, and to one of the highlight ports of this cruise, at Dubrovnik in Croatia.

Life on board this beautiful ship was the same as on the other two vessels we had already enjoyed. It was perhaps a little shinier and glitzier than Oriana but it retained many of the features that British cruisers enjoy. There was a full wrap around promenade deck to stroll and we made the most of it to stretch our legs during the warm daytimes. Deb and I also enjoyed the privacy of the balcony, but the open deck was our favourite spot to enjoy the sunshine. We stirred occasionally to cool down in one of the swimming pools, or to simply lean on the ship's rails and stare at the water passing by. Our holiday life had changed so much in three years, and cruising both excited us and mellowed our minds from the routine of work.

The only differences we noticed from previous cruises was that there was no mid-morning free ice-cream, and they were using plastic tea pots in cabins instead of stainless-steel ones. We had no real concerns about this, but we did make a mental note to bring our own teapot in the years to come. The buffet was our preferred venue for breakfast and lunch, and perhaps there was slightly less choice than we had been spoiled with before. The American designed ship also used plastic trays with sections for starter and main meal choices in the buffet, rather than the china plates of Oriana and Arcadia, but we never encountered this again on any of the ships.

In the evening, the other people at our dinner table were wonderful and we enjoyed almost every meal chatting and laughing about the cruise. We did try out the alternative venues on a couple of nights, and this was a time when there was no cover charge for the more exclusive choice of menu, and even higher standard of service.

Our evenings were dominated by the main Limelight Theatre lounge shows where it was still the Stadium Theatre Company performing their revues. In the Spotlight Lounge there were cabaret acts throughout the cruise from a male duo called 'Smart Move' that were superb singers, plus Allan Stewart and Helen Jayne as solo vocalists. There was comedy from Les Bryan, and classical recitals by two musicians. Apart from the classical options we made the most of these acts and never went short of something to do.

*Dubrovnik*

Early in the morning of Wednesday 25th June, Adonia made her approach to the port of Dubrovnik in Croatia. This country was ravaged by war from 1991 to 1995 as the Balkan area tore itself apart. This was a war that had its roots in sovereignty and religion, as the mighty Yugoslavia split apart into the different countries that exist there today.

When we visited the country in 2003 it was still recovering, and the scars were visible in the countryside with empty or partially destroyed buildings, and a population that were still angry and suspicious. Croatia was being helped by the rest of the world to grow strong and stable, and holidaymakers were welcomed to help pay for the rebuilding of the country's infrastructure.

The port of Dubrovnik (officially known as Gruz) was an example of a new development, and the first thing we saw was the spectacular 'Franjo Tudman Bridge' across the Drava River. Its construction began in the 1980s, but the war stopped work before finally being completed in 2002. It is named after the country's first President and is impressive to say the least.

The ship would be virtually empty of passengers that day as hundreds of curious cruisers went off on tours to explore a country that is truly beautiful. Our own tour began with a 15-minute drive from the port area to the old town of Dubrovnik. This walled town is somewhere everyone wanted to see, and our coach was just one of the constant queues to arrive and offload their passengers.

Our guide led us across a bridge over an old moat and through one of the huge sets of gates in the towering wall. Inside we spent an hour exploring the buildings, looking at the beautiful harbour area, wandered through inviting backstreets and soaked up the atmosphere. Even the main street (The Placa) is impressive with its marble slabs worn to a shiny finish from centuries of footsteps. As we walked along the marble stone street, we saw numerous small alleys leading away from the centre of the town. Many of them led inquisitive tourists towards the interestingly vowel saving named Srdj Hill, which makes up a backdrop to the town beyond the walls in one direction, with the sea in the other.

Suitably content with our first glimpse of the old town we re-joined our coach and made our way up into the hills and inland. As we drove to our next stop the guide talked some more about her country, and her pride was as obvious as her pain from the recent history. We had a quick photo shot opportunity with a glorious view down over the old town with its red tiled rooves. This gave us a fantastic chance to see the wall around the small closely packed houses, and we almost instantly decided we would have to return one day and walk around on top of that wall.

Our tour then had a stop in a small restaurant where we had a lunch of typical Croatian food washed down by local wines. It was delightful as we sat under a canopy of trees that shaded us from the heat with the sound of a gentle river trickling past our tables. The people of Croatia were proving to be so friendly and really appearing to love having us come to their country.

The last stop was at a fishing village called Cavtat where we had an hour to wander, buy souvenirs and simply soak up the wonderful atmosphere. Deb sat on a harbour wall and paddled her feet in the refreshingly cool Adriatic while we watched some youngsters playing water polo in the clear water.

After a long and tiring but superb day we stood on the deck of Adonia as she reversed out of the harbour, making a three-point turn under the giant bridge before sailing away to the open sea. We had a short journey across the Adriatic Sea overnight to arrive at yet another new port for us. Tomorrow would be Venice, and the ship was buzzing with anticipation from the hundreds of us who had never been there before.

*Venice*

With the buffet being at the front of Adonia, it was packed early the next morning as excited passengers ate their breakfast while watching our approach to Venice. This is a long sail-in beginning several miles out from the city itself, as ships leave the Adriatic and enter a shallow lagoon. Adonia was sailing along the narrow and slightly less shallow shipping lane between islands and sandbanks. In the distance the landmarks of Venice soon appeared, and then the various water transport boats became more noticeable, with ferries and private launches bringing people to work.

As we began to see buildings in more detail, we walked out of the buffet, and merged with the vast numbers of people staring through the glass panels to get the best photo opportunities. The closer you get to the city, the noisier the sounds of boats become until reaching a crescendo of engine roars and splashing.

Although we had never been here before, Deb had researched Venice and we recognised iconic landmarks as we approached the already crowded St Mark's Square on our starboard side. Adonia towered over the buildings as we edged past the entrance to the Grand Canal and continued up the Giudecca Canal towards the cruise terminal. It quickly became apparent just how much the transport system relies on the canals. There were the relatively large green public transport boats (called Vaporetti) ploughing through the water between the various waterside stations, plus water taxis and launches, as well as the private speed boats.

Alongside the passenger boats there were other craft with barges carrying the occasional car or small lorry, but mostly they were the delivery vehicles for food, building materials, or just cardboard boxes. Occasionally there were police launches complete with blue lights and two-tone sirens, and later in the day we saw fire brigade launches. On the banks of the canal people walked and waved at us as they crossed bridges over the tens of smaller canals, that are the equivalent of side streets in this amazing city.

Just this sail-in had made us fall in love with Venice, and we had a long day ahead of us to find out more.

We were soon docked at the cruise terminal and we quickly went back to our cabin to have a wash and prepare our bits for a mid-morning tour.

Our choice today was a guided walk through the backstreets of Venice. As we wandered through sleepy squares, that seemingly all had fountains that looked like monuments, our guide showed and described the various churches and architectural masterpieces that are everywhere in this city. There was rarely more than a couple of minutes between crossing over one of the gently arching bridges over the canals. We saw so many different styles of water transport, with wedding parties as a convoy, and even a funeral procession. The waterways are really the equivalent of our streets with all the same traffic jams and frustrated drivers.

Without any warning the background sounds increased, and we rounded a corner and found ourselves adjacent to the Grand Canal and our first view of the magnificent Rialto Bridge. Our route took us over the bridge with a short opportunity to join the vast crowd of tourists looking down at the water scene below, with every imaginable form of boat fighting for space.

Onwards again and the amusing and knowledgeable guide showed us the fish market. It was late morning by now, and I had smelt it long before I saw it.

Many people had warned us that Venice is a smelly city, and that in the height of summer it has a horrible stench. To clarify this from our experience, we have been to Venice on several occasions, at different times of the year, and the only time my sensitive nose detected any obnoxious smells, was this fish market.

… perhaps we have been lucky.

From the chaos of the Rialto Bridge, we carried on through more back streets, and over more canal bridges, until we suddenly popped out into the amazing St Mark's Square.

It is vast, with one huge rectangular space as large as a football pitch with another slightly smaller square at right angles to it. The larger section is surrounded by sensational buildings, some with colonnades, others with cafes and restaurants, and some of these even had pianists or trios of musicians playing classical music tempting tourists to spend an absolute fortune, on a cup of coffee or to nibble a snack.

We were not tempted, or had the time to sample the coffee here.

Then there was the Doge's Palace dominating one long side of the square with sensational architecture featuring a jaw-dropping façade. Next was a clock at the top of a tower with figures that marched around as it struck the time. And of course, dwarfing everything else around it, was the tall Campanile tower. The guide gave us long enough to look at the magnificent scene and quickly absorb the flavour of what was being viewed by hundreds, if not thousands of tourists cricking their necks to stare up at the beauty all around them.

But our time was up, and we were showed onto a water launch that would take us along the Giudecca canal back to our ship in time for a late lunch.

Deb and I were totally gobsmacked by what we had seen of Venice, and having eaten a snack we were off again to spend more time in a city that became a favourite over the coming years.

We got on one of the Vaporetti ferries from near the terminal back to St Mark's Square. Even this experience was special as we stood by the open boarding area of the ferry, and allowed the wind to blow our hair, and the water to splash up over us as we bobbed along the canal.

This time we had as long as we wanted to look at the buildings of the square, and take time to capture memories on our cameras. We wandered through the narrow streets, and crossed bridges again to really see and feel what Venice was all about. It was a mixture of tourists looking for designer label clothes, traditional Venetian masks, or beautiful Murano Glass souvenirs, but the tourists shared the city with locals carrying shopping bags, and going about their typical daily routines.

Part way through the afternoon we found a small bistro style restaurant and treated ourselves to a pizza and a glass of wine. It was delicious, and made us feel even more contented with our visit.

From there we rounded off the day with a visit to the Campanile Tower to look down on St Mark's square where people looked like ants. In the distance we could see our splendid ship, and there were smiles on our faces as we overheard people around us remarking on how wonderful it must be to sail on a ship like that.

Yes, it was!

Deb and I had had enough. We'd been up from about 6:30 that morning, and it was nine hours since we had sat and relaxed our legs. It was time for a Vaporetti ride back to Adonia. We had a cooling drink and then stretched out on the open deck to enjoy the wonderful sunshine. We had breaks from being horizontal and looked around at the views. From one side we could see a train station with some old wooden carriages. As I looked at them in more detail, I was thrilled to notice that some of the carriages displayed signs showing that they formed part of the famous Orient Express. There was also a lot of activity on barges nearby that neither of us could understand, but which would become clear later.

Suddenly, without warning, it started to rain, and it was accompanied by thunder and lightning. Passengers scattered in all directions to find shelter, but five minutes later it stopped, and quickly the ship dried out, and normal activities were restored. We decided we had had enough sunshine, and rested in the cabin before dinner.

Adonia stayed in port until 11:00, and after a wonderful day and a typical evening on the ship, we opened a bottle of champagne to drink on the balcony as we began sail-away. Now one final thrill made the day absolutely sensational. The activities on those barges we had seen earlier, were finally explained. They had been setting up a firework display, and for 15 minutes we were treated to a spectacle that made us whoop in delight. It felt as if the display was just for us on Adonia, and the magic of Venice was completed.

What a superb day it had been, and what a sensational cruise this was turning out to be.

Adonia was on the homeward journey now but we still had three more ports to visit. Rather than simply passing back through the Messina Straits, we visited the Sicilian port of Messina. Deb and I did our own thing and simply strolled around the city for a couple of hours. It wasn't overly inspiring but it was a chance to stretch our legs.

*Palma - Majorca*

Majorca is the largest of the Spanish Balearic Islands. This archipelago is little more than 100 miles off the eastern coast of Spain, and the nearest mainland city is Valencia. There are four main islands in the Balearic group with Majorca as the biggest. There is also Menorca, Ibiza, and Formentera. The population of the island group is round 1,000,000 people, but this is swelled by the tourists who flock there for the hot summers and temperate winters.

The largest and capital city of the island group is Palma which is in the south west of the largest island of Majorca. To be more accurate, we should really call it Mallorca. Palma has a population of more than 400,000. The busy port is rarely without a cruise ship, and the nearby marina is always full of yachts and pleasure craft.

It is a beautiful city, and a magnet for holidaymakers.

Adonia provided our first visit to Palma, but we have stopped there a couple of times since. Strangely we have never had an organised tour here, and preferred to take a shuttle bus each time to the centre of the city, and simply walk around and admire the superb architecture.

So, on Monday 30th June, Adonia was made secure to the docks in Palma for a morning visit. By mid-morning, we had caught the free shuttle bus that had quite a long journey around the harbour front towards the centre of the city. It was obvious from the size and quality of the yachts in the marina, that this city is popular with the very rich, as well as cruise ship visitors. Our air-conditioned coach eventually parked on a purpose-built road where several coaches were stopped. The shuttle simply dropped us off and quickly returned to the ship for more passengers.

Armed with the usual tourist maps, we turned back towards the city where our view was dominated by the massive Gothic Cathedral of Santa Maria, standing next to the Moorish built Almudaina Fortress that was converted to a royal palace.

Before getting to these examples of wonderful architecture, we had to cross a busy intersection on the main island road, and found ourselves on the edge of the Park De La Mer. We didn't go there on this occasion but on a future cruise we took a walk along the lake with fountains, then tree lined avenues with shaded seating areas, and playgrounds for the children.

Back to that first visit, and before climbing up a hill to the side of the cathedral we passed various street theatre shows from human statues. They stood or sat perfectly still in the blazing sunshine to amuse the visitors and hope for a few Euros to be dropped into their collection bowls. The next thrill was an area shaded by the cathedral walls with a small pond where two black swans proudly swam for our delight. To the left of this was a long tree lined water garden. The imagination of the designers of this area amazed me, and all around me the cameras were capturing the visual treats.

Deb and I didn't go into the cathedral, and weren't tempted by carriages pulled by tired looking horses for a ride. We carried on along the road to a square with cafes and bars all around us. I remember a building that was another example of Gaudi architecture, and close by a huge Olive tree that has probably stood there for hundreds of years, with its gnarled trunk and twisted branches providing shade for sleeping cats and dogs.

Our planned destination was a supermarket to get some coke and chocolate for the cabin. Below the shop itself was a basement market with smaller outlets and stalls. There were lots of possible souvenirs down there, and I remember buying a small wooden box with a marquetry picture for my collection. For nearly 20 years that little box has been used to hold my cufflinks, and serves as a reminder of the wonderful places we have been on our cruises.

I think we may have had an ice-cream, or perhaps even a cup of coffee, but it wasn't long before we retraced our steps past even more human statues to where the shuttle bus would be waiting. Soon we had air-conditioned relief from the heat, and our shuttle bus headed back towards the ship.

Just after lunch Adonia let go of the harbour, and we set off again, towards the final stop on the cruise at Gibraltar.

The cruise was nearing the end now, and after stretching our legs in Gibraltar and a look in the shop windows, we turned out of the Mediterranean Sea and sailed toward Southampton, and home.

This was our only cruise on this Adonia, and we had truly enjoyed the experience of having a balcony cabin, and the delights of the Adriatic. Deb and I wanted more of this extra level of cruising luxury, and further visits to the Adriatic were put on the ever growing *things to do* list.

*Return Visits to the Adriatic*

The Adriatic area had really ticked the boxes for us, and we cruised there again several times over the coming years. There were slightly different ports, and we sailed on different ships, but Dubrovnik and Venice remained the highlights and have never ceased to thrill us.

There are differences of course.

Firstly, Dubrovnik plus other Croatian destinations on the cruise circuits have grown up. I said that the people appeared thrilled to see tourists, but this is no longer so obvious. Croatia has gained a special cultural and historical status from many organisations and countries around the world, and money has poured in to rebuild the country's infrastructure, and Croatia is prospering.

When we first stopped at the port of Gruz in 2003 it was obvious that the people didn't have a lot of money. Many of the buildings were old and tattered, many people wore clothes that were past their best, and yes, most people were thrilled by our arrival with bulging wallets.

As the years have passed by, the investment into the country is visibly noticeable. Many of those older buildings have been repaired, and are surrounded by new ones. The roads are packed with expensive cars, and that harbour now has an armada of wonderful yachts for Croatia's growing population of millionaires.

With our cruise ship's early morning arrival, we get a chance to watch the port waking up. A fleet of tourist vessels stream by our floating hotel towards the harbour of Dubrovnik's old town, tempting holidaymakers to part with their Euros, dollars, or any other currency to enjoy the delightful waters of the Adriatic.

Venice remains a spectacle that just has to be seen by everyone at least once. But sadly, our planet is struggling to avoid rising sea levels with unpredictable storms. The city is sinking, and the arrival of gigantic cruise ships create invisible underwater tsunamis that churn up the canal water sending it crashing into the foundations of the buildings.

Several years ago, the city threatened to stop ships over a certain weight from sailing into the city along the main canals. That began a fight between the importance of touristic income compared to the preservation of the city. The introduction of the ban is still going to happen, but they are delaying it until a new route that avoids the Giudecca Canal can be made navigable for the monster maritime spending machines to offload their passengers.

In the meantime, thousands of holidaymakers pour into the city every day, to capture the history and spectacle of this unique place. Little has changed in the 15 years since we first visited Venice. It is still packed with tourists wondering if a gondola ride is worth the money, or if the queue to enter the Doge's Palace will ever get shorter.

Yes, a gondola ride is amazing, and yes, the queue is much shorter if you get there early in the morning.

There are more visitors from China and Japan than I remember from 2003, but that is the case all over the world. They make themselves very noticeable by their insistence to noisily move around in groups that seem to crash their way through the crowds.

They are also the worst culprits of the 'selfie' habit. What is the reason to take a photo of yourself with a sensational building, or bridge, or even shop windows, that are partially obscured behind you, while pulling strange faces? Even worse is the latest version of selfies, where these excited people use a video camera pointing backwards over their heads to capture shaky images of the amazing scenes that they have just passed by.

No matter how much these people might annoy me with their lack of consideration for other tourists around them ...

... I still love Venice.

# History 2002 - 2006

At the beginning of the 21$^{st}$ Century, the cruising industry was rapidly expanding worldwide, and where there is a growing market, companies who want to succeed have to grow accordingly.

One way of expansion, is to buy out smaller companies, and during the late 1990s, Cunard attempted to take over P&O, but the offer was rejected. Sadly, rather than creating a single major British cruising organisation, predatory cruise companies from around the world began to take a serious interest in the British cruise industry. Royal Caribbean attempts were initially fought off, but in 2002 the Carnival Corporation made an offer for both P&O and Cunard that could not be rejected.

This huge American mega organisation has spread its cruising wings throughout the world, and as well as its own vast fleet of Carnival branded ships, it also controls:

> Holland America Line
> Princess Cruises
> Seabourn
> Cunard
> Aida
> Costa Cruises
> P&O (UK)
> P&O (Australia)

Carnival is the largest cruise organisation in the world and in 2020 they had around 90 ships capable of carrying a total in excess of 200,000 passengers.

The next largest cruise organisation is Royal Caribbean with five different companies around the world. But they only have about 40 ships.

That takeover was seen as a disaster by the loyal British P&O passengers, but all companies have to grow, or risk being left behind. That growth needs money to invest and Carnival offered the chance of that money.

Initially there was little difference for the P&O passengers, but little by little small changes were being made.

P&O, and all the other cruise lines mentioned, still have their own identity, and initially there were no obvious changes for passengers. But as time went by it was becoming clear that the influence of Carnival meant things were changing. During the 20 years we have been cruising, those subtle changes have become quite significant.

One of the regular comments quoted by P&O management was about the very important and special British '**P&O ness**' that passengers talk about, and enjoy so much.

Sadly, I think that is changing to a far more American style of '**Carnival ness**'.

In 2005 one of the first obvious benefits of being part of Carnival was the launch of another brand-new ship. She was called Arcadia ...

... yes, another one.

It appears this ship was originally planned for the Cunard fleet and rumours suggest she would have been named Victoria, but for some commercial reason, Carnival decided to put the P&O flag on her. This new Arcadia was a little larger than the Oriana and Aurora but with a comparable passenger capacity nearing 2000. A very important feature was that Arcadia was the first in the P&O fleet to be an 'adults only' vessel. She became one of our favourites especially as there were many more balcony cabins in our price range.

In that same year, as Arcadia arrived, the Adonia completed her brief spell with P&O. It was time to say goodbye to her, and this rather lovely vessel returned to her previous life as the Sea Princess.

*Sadly, Sea Princess became a casualty of the Covid pandemic, and in 2020, Carnival sold the her to Sanya International Cruise Development. Her new name was the 'Charming', but what her future will be, is unknown.*

2005 was a busy year, and there was another ship swapped from the Princess fleet to P&O. The much smaller Royal Princess was launched in 1984 but was now renamed Artemis. It was a replacement for the much-loved Victoria, and was small enough to visit some ports where the bigger vessels just couldn't get alongside. Artemis became the oldest vessel in the fleet with a passenger capacity of around 1100 people.

The next change of direction within P&O came in 2006 when they decided to change the country of registration for Oriana to Bermuda rather than Britain. Other ships in the fleet followed this lead and the company had to work hard to dispel rumours of becoming even less British, and said the move had been made to allow P&O to join the lucrative market of providing weddings at sea.

# 'Captivating Canaries' Cruise - 2004

After four years of cruising in the Mediterranean, Deb and I decided we had to explore somewhere else.

So, on 5th July (our wedding anniversary) in 2004 we boarded Oriana for the third time. But instead of turning left at Cadiz, we continued southwards to the Canaries. Our adventure was called *'Captivating Canaries'* and we would visit four of the Atlantic Spanish islands of Lanzarote, Gran Canaria, Tenerife, and la Palma.

The Canary Islands (or Canaries) are under Spanish sovereignty who refer to them as 'Islas Canarias'. This archipelago has seven significant islands and a few smaller ones. From west to east the main islands are: El Hierro, La Palma, La Gomera, Tenerife, Gran Canaria, Fuerteventura, and Lanzarote.

Around 20 million years ago a weak point on the sea bed became a giant pimple, that erupted and spewed volcanic material into the water above. This was the beginning of the Canary Islands as that unstoppable torrent of magma created a new feature, that grew through the 4000 or so metres of water until it finally emerged from the sea and became Fuertoventura. Over many years the cooling air slowly solidified the lava and stemmed the flow of volcanic magma, and the island became what we see today. But nearby other gushing flows of the earth's molten material were exploding into the sea creating further islands. The different islands that attract tens of thousands of holidaymakers each year were formed one by one over millions of years, with the newest ones on the west of the archipelago with El Hierro being just over a million years old.

The Canary Islands are about 600 miles from the port of Cadiz which we had stopped at on the journey south, and about 60 miles from the nearest land on the Moroccan coast.

The islands are classed as being in the Sub-Tropical Region, and have a pleasant climate with annual temperature variations of between 18° to 24°C. Except in the depths of winter there are very few rainy days, and even then, the rainfall is low. A lot of retired British people spend the winter in the pleasant warmth of the islands when accommodation is relatively cheap. Tourism makes up about 80% of the islands' economy with the rest coming mainly from bananas and a few other crops.

It was good to rekindle our love of Oriana which was being commanded by the familiar Captain Hamish Read. It had been a two-year break from this ship and we quickly relaxed into it again.

There were no obvious differences from our previous cruises, except the lack of paper streamer sail-away, but perhaps the cabin steward appeared to be a little less friendly, as the number of cabins he had to service was increasing, and there was definitely no more free morning ice-cream.

Although the cruise was destined to explore the Canaries, the journey south began with three stops on the Atlantic Coastline of Spain and Portugal.

*La Corunna*

The first stop was La Corunna on the extreme north western tip of Spain. It is a part of the larger region of Galicia and very much the Celtic area of Spain. As well as having Celtic influences, it was also popular with the Phoenicians and Romans. Earliest records show that the Romans decided to take a serious look around Galicia in the 2nd century BC and discovered some interesting minerals. The city was known as Brigantium during this period and even hosted Julius Caesar in the year 62 BC.

In those long-ago times, the Romans would have seen many of the local people working as fishermen, but things were about to change with the port making an ideal location for sea trading. There is even a lighthouse constructed as far back as the 2nd century AD and known as the Tower of Hercules.

Time for a change came when the Phoenicians strolled across Europe and invaded the area in the 8th century AD. Obviously the Roman influence had toughened up the locals and they did their best to put the Phoenicians off. As well as not being welcomed, the weather may have been a little cool for the Phoenician tourists, and they didn't stay very long.

As Spain became a major sea-faring nation, the port became a regular starting point for explorers.

One last memorable moment to give you is that in 1588 the Spanish Armada left from the nearby port of Ferrol. It sailed towards Britain with 130 mighty galleons, but as our proud history tells us, it was defeated and only half of the fleet ever made it back to Spain.

... "**Well done Sir Francis!**"

Let's fast forward to 2004, so what did we think of La Caruna, and how did we spend our time there.

The view from the ship was dominated by a marina of yachts with typically four-story buildings beyond the water, and many were pastel shades of pink, and orange. The cruise ship terminal was an easy stroll from the commercial area of the city, so our plan was to simply stretch our legs and look around. Sadly there was a light drizzle, but undeterred, we set off to explore.

After perhaps a ten-minute walk around the dockside, we came to some very pretty buildings that often had ornate ground floors with columns and arches forming a covered walkway, with shops or offices behind them. The first and second floor facades had quite large traditional windows, but the third floor was regularly fronted with balconies or what appeared as full width conservatories. The windows were often made up of lots of smaller panes of glass, and this is supposed to look as if the buildings are covered in crystals, and the city is often referred to as the 'Crystal City'. It was quite attractive, but I couldn't personally see any obvious similarity to crystal.

As with so many Spanish towns and cities, La Coruna has an abundance of narrow streets, some with steps leading up to the higher areas of the city. We found the 'Maria Reta Square' with a beautiful town hall topped with three red tile roofed towers making up its third floor.

By now the light rain was beginning to soak into our clothes, so the beauty of this peaceful place was losing its attraction, and it was time to return to Oriana. Perhaps in hindsight we should have booked a tour to see a little more of what La Coruna had to offer.

*Lisbon*

Oriana set sail again at midday, and by the next morning we were making our way up the River Tagus towards the beautiful Portuguese Port of Lisbon.

The sail in along the River Tagus to the Capital City of Portugal is spectacular. The highlights begin with what looks like a fairy tale castle called the Belem Tower. A few minutes later is the huge rose-coloured stone 'Monument of the Discoverers' celebrating the famous sea-going heroes of Portugal. A statue of Henry the Navigator stands at the front of what looks like the prow of a ship. He is holding a small Caravel sailing ship in his hands as he seemingly looks toward far off lands.

As that monument was left behind, we began to hear a strange buzzing sound, that grew louder. It was the sound of the cars and lorries crossing over the wonderful 25th April suspension bridge. The name is to remind people of the 'Carnation Revolution' on 25th April in 1974 when the regime of the Estado Novo was overthrown. The title 'Carnation' is used as there were no gun shots fired and local people put carnation flowers down the barrels of the soldiers' rifles.

Anyway, the bridge is a reddish colour and looks very similar to the Golden Gate Bridge in San Francisco Bay, and the buzzing noise is because the road is made of a metal grating. The hundreds of cars crossing it from the city of Lisbon towards the south rumble on the grating and create the fantastic buzzing sound like a million swarming bees. Making it even more visually spectacular there is a monument on the hill to the southern side of the bridge that is topped with a statue resembling the famous Christ the Redeemer one in Rio de Janeiro.

Once you have passed beneath the bridge, it was just a few minutes before the cruise terminal appears, and it is situated very much in the centre of the city.

Lisbon (Lisboa in Portuguese) is reputed to be the second oldest city in Europe (behind Athens) and built on a series of hills, and it suffered serious destruction during an earthquake in 1755. Over the centuries it has been rebuilt, and there are many different styles of architecture to excite the eye.

We have enjoyed a stop at Lisbon many times and looked around the small but beautiful city on various tours, or just used a quaint old tram that rattled on the cobbles, or often simply on foot. It has some wonderful architecture, quirky narrow streets with ceramic tile walled houses, wide busy avenues, huge squares with statues, and open-air cafes where you can sit and drink the most amazing cinnamon flavoured coffee while savouring a delicious 'Nata' cake. Officially called *'pasteis de nata'*, they are custard tarts, but so much tastier than those you can get in Britain.

Lisbon may be one of the smallest capital cities in the world but it is a wonderful city. It has a lot of history and architecture for visitors to enjoy and plenty of shops where you can spend your money. It is definitely not a port where you stay on the ship.

After having numerous pleasant visits to Lisbon, it has become a bit of a favourite. There have been some changes over the 20 years, and the most significant is a new Cruise Terminal.

When we landed here in the year 2000, the terminal was a simple dockside quite close to the 25$^{th}$ April road bridge. In the last couple of years, a new terminal has been created almost in the centre of the city within walking distance of Black Horse Square and the shops.

Having explored the city quite seriously on our visits, our time in Lisbon is now very much a place to stroll and look at the familiar sights, look for souvenirs or simply have a cup of coffee. Being at the beginning of many cruises, we also use it to top up our chocolate and soft drink supplies.

*Cadiz*

From Lisbon Oriana sailed south to the third port on the Atlantic coast, and this was Cadiz.

The port of Cadiz is very cruise ship-friendly, with just a couple of minutes' walk to the dock gates. Once through the gates, there is a busy road to cross, but that brings you within a short stroll of the city's popular sights. One of the first delightful views is the imposing 'Monument to Cortes' with a tall stone pillar guarded by a pair of stone horses and their riders. The monument was built in recognition of the first national 'Cortes' (Spanish name for the governing assembly), formed in 1812. Below the pillar is a symbolic empty presidential throne to signify that a president was no longer in charge. In front of the main sculpture is a common sight throughout European cities of an 'Eternal Flame' burning.

Behind this monument there is a small park giving the visitor a chance to sit, before moving into the narrow streets that crisscross the city. Many of the streets have shaded residential properties with flowers growing in pots on their balconies. Elsewhere the streets provide a vast shopping choice, with some dedicated to fashionable outlets while others concentrate on souvenirs, tempting bars or cafes plus the day-to-day needs of the population.

At the end of the streets you often come to a small square, or Plaza, where there always seems to be a fountain, and crowds of tourists enjoying the peaceful atmosphere while staring at the architecture.

It is not a large city, and within minutes you are most likely to enter the *'Plaza de la Catedral'*. The cathedral is a wonderful sight with its tall towers and impressive golden dome. That dome can be seen from all over the city, and even several miles out to sea as well.

Another short stroll and you will come to the waterfront on the other side of the city from the docks. This area gives the visitors a chance to stroll along the wide pavements while staring one way to sea, and the other at the remains of the city wall and the delightful mixture of old and new buildings of Cadiz.

If a city stroll is not your thing, tours from the ship will take you to small villages that allow the visitors to see and sample the quieter traditional life. Jerez de la Frontera is where tourists can taste the local sherry (Jerez), and a little further away is the hillside village of Arcos de la Frontera. These small villages are magical experiences, and regular visitors to Cadiz often head for them to avoid the commercial 'sameness' of the city. Another very popular tour involves quite a long drive to the major city of Seville.

Cadiz hasn't changed much over 20 years. It is a beautiful old city, and we have become comfortable to simply walk around. There are lots of places to enjoy a coffee or a beer, and it was the first place we ate Churros, which are sweet doughnut style treats. We try to have some wherever we can, and can even get them now in nearby Truro on market days.

The stop in Cadiz is another port that is often at the beginning of a cruise, so perfect to get those forgotten bits, such as nibbles for the holiday to come.

Depending on the next destination, visits to Cadiz are often just a morning, but in 2004 our visit to Cadiz had been for a full day. After a warm and sunny day Oriana set off southwards for the main attraction of the cruise. There was a day at sea before we arrived at the first of our Canary Island Ports.

*Arrecife - Lanzarote*

Our island adventures started around 8:00 am on 11th July as the Oriana made her final approach to the port of Arrecife on the southern coast of Lanzarote. The day began a little cloudy, and a cool breeze was blowing, but the temperatures would get up to 23° as the day progressed. It wouldn't be that hot where we were going, as our tour was taking us up to the 'Timanfaya National Park' and the amazing 'Fire Mountains'.

Lanzarote is one of the newer islands and volcanic activity is still going on. The most significant event was over 300 years ago when massive eruptions over a huge area of the island created much of the current landscape. Volcanic activity continues and eruption after eruption has produced a vast area of land that is often said to look like a lunar landscape. It includes a number of mountains that are referred to as the Fire Mountains, because the grumbling volcanic indigestion is ever present not far below the surface. The area was designated a National Park in an attempt to conserve the striking rocky formations that nature has produced.

Our tour took us up some 1600 feet near the top of one of those mountains where it was distinctly cloudy and rather cold.

Fortunately we had all been pre-warned of the likely change in temperature, and there was the rare sight of cruise passengers wearing substantial layers of jumpers and jackets.

The next few minutes were rather strange but very enjoyable as we began to realise just how close the volcanic activity is to the surface. Firstly, we witnessed seemingly sensible grown men pouring buckets of water down a crack in the ground. They then stood back quite quickly before there was a hiss, then a roar followed rapidly by a gush of steam from that crack. With gasps and applause from the watching audience the trick was repeated a couple more times.

Next these same men displayed their version of Boy Scout skills creating fire from a pair of twigs. Instead of twigs, they simply took an armful of grass and shoved it down a hole. After maybe a minute smoke began to rise, and seconds later a blazing inferno erupted.

In a nearby café we had a cup of tea and had the opportunity to stare down inside a barbeque, where red hot coals just a couple of feet down were being kept warm by Nature.

After the demonstrations we returned to the coach for a drive down through the volcanic lunarscape created by that eruption three centuries ago. The drive through the National Park is incredibly spectacular, and the tour designers had enhanced the experience with a soundtrack of classical music, as the coach slowly wound its way along the one-way route. The rock formations are almost touching the coach in some places and weird shapes fool the eyes into seeing faces, or shapes of animals in the solidified lava. I don't know if they still do the same tour today, but to be honest after about ten minutes I had seen enough grotesque sculptures and lava to last me a lifetime.

At odd moments our view allowed us to see further away and I was amazed to see camels carrying tourists across the landscape. They might be known as ships of the desert but I had no idea they managed to swim to the island from nearby Morocco.

With the volcanic drive-through complete, we moved on to see how time and the weather has started to wear down the very hard volcanic stone, and arable conditions have begun to be created. It is difficult in the windy environment of the Canary Islands to stop any useful soil from being blown away, but the ingenuity of the farmers has found a way of preserving the small amount available.

On the barren landscape we began to see crescent shaped walls made by some of the abundant rocks. This wall created a wind break against the prevailing wind and behind it the farmers gathered as much soil as they could to form a little sheltered patch of garden. There were hundreds of these crescent patches of garden and as we got closer we could see vegetables growing. As we came to a sheltered hillside it was obvious that nature had moved on, and there were far more crops where soil had taken over from lava.

This was our next destination at a vineyard. Here we took a quick look at the wine making process but also a significantly longer period actually tasting it.

On balance I didn't find the wine was that nice but I tried not to be rude, and accepted the little glasses that kept appearing. The experience was made slightly better by the nibbles of local bread and other tasty bits and pieces.

Suitably refreshed, and having made use of the toilets of course, we returned to our coach. One or two of the passengers bought a few bottles of the wine to take home so I suppose the farmer was happy with our visit. It was time to make our way back down from the mountain area to the coast and our ship again. The morning had been quite a set of experiences but now we were content to get back to the warmth at sea level and have lunch back on-board Oriana.

Once fed, we decided to take a look around the town of Arrecife. Unfortunately, our timing was a disaster as we encountered the Spanish custom of a post lunch siesta. There were a few smaller shops open to buy an ice-cream and the occasional café for a coffee, but souvenir outlets were sparse. We did consider the options of waiting around, or coming back later, but on balance we decided the ship was a more inviting place. We had soaked up far too much of the hot sunshine for the day, and Oriana had delightful air conditioning available.

Lanzarote had been something different with a look at its volcanic history, plus how the landscape has slowly been changed to allow agriculture to begin. A lot of passengers did the same tour as us, but the island has more to offer. Up in the mountains are the Cuevas de los Verdese (Green Caves) formed from a collapsed lava flow tunnel. For those that didn't find volcanoes very interesting, a couple of museums gave a culture boost while finding out a little about the island's history. Various other attractions were available, but one of the most popular choices was to simply go and relax on a beach.

Late in the afternoon, all of Oriana's passengers had returned safely, and Captain Reid announced that we were ready to set sail again. Overnight we would be making the short 200 nautical mile crossing to our next stop at the port of Las Palmas on the island of Gran Canaria.

*Las Palmas – Gran Canaria*

Our second Canary Islands stop was Gran Canaria which is nearly twice the size of Lanzarote. Our port for the day was the island's capital of Las Palmas on the north-eastern coast of this almost circular island. It has a population of less than a million people which makes up about 40% of the total population of the Canary Islands.

Here is a little historical fact to thrill, or bore, friends with. Christopher Columbus anchored in the Port of Las Palmas and spent some time on the island on his first trip to the Americas in 1492.

Well, our slightly less historic day on the island was on Monday 12th July 2004. The weather would give us a pleasant temperature of around 23°C with light winds to give a little relief. We had a tour booked so had breakfasted early and were in the theatre by 9:00. Our morning adventure would start with a guided walk around Las Palmas before going on a scenic drive to the Bandama Crater.

We had a rather pleasant morning beginning with a stroll around Las Palmas in the glorious sunshine. The city has a modern feel about some of its architecture but there are also many older buildings as a reminder of its history. There are museums for those who want to learn more but Deb and I were perfectly happy with our walk being restricted to external views. One beautiful building was the Columbus Museum in a quiet square, and its three-storey building's frontage is a mass of shuttered windows with balconies on the upper level. There is also an ornate gateway style door with statuettes and carvings around it.

Of course there was also an obligatory visit to the cathedral. All guides around the world insist we look at their cathedrals, mosques, or temples, and although I often find them beautiful and architecturally amazing, I get no spiritual thrill from them.

One place where we spent quite a while was the Pueblo Canarias which is a park designed for tourists and locals alike. The quiet green oasis is a mix of different areas including flower gardens and a woodland, plus cafes and places for concerts.

We came across a statue of what looked like a pile of rocks with one man attempting to pole vault very badly from the top, and another seemingly falling head first. Our guide explained that this was dedicated to the proud local men who preferred to commit suicide by jumping off the cliffs rather than be killed by Spanish invaders.

Now it all made sense.

In amongst the peaceful patches of greenery and tropical flowers there was also a wonderful mosaic paving, and concrete recliners to rest on, which were actually more comfortable than the description might seem.

In the wooded area we had a bit of a shock to see men climbing up what are called Dragon Trees to perform various pruning and tree surgery activities. The men were dressed in full safety kit with hard hats and ropes to stop them falling …

… or perhaps to swing around on to amuse the visitors.

Deb attempted to make friends with a local scrawny cat, but obviously her charms were not enough, especially as her sweet talk was in a foreign language. Unable to attract the local wildlife we helped the economy of the island instead with an ice-cream.

After our few minutes of free time in the park we went to our coach for the short drive out of Las Palmas towards the volcanic Bandama Crater. The drive took us some 600 metres up from sea level to a viewing point of this gigantic Caldera. It looks like a vast bomb crater that is 1000 metres across and 200 metres deep. The nearby volcano created it when it belched up millions of tonnes of molten magma and rocks, that crashed into this probably once quiet spot. That volcano is now well and truly dead and the crater has slowly overcome its trauma. It is alive again with birds singing in this delightful green and vegetated scene that disguises the power and violence that created it millions of years ago.

It was the end of our tour, and although we hadn't seen much of the island, we had experienced a city that has a mix of old and new architecture, as well as the thought-provoking spectacle of the Bandama Crater. As the guide gave us a little more information about the island, our coach took us back to Oriana for lunch.

I know we should have tried to see more after lunch, but the lure of warm sunshine was enough to avoid doing anything else active for the day. The sunny deck and delightful background music from the ship's band (Natural High) was more than sufficient to waste away the afternoon in Gran Canaria.

Other more adventurous passengers enjoyed various tours from the ship, and many were attracted to the island's beautiful golden sandy beaches. The local tour sellers tempted some to surf or snorkel as an alternative to simply laying on the sand. Elsewhere people took boat trips around the coastline, or simply stuck to the land and cycled over the different terrains. Those needing more cultural knowledge spent time in the various museums. And finally, the island offered numerous places to just enjoy nature in the hills or around its coast.

*Our Dinner Table Friends*

After our first cruise when we requested a small dining table for four, we have always opted for larger tables to have the company of more people to eat with. Sometimes there have been eight and even ten of us on a table, and we have almost always enjoyed meeting new people, and making temporary friends while enjoying our delicious evening meals. There was only one occasion when a couple really didn't gel with our quite open views, and we requested a move of table, but that was once in over 20 years of cruising.

On this cruise we had a table for six with the company of Jim and Margaret plus Mike and Anne. As well as dining together almost every night, we also met up for the late-night Syndicate Quiz to confuse our minds while we sipped a nightcap or two.

Jim and Margaret were from Scotland, and when ashore, we regularly found Jim standing outside a shop while Margaret was inside looking at handbags or shoes. Margaret loved shopping, and Jim loved making her happy by paying the bills. The couple continually appeared confused about what was happening on the ship, and it took a few days to realise that they never read the daily newspaper with information about entertainment and activities. Apparently, Margaret always picked up the paper each night and immediately threw it away.

As the cruise was coming to an end Margaret began to panic about Customs officers stopping them on our return. It wasn't that they had anything to hide, it was just the fear of being stopped. On the day we arrived back in Southampton as we walked through the arrival hall, Deb and I had a giggle as we spotted the couple, who had indeed been stopped, and their suitcases were being searched. I think Margaret's inward concerns must have shown up on her face as a look of guilty panic to the Customs team.

Turning to the other dinner table couple, Mike was a retired naval officer and always showed a deep love for Anne. She was unfortunately suffering from a life changing, and life shortening illness. Anne openly discussed her illness but she nearly always had a smile on her face. Mike and Anne were making the most of the time they had left together, and we often found them cuddled up on the promenade deck, enjoying the evening warmth watching the sunset. Occasionally we had a drink with them to share the magical sunset moments, but sometimes it seemed rude to interrupt their personal moments of reflection.

Over the years we have made many wonderful friends on our cruises. They have come from so many different backgrounds with a wealth of knowledge and life experiences to share. At one end of the scale there was a retired orthopaedic surgeon, and another was a millionaire businessman who had just married his secretary. On those same tables we also smiled and laughed with a cleaner, and an ex-merchant seaman who was injured during the war when a German fighter plane targeted his ship.

These people all became temporary friends for a couple of weeks and added so much to the pleasure Deb and I have gained from cruising.

*Santa Cruz – Tenerife*

After leaving Las Palmas we sailed some 200 nautical miles west overnight towards Tenerife. It was around this time in the cruise that I began to realise just how close together the islands of the Canaries actually are. Oriana has a maximum speed of around 24knots and usually comfortably purred along at around 20knots. With around 14 hours during the evening and night to reach Tenerife, Oriana was able to relax her engines and have a gentle stroll across the ocean to her next port.

I wasn't really worried about the speed as the sea was quite calm and the overnight journey was rather smooth. The only negative aspect was that perhaps we could possibly have had longer in the previous port.

Anyway, by the time we drew open our cabin curtains we were almost along-side at the port of Santa Cruz, on the north-eastern coast of the triangular shaped island of Tenerife.

This is the capital city of the island of Tenerife which is the largest of the Canary Islands with a population of some 900,000 people. It attracts around 10 million tourists a year and many of the younger visitors enjoy the nightclub venues and sandy beaches on their party style holidays.

The majority of Oriana's 1,800 passengers were perhaps not quite so interested in that aspect of the island.

Deb and I were on a tour of the highlights of Santa Cruz plus nearby attractions, and we had to be ready to leave before 9:00. Hence we were out of bed quickly to choose suitable clothes for another hot day that got up to 26°C. There was plenty of time for breakfast before cleaning our teeth, grabbing cameras and water and going to the theatre to get our coach tickets.

It turned out to be a really good morning that started with the coach dropping us off for a stroll around parts of the city before the sun became too hot. Santa Cruz struck us as being quite a modern city with some abstract architecture and busier roads than we had seen on the other islands.

The finale of our walk was a botanical garden. The guide gave us an introduction but we were soon left to explore on our own. It was an amazing 45 minutes with flowering plants giving us a colourful visual thrill as well as the continual perfumed treats. Giant cacti reminded us that the island has an almost tropical climate, and trees towered over us to give shade from the sun which was now seriously hot. In this shade there were often benches to rest our legs while we absorbed the beauty of the flora as well as a number of sculptures.

Back on the coach again we drove out of the city and the guide earned his tip as he talked about the island, pointing out various landmarks as well as talking about the people, history and economy. One place that caught my attention was a banana plantation and I hoped we were going to have a stop. Perhaps bananas on Tenerife are not seen as that unusual, or there was no time, but we kept moving. The drive took us to a seaside village called Puerto de la Cruz where we had an hour's free time to explore the beach and shops.

... ice-cream time!

For a change we went out again after lunch on the ship. The intention was to walk to a shopping complex that we were told was just a little way from the docks. It was hot but we hoped to find somewhere to buy souvenirs so off we went.

Well, about 20 minutes later there was no sight of a shopping complex. It was really hot by early afternoon and we had stupidly not taken a drink with us thinking the walk was not long. De-hydration was setting in and we realised why so many Spanish decide on a Siesta in this *'Mad dogs and Englishman'* period of the day.

We turned around and made our way back to Oriana for a cold drink and a lie down in the air-conditioned cabin.

Even after stupidly considering the walk, our day on Tenerife had been enjoyable.

*Evening Entertainment*

We had been cruising for four years by now and still made a point of getting to the shows or the cabaret artists most evenings. About the only thing we avoided were female singers. Nowadays the P&O ships all have the 'Headliners' theatre troupe across the fleet, but back in 2004 each ship had their own group of singers and dancers.

The shows from the Oriana Theatre Company were still new to us and each year there seemed to be new ones to enjoy. On this 13-night cruise they put on seven shows although one was simply a series of songs and the other was a short event outside on party night. They weren't always in the theatre as they also appeared in the Pacific Lounge at the other end of the ship when one of the cabaret acts was starring in the main venue.

On the theatre company's night off the cabaret acts included a Welsh Female vocalist called Diane Cousins. We never saw her act but did have a chat to her over a glass of wine one night. There was a violinist called Gary Lovini that we also avoided, and a male singer called Paul Emmanuel who was very good for both of his shows.

The final visiting artist was a comedian called Jimmy Cricket. We recognised him from various appearances on television and so we went to his first show. The act was the same as we remembered from many years previously. It wasn't overly funny the first time and now it was dire as his passing years had slowed down the patter and perhaps clouded his mind a little. We avoided his second show.

There were classical recitals in the Curzon Room for those who preferred more serious music. Incidentally, that room was eventually converted into a Speciality restaurant.

Various pianists, duos, trios, and bands also entertained us in the different venues, but our favourite was Natural High that played a mix of modern and ballroom tempo sets. They were really rather good and were the resident band on board Oriana for several years. One of their highlight shows was the deck party with streamers cascading down for the finale session that heralded conga dancing and almost all of the passengers joining in with the patriotic songs.

While singing and dancing kept us happy each night in the theatre and the Pacific Lounge, the entertainment team also ran quizzes, Karaoke, and game shows each night. There seemed to be more going on back in 2004 than today, but perhaps it is just because we have grown choosier and avoid the acts and shows that don't fit with our tastes.

*Santa Cruz de la Palma – La Palma*

Oriana stayed in the Tenerife port of Santa Cruz until midnight before setting off west again for the final Canaries Island on our trip. This was a short 110 mile hop to the smaller island of La Palma and the port of Santa Cruz de la Palma.

These people really like the name Santa Cruz!

The island of La Palma has a population of less than 90,000 people and is situated in the north western area of the

Canaries Archipelago. It's more fertile than the other islands and doesn't rely as much on tourism...

... or is it just less popular!

Anyway, we arrived at the port of Santa Cruz de La Palma on the eastern coast of the island, and were tied up to the dockside before 8:00 in the morning of 14th July. The day would be hot with the sun warming up to around 26°C again. We had no official tour booked today so it was a leisurely rise before breakfast.

While we waited for the groups on tours to leave the ship, we had plenty of time to look at the views. Across the harbour was a beach with slightly less than attractive black sand formed from volcanic rock. It seemed popular, with quite a few people laying on their towels during the day or having a swim in the calm and presumably warm water.

By mid-morning we had prepared ourselves and set off down the gangway for a walk around the island's capital city.

It obviously didn't leave a big impression on me as I remember very little. It was quite pretty with Mediterranean style narrow streets and pastel-coloured painted houses. Many of them had wooden balconies on the higher floors reminding me of the Northern Spanish city of La Corunna.

The whitewashed Church of El Salvador caught our attention at the top of a flight of stone steps. The entrance area walls were of bare stone with a contrasting dark wooden panelled door.

The bell tower was also bare stone to make the building a little more interesting to look at compared to some of the churches we come across.

We had a map tempting us to visit various places and we found a fountain with cherubs and scallop shells in the middle of the Plaza de la Constitucion, but it was not so impressive without any water. I am sure some of the passengers went to visit the nearby Maritime Museum, but it was not for us.

After exploring the shops and waterfront we strolled back towards the ship. La Palma had lots of delightful scenery and places to visit but we had reached a point where we needed a rest. Our cruise around the Canary Islands was coming to an end and we wanted to make the most of the sunshine on our beautiful ship. Natural High were on deck playing memory jerking background music as we sipped cool drinks and relaxed on our loungers around the pool for the afternoon.

At 5:30 in the afternoon Deb and I were having a drink in the Lord's Tavern and competing with each other in the Individual Quiz. Captain Reid interrupted proceedings to announce that everybody was back on board and we were just about to say goodbye for now to the Canary Islands.

*Funchal – Madeira*

It was Thursday 15th July 2004 and after a gentle overnight journey north for some 240 nautical miles we woke up to find ourselves entering the harbour of Funchal. This is the capital of the Portuguese island of Madeira, and it was our first (of several) visits to this delightful place.

It was to be another hot day with just a gentle breeze, and we were on a morning tour called *'Flowers, wicker, and wine'*. It meant an early start and by 8:45 we were sitting in the theatre with our little stickers waiting for the call to our coach. Like so many of our tours, this was one that looked at various aspects of the island, and as the names suggests, it included a little wine tasting.

Our guide was a very talkative gentleman with an amazing knowledge of the island's botanical life, and we were constantly treated to the Latin names of trees and flowers that we passed. I am not totally sure that the majority of passengers appreciated his expertise and would have been quite happy with the 'day to day' names of the plants.

The coach took us through the streets of the town before stopping at an embroidery workshop to see the traditional craft of lace making. Of course, the quick look around the workshop ended with a chance to look at the finished items, and to buy a souvenir. We were impressed by the beautiful results of many hours of work, but the prices were equally impressive, so we didn't add to our souvenir collection here.

Driving up towards the higher area of the island we passed close to the cable car, and Deb jokingly attempted to interest me in a ride on it. As well as a fear of flying I am less than happy with any transport that involves a gap between my feet and ground level, so just the thought of a cable car ride made my legs quiver.

The panoramic drive allowed views of various churches, gardens, and the views down to Funchal and the coastal areas below us. Our only stop in this area was at a wicker and cane factory where toilets were available while we pretended to look around the shop. There were hundreds of different shapes and sizes of baskets on display, and several of the group were tempted to open their wallets. To us the most amazing sight was the range of huge wicker sculptures of different animals, and even a virtually life size motorbike and a huge Viking ship.

Back on the coach again our guide continued with his botanical lesson as we savoured the beauty of the island. We realised that back home Britain was approaching its best with summer flowers and tree foliage, but Madeira had already peaked several weeks earlier. It was still wonderful, but it made us realise that a visit in the Spring might be even more spectacular.

Having enjoyed the views and botanical delights of the higher areas of the island we moved back towards the town of Funchal. The coach dropped us off within walking distance of the huge market where our senses were tickled by the sights and smells of flowers, vegetables, fish and meat, as well as more examples of wickerwork, plus lace and leather goods. Perhaps a market doesn't inspire every visitor, but Deb and I found it fascinating.

It was time for the last stop on the tour and that was at a wine lodge. We thought we might be seeing something of the production stage, but as we entered the San Francisco Wine Lodge we were immediately sat at long tables. A series of small glasses of wine arrived with a quick description, and the group of Oriana's passengers began a rather rapid tasting session. The majority of us enjoyed a mild alcoholic buzz but few bothered to purchase any of the quite expensive wine that was on offer.

That was the end of our tour and the coach picked up the slightly tipsy group again for the short ride back to the dockside and Oriana. It had been a delightful look around just a little of the island, but now it was time for lunch.

Madeira was the final chapter of our cruise. Late that afternoon (15th July) Captain Read gave the order to set Oriana free, and she was let loose by the stevedores of Madeira. We began the two-day high-speed dash back to Southampton, and home.

## 2005 – 'Renaissance and Rivieras'

Sunday 10th July 2005 and we were boarding Oriana for our fourth annual holiday on this wonderful ship. After the previous year's adventure to the Canary Islands, we were returning to the Mediterranean Sea.

Deb and I had just celebrated our 30th Wedding Anniversary, so this was a belated present to ourselves. This year we would return to a number of ports we had visited already, but there were also two new ones to add to our growing list of experiences.

This was the year we changed the way we travelled to Southampton before a cruise. Instead of driving on the morning of a cruise, we made the journey the day before. We then stayed overnight close to Southampton, before a short drive to the cruise terminal the following day.

There was no intention in 2005 to make this a permanent change of travel arrangements, it was planned so as we could meet up with our daughter and son in law to be, who were now living near to Southampton. It allowed us to meet up with them on the night before our cruise, and although just a fleeting visit, it was so good to catch up.

Our overnight stay was at a little bed and breakfast outlet in a place called Otter's Green. This left us little more than 45 minutes to get to the port, so we spent a leisurely morning before making our way to what was then called the QE2 Terminal for our usual early boarding.

Incidentally, when the QE2 eventually completed her cruising life, this terminal was renamed the *'City Terminal'*.

Anyway, travelling to Southampton on the day before our cruises would become the normal arrangement for the next 15 years. It eased any concerns about arriving late due to traffic issues, and also felt like we were extending our holiday by a day. To begin with we continued to use parking facilities organised by P&O, but as the years passed, we booked *'cruise and stay'* packages with hotels in or around Southampton.

Our cabin on this cruise was a standard outside one on our favoured port side, and we were quickly unpacked and exploring the ship. Late in the afternoon we had the muster drill and soon Captain Mike Carr was announcing our departure. There were no streamers this time, but we still had a band to play us off as we sipped our glass of champagne on Promenade Deck.

The dinner table was for six and we shared it with a honeymoon couple, and a pair of sisters. It was yet another friendly and talkative fortnight's dining experience with good food, and plenty of wine.

Our cruise began with three full sea days, and it was terrific weather from the first day. We made the most of the warm sunshine to give some colour to our pale skin. Deb also took advantage of the quiet swimming pool to keep her fitness levels way above mine.

*Barcelona - Spain*

On Wednesday 14th July we arrived in Barcelona for our third visit to this delightful Spanish city. On the previous cruises, we had explored the city on organised tours, but this time we decided to do our own thing.

The sunny morning began with a shuttle bus trip into the city centre without any thoughts of what to do. After a brief discussion, we made an instant (and stupid) decision to try and get to the top of Mont Juic. The plan was to walk to the funicular train station for the ride to the top of the hill, but we discovered that the train was not running that day. Not to be beaten, we decided to walk.

... what a bad mistake

It was hot, and it is a long way, and not really signposted.

After half an hour (or more) we gave up. The scenery wasn't overly exciting except for the odd glimpse down at the city, and we had no idea where we were, and how much further we had to walk. The final straw was a lack of water, and we were dehydrating rapidly. Retracing our steps, we managed to find a drink, and made our way to La Ramblas to remind ourselves about the street theatre, and the vast range of stalls. At least our visit to La Ramblas cheered us up after our disastrous walk, and the morning in Barcelona ended well.

Deb and I were back on Oriana for lunch, and then enjoyed the sunshine until it was time to set sail again.

*Cannes - France*

From Barcelona we sailed a relatively short distance overnight for our first visit to Cannes. Oriana was too big to dock at this small port on the south-eastern coast of France, so it was tender time.

Our day was quite busy with a morning tour taking us to Nice. After a pleasant 30 to 40km coach ride along the delicious coast, we set off on a walk along the 'Promenades des Anglaises'. Our guide chatted to us and pointed out the landmarks as we strolled in the sunshine. We mingled with the hundreds of tourists walking up and down, and looked down on hundreds more enjoying the sandy beaches.

We were given a few minutes to look around an open-air market before boarding a little land train for a panoramic ride around Nice. After an amusing look around the streets, our little train with its bell constantly ringing, climbed up to the Castle Hill Park. Here was a chance to stretch our legs with some wonderful views of the city below, and the beautiful Mediterranean Sea of the 'Baie des Anges' (Angel Bay).

With the bell ringing again, we retraced our journey down, taking in the sights of the park with its monuments and fountains. The sun was really hot, and it was a relief to get back on our air-conditioned coach for the return ride to Cannes.

After lunch on Oriana, we took a tender back to Cannes again. This time we simply walked around the shops, and gardens around the tourist trap Film Festival area. The delightful park area had busts of famous French people, surrounded by superb displays of flowers, plus handprints of film stars set in the concrete of the pathways.

Of course, we walked up the red carpet covered steps to the 'Palais des Festivals' building and absorbed the busy atmosphere. It was obvious that we were sharing this iconic place with hundreds of tourists getting a feel of one of the most famous locations of the film world.

Tired, but happy, we headed towards our ship with quite an exciting tender ride. The tide had turned, and quite a strong wind was whipping up the sea to create a bumpy few minutes with waves breaking over the little boat. We heard later that the wind was concerning the ship's officers, and there was a suggestion that tendering would have to be abandoned.

Luckily there was no reason to do this, and before dinner with all the passengers safely aboard, Oriana set off again to sail further eastwards across the Ligurian Sea to a port in Northern Italy which we hadn't visited before.

*Livorno – Italy*

On the north-west coast of Italy, virtually due east of Nice, is the port of Livorno. It is not an inspiring port, but is one of the places used to take cruise passengers to the tourist hotspots of Pisa and Florence. We had been advised to visit one or the other, and not try to combine both, and we opted for a day in Florence.

There was quite an early start for our tour as the journey was over 50km. Fortunately the highway route enabled the passengers (or those awake anyway) to catch a glimpse of the famous leaning tower of Pisa in the distance.

The sun was already scorching us as we left the coach in Florence for the walk into the city. This city is wonderful, and our enthusiastic and knowledgeable guide brought the history and culture to life as we strolled from vast squares, through narrow streets to sensational architectural buildings. We were shown a tide mark on a building showing how deep the waters were in a flood in 1966. It was about ten feet above the ground, and the raging torrents killed over 100 people, and the damage to buildings and artwork was catastrophic.

The churches, towers, and major buildings are stunning. Add the monuments and statues to the architecture, and it is difficult not to be impressed. Of course, one of the most famous things to see in Florence is Michelangelo's statue of David. Completed in 1504 this marble statue is over five metres high, and originally planned to be displayed on the roofline of the cathedral. This idea was abandoned, and the nude figure is displayed instead in the Galleria dell' Accademia. We didn't have the time to queue to see the proper statue, but fortunately there is an identical one outside in the Piazza della Signoria. We all joined a vast crowd to take a good look at the biblical David with huge hands, but perhaps less than impressive items of manhood.

Our walking tour took us to various civil and religious buildings for a couple of hours, and then we were let loose on the city by ourselves. The guide gave us a few suggestions of what to do, and where to find the best food. Deb and I set off, and our first thoughts were to find some food. The choice was vast, but we eventually settled on a small café where we had toasted panini and a glass of red wine. It was so delicious, and the service was wonderful, so we had a rather guilty cake to finish off our snack.

Back to the streets again and we retraced our steps to the Piazza della Signoria and the Uffizi Palace. We didn't go inside but were more than happy to look at a series of statues of artists, philosophers and scientists lining the courtyard. The experience was enhanced by a classical guitarist busking. This was one of the few moments when I considered purchasing a busker's CD, but sadly I didn't bother.

After consulting our map, we set off again through the streets and came to the iconic 'Ponte Vecchio' (old bridge) over the River Arno. The bridge is beautiful, and we captured some wonderful images before walking across it. There are shops on either side, but they concentrate on expensive jewellery and gifts way outside of our budget. Window shopping was perfectly sufficient for us.

With our minds full of images of statues, Campaniles, Cupolas, ornate facades and bronze doors, we made our way back to the 'Santa Croce Piazza' where we had started. We sat on the steps of the church and waited for our guide to gather us together for the walk back to the coach.

On the drive back, many of us contemplated the wonderful day by closing our eyes, and nobody bothered to mention the sight of Pisa in the distance.

As Oriana set sail again, many of the passengers enjoyed the warm evening out on the Lido Deck for a party with streamers, glasses of wine, and a show from the dancers and singers. It had been a lovely day, and our mental diaries already had a return visit to Florence pencilled in.

Well, that return visit took a long time, and it was 2018 when we finally went back to the Port of Livorno. This time we began the day by going to Pisa. It is a special place and well worth looking around.

*... and yes, of course we took each other's picture while pretending to hold the tower up.*

From Pisa we moved on for a second visit to Florence. We began with lunch again before spending the afternoon wandering through history, absorbing a little more of this wonderful city's beauty, and ate a delicious, huge ice-cream.

*Rome and Naples*

Back to 2005, and our cruise was half over by now, and Oriana went south towards Civitavecchia, and a second visit to Rome.

This time we opted for a simple 'Rome on your own' experience. Most of our time was spent on a 'Hop on Hop off', sight-seeing bus tour. We sat on the top in the blazing sunshine and absorbed many of the spectacles that Rome has to offer. Our only stop was to get off and explore the Coliseum. It looks huge from the outside, but once inside it feels even bigger. The experience was amazing and it really did trigger thoughts of what it must have been like with thousands of spectators shouting and baying for the blood of the fighters.

Our day was rounded off with a quick stop at the Trevi Fountain to throw a few more coins in, and a few minutes looking at the magnificence of St Peter's Square before taking our bus ride back to Oriana.

The next day we were docked in Naples for the second time, and as we promised ourselves in 2001, we concentrated on getting a longer look at Pompeii.

We took a short taxi ride to the Naples railway station and caught a train to the station right outside the entrance to the Pompeii site. This was the Circumvesuviana train service which goes back and forth along the Amalfi coast from Naples to Sorrento. The cost of the trip was really cheap, and when I checked the prices in 2018, it was €2.20 each way. If you want to go from Naples to Sorrento, it was only €3.60 each way. This is significantly cheaper than anything offered by P&O.

Anyway, on that day in 2005 we had a superb morning at the Pompeii site, and really got a proper look at one of the most amazing spectacles we have seen anywhere in the world.

The journey back to Naples was slightly less pleasant as we realised the impact of migrants affected Italy as well. There was a mum, dad, and baby group begging on the train. We stood out as tourists and were getting a lot of attention from them. Fortunately, the train guard sat by us and made a point of telling these people to "**go away**" … or something like that anyway.

Safely back in Naples we walked back to the dockside which was only a 20-minute stroll. This wasn't to save money, but to avoid the maniacal driving of the Italian taxi drivers.

When Oriana set off again that evening, Deb and I decided we still had unfinished plans for Naples, but it would be three years before we managed to get back.

*Sicily, Majorca, and Gibraltar*

From Naples, Oriana sailed overnight to the Italian Island of Sicily, and the Port of Cagliari. We were there early on Tuesday 19th July, and yes, it was another hot and sunny day.

We were tired after a busy few days, and decided not to bother going ashore. Hence it was a relaxed day on Oriana enjoying the chance to lay in the sun.

In the evening we set off towards home.

The next morning we were docked in the city of Palma on the Island of Majorca. Strangely we have never bothered with a tour here, and as with our first visit in 2003, we took a shuttle bus into the tourist area. The architecture is amazing, and can never be ignored, but we simply headed for the shops.

Thursday 21$^{st}$ July and Oriana arrived into Gibraltar at lunchtime. Deb and I remained boring, and walked into the shopping area to look for bargains. I know a lot of British are patriotic about Gibraltar, and rave about visiting it, but it doesn't inspire me very much.

It is often the final stop on a cruise, and I suspect it sub-consciously tells me that the holiday is almost over. Perhaps one day we will get the urge to take a tour again.

Well, that was it. Oriana left Gibraltar late in the afternoon, and headed out of the Mediterranean and then northwards.

Once again, we had had such a lovely holiday on a ship that really was a favourite. We didn't know it at the time, but it would be several years before we spent more than a weekend break on Oriana.

It was time to sample some of the other ships in the P&O fleet.

## 2006 - The Azores & the Canaries

There was a major landmark moment in early May 2006 when our daughter was married. The ceremony and reception were held in a hotel in Southampton, which at that time was called the 'De Vere'. It is close enough to the harbour side to see the cruise ships, and its Pyramid shaped atrium is a landmark we always look for as we leave on a cruise. With the cost of the wedding denting our bank balance, we had no plans for a cruise that summer...

... but we spotted a last-minute offer that was too tempting to ignore

This holiday would be our first trip on the Oceana which came to the P&O fleet from the Princess line in 2003.

It was a sunny Saturday 17th June 2006 when we arrived early (as usual) to board Oceana. Our cabin was basic, but had a pleasant balcony to enjoy the sunshine over the days to come.

Oceana was the sister ship of Adonia, that we cruised on in 2003, and apart from some minor differences, and variations of room names, she was virtually identical.

Our captain was Alastair Clark, and this was the first time we had encountered him, but he would be the master of the ships we sailed on in the years to come. The cruise was simply called *'The Azores and the Canaries,'* and as far as I can remember, this was the first we experienced without a slightly interesting or romantic title.

Late in the afternoon we had the Muster Station drill and heard Captain Clark's voice for the first time. That was followed by sail-away when we stood on the upper deck with our first glass of champagne as we listened to the band playing below. Soon we were waving to total strangers in the Mayflower Terminal viewing gallery as we slipped away from the dockside, and set off down the Solent. After a couple of minutes, we spotted the De Vere Hotel atrium to remind us of our daughter's wedding just seven weeks before.

Our unexpected cruise had begun, and it would be a two day and night trip to our first port in the Azores.

*A little bit about the Azores*

The Azores are about 1300 miles south west of the tip of Cornwall, and about 900 miles west of Lisbon. Naively I thought the Island group of The Azores was much further away in the middle of the Atlantic Ocean, but in reality, it isn't as far south as the Canaries.

The Azores are another archipelago of islands in the Atlantic Ocean, and is a region of Portugal.

There are nine major islands spread out over an area from North west to South East, of about 350 miles. The islands are in three groups and named from west to east as:

Western group - Flores, and Coro

Middle group - Faial, Pico, Sao Jorge, Graciosa, and Terceira

Eastern group - Sao Miguel, and Santa Maria

Similar to the Canaries they were formed by volcanic activity millions of years ago and first discovered in 1432 when the Portuguese explorer, Goncalo Velho Cabral, found the island of Santa Maria. The other islands were discovered over the following 25 years by various other Portuguese and Dutch explorers. Initially uninhabited the islands slowly became populated by mainly Portuguese, French, and Flemish.

The major cities of the island group are Ponta Delgada (Sao Miguel Island), Horta (Faial Island), and Angra do Heroísmo (Terceira Island). The total population of the islands is around 250,000 people.

The climate is mild with summer temperatures peaking at about 26°C but it could just as easily be as low as 15°C. In the winter the lowest temperatures are around 11°C and up towards 17°C. It is changeable with rain coming and going, so this is not a place for a holiday if you want guaranteed sunshine and warmth.

That's enough of the basic facts about the Azores so let's return to the story of our cruise in 2006.

*Ponta Delgada - Sao Miguel*

Oceana had sailed at over 20 knots for two days as we made the 1300 nautical mile crossing from Southampton, across the Atlantic towards the Azores archipelago. The weather had been very kind, allowing us to worship the warm sunshine immediately. During the evenings, the sunsets had been spectacular and sometimes the different shades of red and orange were almost as if the sky was full of volcanic lava, and the calm sea seemed to be alive with the glowing reflections of nature's goodnight message.

At lunchtime on Tuesday 20$^{th}$ June the ship was tied up alongside the docks at Ponta Delgada on the island of Sao Miguel. It is the largest island of the archipelago, and lies in the east of the group. Its population was around 140,000 people, with about a third of them living in or around Ponta Delgada, which is the capital city of the Azores.

Our first impression of the island was a typical volcanic mountain vista with lush green vegetation in the distance. The city itself was mainly two or three-story buildings with the occasional taller complex. Most buildings were white with lots of windows facing the waterfront.

We had an afternoon and evening at this port, and as we looked down at the quayside from our balcony, we could see a long line of coaches and minibuses waiting to take Oceana's passengers on their tours. We probably had the entire fleet of the island's coaches and minibuses that afternoon.

Deb and I had already finished our lunch and we were ready for our tour called 'Crater Lakes'.

The guide described the city of Ponta Delgado as we drove through the streets towards the hills in the distance, but our first stop was a ceramics factory called 'Ceramica Vieira'.

When I say 'factory' I really should add that it was little more than a shop with a couple of backrooms where pottery was being created and finished before ending up on the shelves. Our coachload of over 40 tourists walked in a snake-line as we were ushered through the premises with quick descriptions of the process going on before us.

Yes, it was a little crowded, but still an interesting look at how various ceramic items were first created on the potter's wheel, allowed to dry before being baked in the kiln, and then painted. We were given total freedom to get close and look at whatever we wanted. One of our party was using a video camera to capture the actions of a young lady, who was painting little terracotta-coloured leaves onto white mugs. He was ever so close to her, and probably making her feel very uncomfortable as she went about her delicate brushstrokes. I remember this instance because I was on the other side of the room taking a photograph of the scene, and I was just as close to the very artistic and embarrassed young lady.

All too often the souvenirs we pick up on our travels around the world could have come from anywhere on the globe, but on that day, we were able to buy something locally manufactured from the raw clay. Our purchase was a white lidded pot with a hand painted blue and yellow leaf design. We try to buy things that will be used, and this one sits on our kitchen windowsill to hold the used tea-bags before they go to the compost bin.

From the ceramic factory we carried on into the countryside and stopped next at a pineapple farm. Now, this was quite special and opened my eyes to something I had never thought about too much before that visit.

Just a single pineapple fruit grows from a plant, and it can take more than two years for that plant to initially flower and then to bear and ripen its fruit. The farm we looked around was using several huge greenhouses, and each one had the pineapple plants at different stages of their life cycle. One of the glass hot-houses had juvenile plants that were little more than little green leaves. Another had plants with small fruits, and then others with almost fully-grown fruit. The farmer talked us through the process to the harvest stage and then described how once a greenhouse was harvested, it would be emptied, and then planted out with cuttings from the old plants. The process would then begin all over again. I was amazed that these delicious fruits, that can cost less than £1, actually take over two years to grow before being picked, packaged, and shipped thousands of miles to our shops.

Sadly, there were no samples of the fruit offered to us, but I think most of the Oceana passengers enjoyed this visit very much.

It was time to move on again, and the coach was taking us towards the main highlight of our tour.

As we climbed upwards through the lush landscape, the guide stopped the coach for us to look at the beautiful views towards the coastline of Sao Miguel. It was here that Deb and I began to notice an abundance of hydrangea bushes. They seemed to be everywhere, and in fact they appeared to be used as informal hedges. When the guide was questioned, he said that the plants grow wild all over the island.

At home we pay good money for hydrangeas but here they grow naturally and have no value.

Anyway, after a further short coach ride, we arrived at the edge of a vast volcanic crater from where we could look down on the small town of Sete Cidades. The little town however, was not what we were looking at. Instead it was the massive lake (or lagoon) that filled the majority of the crater.

The view was stunning.

The crater is some 3 miles across, and most of it is made up of the lagoon. It is actually two separate lakes and the water in the largest lake is a deep blue colour. The other smaller lake is separated from the other by a wall and the water has a greenish colour. The different colours are apparently created by the larger lake reflecting the blue of the sky, while the other reflects the green of the lush vegetation that virtually encircles it.

I prefer to think that it is all due to the magic of the legend of love and tragedy that our guide told us.

After a wonderful afternoon tour, we were soon back on the Oceana. From our balcony we were able to look down to the quayside, where the final coaches were dropping off the satisfied passengers. There was a long line of tired explorers stretching back over half the length of our ship as they queued to climb the gangway and pass through the security scanners. The afternoon was drawing to an end, and it was time to have a shower and prepare for dinner.

After another delightful meal we took a look at what entertainment was available. That night one of the ship's main attractions was television coverage of a World Cup football match between England and Sweden.

Deb detests football, and I have to admit that I wasn't interested in watching football as my evening's holiday entertainment. Instead we went for a walk along the quayside and enjoyed the evening fresh air for three quarters of an hour, before going to the late show with the Oceana Footlights Theatre Group performing 'What a Feeling'.

By the time we left the theatre, Oceana was just setting sail again for the short overnight 150nm journey to our next stop at the island of Faial.

Oh, and if you are in the least interested, England drew with Sweden 2 – 2 with our goals coming from Joe Cole and Steven Gerrard.

*Typical Dinner of that Time*

Dinner that night offered the usual selection of tasty dishes:

### Starters

*Goat's Cheese and Hazelnut Soufflé*
*Duck Terrine*
*Squid, Octopus and Shrimp Salad*

### Soups

*Beef and Vegetable or Chilled Gazpacho Soup*

### Main courses

*Grilled Seafood Brochette*
*Roast Turkey with all the trimmings*
*Fricassee of Veal in Puff Pastry*
*Venison*
*Pheasant and Mushroom Pie*
*Mushroom Risotto.*

### Sweet courses

*Treacle, Coconut, and Lemon Zest Tart*
*A Trio of Chocolate Mousses*
*Strawberry Shortcake*
*Mandarin Compote*
*Raspberry Sorbet*
*Various flavours of ice-cream.*

*And of course, there was cheese and biscuits, with tea or coffee, and macaroons to end the feast.*

This was typical of a dinner menu ten years ago. I am sorry to say that a modern dinner menu has fewer choices and the dishes are far more straightforward. Dinners on a cruise were exceptional when we started our sea-going adventures, whilst today (in my view) you have less choice and a lower level of service.

You have to pay a supplement and dine in the select outlets to get the quality, and sadly the standard of service that we used to get.

*Horta – Faial*

Faial (often called Fayal) was the second of the Azores islands we visited. It is in the central block of islands and is quite small with a population of around 15,000. Being small meant that it didn't have a harbour big enough to dock our ship, so it was a 'Tender' day, and Oceana was anchored off-shore in a sheltered bay.

Deb and I really enjoy the Tender Ports. There is an extra bit of excitement on a smaller boat that bobs up and down on the waves, and when the sea is a little rough it can be a bit of a roller coaster experience. That was not the case that day when the sea was calm for the short crossing to the town of Horta.

We were at anchor by 8:00am and the weather was overcast. The temperature eventually managed about 20°C so not the hottest we have enjoyed, but perfectly fine for sight-seeing.

There was time after an early breakfast to look at the views of the island before going to the theatre to get tickets for the day's tour.

The island's volcanic roots mean it is dominated by mountains that were covered in the early morning mist. The town of Horta was quite close to where the ship was anchored and we could see the large yachting marina inside the breakwater. Behind the yachts there were lots of white houses and apartment blocks with red roofs. On the outskirts of the town there were some impressive villas partially hidden by deep green trees.

The chosen tour for the day was called 'Caldeira Volcanoes' that would give us a panoramic coach drive around the island culminating in a visit to the 'Cabeco Gordo' (Portuguese for Fat Mountain). Our crossing on the tender was perfectly smooth, and when we got to shore there was a wonderful photographic moment to capture a picture of Oceana at rest in the bay.

A coach was waiting for us on the Esplanade that ran along the waterfront. Nearby was the apparently famous 'Peter's Café Sport' that housed a scrimshaw museum. The guide told us that people who do not visit this café have not really visited Horta.

… we didn't bother with it.

On board the coach the guide gave us a welcome and introduced us to the island as well as pointing out what we would be seeing on the tour. We drove away from the quiet harbour-side area of the town and were soon out in the countryside. The journey climbed steadily up into the hills and Deb and I quickly began to see hydrangeas again.

We stopped at a beautiful spot to look down towards the town of Horta. From there we could see both sides of the island with long stretches of the black sandy beaches that were so common on the Atlantic islands. The coastal area was a patchwork of fields of varying shades of green with occasional hamlets of the white houses with their red roofs. Where we stood there were bushes and trees plus the hydrangeas seemingly in every direction.

Moving on again we came to a part of the island that was seriously altered by a volcanic eruption in 1957. The volcano of Capelinhos destroyed wide areas of vegetation but more amazingly the lava and ash actually created a half mile stretch of new land from the sea. A lighthouse once stood on the cliff edge but it is now some distance from the sea and buried by ash to the second floor. It is a dusty slippery landscape to walk across, but the views of cliffs made from layer upon layer of volcanic rocks are spectacular and worth it.

From a truly thought-provoking spectacle created by nature just a few decades ago, we drove further up to the top of the Cabeco Gordo which is the highest point on the island. The intention of our visit here was to look down into the crater of this extinct volcano. Unfortunately the mist was completely blocking any views so our guide had to do his best to describe what we would have seen. Many of the disappointed passengers wandered away as he described the steep sided crater with lakes at the bottom.

… but nature had one last twist for us

Suddenly those of us still listening were given a treat as the mist mysteriously rolled away and gave us a brief few second's view of the crater. As described, it was a lush green colour mainly covered in grass but with several wooded areas. Yes, we also saw at least one small lake in the bottom and excitedly we shouted across to the other passengers to come and take a look …

... they were too late

The blanket of mist returned and they never saw anything. Even the few of us that did catch a glimpse struggled to get cameras out in time to capture a picture.

Slightly chilled we climbed aboard the coach again and began the drive back down to Horta. On the way we made one last stop at a statue of Mary, that looks down at the sea supposedly watching the ships leaving the island for America.

Several of our tour group took the opportunity to have a walk around Horta when we got back to the quayside, but most (like us) caught the first available tender to return to Oceana. We had enjoyed the morning but the weather was just a little chilly to wander around in our shorts and tee-shirts so the ship was more appealing.

Late in the afternoon it was time for Captain Clark to give the order to pull up the anchors and set sail south-eastwards towards our next port, and this was a moment when we said goodbye to the Azores.

*Madeira and Canary Islands*

With the Azores suitably explored, Oceana made her way to Madeira for a second visit to this beautiful Portuguese island.

After a quiet morning, our afternoon tour was one of those *'must do experiences'*. It involved me braving the cable car ride up to the hill above Funchal, before the return downward trip on a wicker toboggan. Although I detested the trip in the cable car, we did get some wonderful views, and the toboggan (while not a white-knuckle rollercoaster ride) is something everybody should try.

Back at the bottom we had a few minutes exploring the huge covered market before our coach returned us to Oceana. The weather was warm and we made the most of the sunshine on board the ship. Late in the afternoon, while we challenged ourselves at the Individual Quiz our captain announced that Oceana was ready to set sail again. Overnight we would be sailing further south for the first of our Canary Islands stops.

The next two days were return visits to a couple of Canary Islands. The first was Santa Cruz on the island of Tenerife, and the second was at Las Palmas on the island of Gran Canaria. Oceana then turned northwards, but before we arrived back in Southampton, there were two new ports to visit.

*Praia da Rocha - Portugal*

After a day at sea, we arrived at the Portuguese port of Praia da Rocha. It was Tuesday 27th June, and this would be our only visit to the Algarve area of Portugal.

… it was somewhere we decided would **NOT** feature on our *'must return to'* list.

It was a tender port, and with no tour booked, our plans were to go ashore at our leisure, and take the shuttle bus to the nearby beach area.

Our journey to shore was a lovely calm boat ride but that is where our pleasure ended. A shuttle bus then took us a couple of miles to the sea-side town and we strolled towards the beach along a narrow street. It was quite early in the morning and the shops (such as they were) were just opening. They were all tourist based selling the usual beach paraphernalia, or cheap imported souvenirs. At regular intervals there were cafés where the menu boards offering all day 'Full English'. If it wasn't a café then it was a bar, and several of these were Irish themed.

To be honest, this could have been a typical British seafront shopping street... but warmer.

We were far from impressed and didn't even waste our energy getting to the beach. The only thing we bought was an ice-cream to cool us down before turning back, grabbing the first available shuttle bus and then a tender to the ship.

I am sure many of the passengers enjoyed the experience, but this place was not for us.

After leaving Praia da Rocha on Tuesday evening, Oceana made a short overnight sail up the coast of Portugal. The next morning we woke early to watch the sail in along the River Tagus to Portugal's beautiful capital city of Lisbon.

This is without doubt one of our favourite destinations.

I have already talked about Lisbon so I won't dwell too much except to say that we had a lovely morning in the city. The weather was superb, and as well as a walk in the sunshine while we explored the shops, we took a ride on one of the old trams for a different view of the touristy areas as well as the narrow backstreets.

*Vigo - Spain*

Thursday 29th June 2006 and by just after 8:30 in the morning we were tied up alongside the dock at the Spanish port of Vigo. This port on the north-westernmost lump of Spain, is just a few kilometres north of the Portuguese border. It is in the region of Galicia and has a population of a little fewer than 300,000. The city has a large fishing port, but its economy is primarily based on car manufacturing and tourism.

This was the last place we were visiting on this very enjoyable cruise. The weather was being good to us yet again with light winds, clear skies, and a warm sunny day. After our typical breakfast in 'La Plaza' buffet, we made our way quickly to the theatre to get our stickers for a tour called 'The Border Country'.

Our tour started with a brief history of the city from our guide as the coach took us through the highlight areas around Vigo. It then climbed away from city centre for a stop at 'El Castro Monte', which is a park high above the city with sensational views down to the sea. The peaceful park had pathways taking us to different levels with statues and a lake with fountains. At the lowest point of the park was another water feature including a monument created with three anchors. This maritime memorial was presumably in recognition of the city's involvement with fishing.  Down below we could see the gleaming white hull of Oceana, and in the distance a vast area of commercial oyster beds.

From the hilltop park we returned to the coach and drove a short distance to cross the River Minho which serves as the border with Portugal. This was to visit the town of Valenca do Minho, with ruins of the old fortress including fortifications, and cannon positions pointing back across the river to Spain. Along with more history about the area, our guide pointed out a rather attractive metal bridge across the river that was said to have been built by Mr Eiffel.

The town of Valenca itself was quite small with a population of around 14,000 and we had time to explore the quiet streets, and the beautiful little white washed walled church of Sao Teotonio.

Our morning out had been very good with a gentle exploration of the countryside on the borders of Spain and Portugal. We were back on Oceana in time for lunch, and then we enjoyed the last day of warm sunshine on the open decks of the ship.

The evening was Formal Dress code and the six of us on our dinner table dressed up in our finest for the last time on the cruise. The evening entertainment featured the comedian (Mike Hammer) and a Supremes tribute group of three ladies called 'The Degrees'. We also watched a few minutes of the ballroom dancing in Harlequin's, but we were not sufficiently confident to get involved very much. By now Deb and I had decided it was time to learn the basics of a waltz, quickstep, and cha-cha, and over the years we have mastered enough to join in and enjoy ourselves on the dance floor.

The next morning, we bounced along the air-bridge in Southampton, and after another wonderful adventure, it was time to return to work, and start to look at the brochures for next year.

*Final Thoughts on the Atlantic Islands*

We have visited the Azores and Canaries a number of times over the years, including fleeting visits at the beginning or end of our world cruises, and there have been noticeable changes.

The lure of generous cruise passengers has resulted in masses of development of port areas to ease the embarkation and disembarking process of the modern giant ships. The longer the passengers have on shore, the more they can spend. Where a single ship might have been in port around the time of our first visit, it is often multiple ships nowadays.

We recently returned to Ponta Delgada in the Azores and the dockside was totally unrecognisable. What had been little more than a harbour wall and road has been replaced by a custom-built terminal with buildings, cafes, bars, and souvenir shops.

The islands have visibly changed with obvious major investment in apartments and hotels plus restaurants, cafes and shops to attract tourists to visit the islands throughout the year. And there is more to do, with a far greater choice of tours and places to see, and spend money.

Perhaps some of the simplicity and innocence of the islands has been destroyed as they increase ways of extracting money from tourists. But if the opportunity is available, why turn down the income?

That investment can come from unusual sources. The waterfront of Funchal (Madeira) now has a huge hotel and leisure complex that was financed by the Portuguese footballer Cristiana Ronaldo. Without a doubt Madeira has opened its arms to tourists, and especially cruise ships. It has become a major venue for New Year's Eve with midnight fireworks that are simply stunning when viewed from the numerous ships that arrive there each year.

Sadly, we have not experienced New Year's Eve in Funchal...yet!

A fortnight sailing around the Atlantic Islands is a pleasant alternative to the Mediterranean, but something was niggling me for quite a while. The experience was different to the Mediterranean cruises, there was something missing, but I couldn't put my finger on what.

It was several years later from our first visit, when I realised the answer.

These islands didn't have the centuries of history that mainland Europe experienced. The mighty Romans and Ottoman armies spread across Europe and enjoyed pillaging and then civilising the countries as far as the Atlantic coast. They rarely found reasons to go further, especially as it might have required significant investment in maritime transport. And what did the islands in the wild Atlantic have to offer that the mainland Europe couldn't provide?

The people who did leave mainland Europe to find a new way of life some 400 to 500 years ago, weren't invaders. They probably sought a new start, and the discovery of fertile soil and a temperate climate were perfect. Perhaps they also looked forward to a quieter and less stressed lifestyle compared with mainland Europe. Their focus was all about creating what was necessary to survive.

Hence, they didn't need to build castles to protect themselves, and there are no Roman amphitheatres, or Moorish forts. Neither did they have the vast wealth, or vanity, to build palaces and huge churches. They certainly did have the architectural knowledge and construction skills to create towns and houses in the style of their forefathers, but building designs were all about necessity, and were less flamboyant than we have seen evidence of in Italy, Spain, or Portugal.

So, the Canary Islands for the holiday makers, are all about superb landscapes and beautiful beaches. They are different. There are no major historical building masterpieces, but they still have the attractions to encourage visitors to come to the islands for holidays. And tourism is probably the only major factor that has created a need to change the islands' ways of life.

Even if the islands lack serious history, Deb and I have still really enjoyed the holidays.

We always enjoy seeing different places, and these islands opened our eyes to barren volcanic landscapes that are just a few miles away from fertile tropical farms and delightful golden sandy beaches.

Perhaps there are some negative thoughts about the actual cruise as we spent far too many days visiting ports on the mainland Atlantic Coast, when we could have spent more time actually on the islands. The night-time crossings from one island to another were also at very low speeds and I suspect with a bit of planning we could have had more evenings in the ports, and perhaps even an overnight stay.

The way the cruises were organised we never really knew we were visiting islands. It was no different to being in the Mediterranean, we went to sleep after a day in one port, and woke up the next morning in another port. Perhaps changing schedules slightly, might make the cruises more fun by occasionally leaving an island late at night, allowing a late morning sail in to the next island. Then we could have looked out for a spot of land on the horizon and watch it grow into our new destination.

Of course, this is all hindsight, and now more than a decade later, the same thoughts apply to the cruises we have been on recently. All the ships are sailing much slower and a typical 14-day cruise visits fewer ports than similar cruises ten years earlier. Certainly, there is typically less time in the ports so exploring new destinations is rushed. It is all about reducing the running costs by saving fuel and paying less port charges.

What a pity we all want cheaper cruises.

Anyway, we enjoyed the 2006 adventure and our love of cruising had not diminished. The brochures were soon laid out on the table again.

*More about Oceana*

She was built by Fincantieri in Monfalcone, in the extreme north east of Italy near the border with Croatia. One of the popular Sun Class design of cruise ship, she was launched in the Spring of 2000, and initially sailed under the Princess flag as Ocean Princess. In November 2002 the ship was transferred to the P&O fleet and renamed Oceana.

Oceana was similar in size to Oriana with 10 passenger decks, catering for a little over 2000 passengers. There were 12 bars and four restaurants, plus a gym, sports court, casino, golf simulator, a spa, three swimming pools, and a 530-seat theatre.

Over the years we returned to Oceana twice more, but they were both last minute breaks rather than our primary annual holiday.

She was a ship we were comfortable on, but the decision was made to predominantly use Oceana for fly cruises out of Malta for the summer, so we only used her during the short winter season when based back in Southampton.

In 2019 the plan was for Oceana to continue fly cruises but this time with Dubai as its temporary home port. Our last cruise on her was in October 2019 when we returned to the Canary Islands again. This turned out to be the last chance to enjoy this ship, as the Spring of 2020 saw the outbreak of Coronavirus when cruising worldwide was abandoned.

Sadly in 2020 the world of cruising suffered turmoil because of the Coronavirus Pandemic. The Carnival Cruises corporation had no income, and had to sell off less economical ships in their fleet. That sell off concentrated on older and smaller ships, and Oceana was one of the casualties. Carnival Cruises sold her off to a Greek company, and was renamed as 'Queen of the Oceans'.

# New Ship and New Destination

It was still 2006, and we had celebrated our daughter getting married, and had a holiday to the Azores, but we were tempted by another offer on the internet.

We found a three-day cruise on a ship we had not been on before, and the price was a bargain.

The cruise was a long weekend on P&O's Aurora. We were simply sailing from Southampton up the North Sea to dock in Zeebrugge for a day, and then return home.

*Aurora*

Aurora was built in Germany at the Meyer Werft shipyard and was purpose built for P&O as a sister to Oriana. Aurora is able to accommodate around 2000 passengers, and entered service early in the summer of 2000.

My personal belief is that Aurora and her older maritime sibling Oriana, changed the British cruise market, and introduced a new generation of passengers to this style of holiday.

At a distance the two ships looked externally very similar, and have the same fundamental layout inside. But, five years newer, Aurora's design matched the demands of the new market, and had far more balcony cabins to introduce the luxury of a private space in the sunshine for passengers willing to spend a small amount more.

Incidentally, we saw Aurora in the distance while we were on Oriana on our very first cruise.

## A Different Cruise Experience

It was on Saturday 7th October 2006 that we arrived at the docks in Southampton to board Aurora. At the time we had no idea that this ship would become very special to us.

The weekend taster cruise was a new experience. If our memories are correct, we had to park the car ourselves, and then carry the suitcases into the arrival hall while we checked in. As we waited in the very long snake of waiting passengers, we realised that this cruise had attracted a lot of different people, compared to those we encountered so far on the longer cruises. There were several groups of passengers in fancy dress, and obviously using the cruise as Stag and Hen parties.

Deb and I had some initial concerns about just what we had got ourselves into, but we were quite sure we would have a good time as usual.

We think we opted for an inside cabin on this cruise, but the experience was only meant to be a short break, and a chance to experience a different ship. Inside the ship we felt comfortably familiar, as the lifts and corridors were almost identical to Oriana. With our very small amount of clothes tucked away in wardrobes and drawers, we set off to explore the ship.

The theatre at the front end was very similar to that on Oriana, but when we watched the shows we realised the stage had several special features such as a revolving area, and various hatches to allow people and objects to appear, or disappear, during the performances. There was an alternate show lounge (Carmens) at the back of the main entertainment corridor, plus a disco room in the centre.

There were two main dining rooms, plus a buffet that had an area for the evenings to have an extra special meal. There was also Café Bordeaux that was a bistro for 24-hour snacks or more substantial meals. Around every corner there appeared to be lounges with different atmospheres. The Sports Bar was noisy and vibrant, and when that became too much for us, we could always relax in the nearby Curzon bar for a quiet chat.

There was also a cinema, plus a nearby library with loads of books to choose from. This room also allowed passengers a chance to sit in comfortable chairs and read in peace, or alternatively use the computers.

Just outside the library was Raffles that was the coffee bar. This area had some delightful squishy chairs and settees to sink into while enjoying a cup of coffee, and perhaps a couple of Belgian chocolates from the counter displays.

At the top of the ship at the front was the traditional observation lounge called 'The Crow's Nest' with lots of comfy seats again plus a bar serving coffee or alcohol all day.

Outside there were three swimming pools, of which one had a glass roof that could be opened in good weather, or closed if it was cool and damp. Unlike some ships there was plenty of loungers to relax on around the pool areas, or quieter spots for anyone wanting a chance to doze.

Aurora instantly felt comfortable, and by the end of the first evening we were sure we would be enjoying the cruise.

*Zeebrugge and Bruges*

Somehow it managed to take the whole of Saturday to sail the quite short distance to the port of Zeebrugge. The port's name translates as 'Bruges at Sea' and is the coastal commercial port, and cruise terminal for access to the city of Bruges. It also has a busy ferry terminal and is renowned for a major disaster in March 1987, when the bow doors of a roll on roll off ferry were not secured and the vessel capsized. There were 197 deaths, and the tragedy initiated new and more stringent rules for these types of ferries.

Anyway, many of our ship's passengers were taken by a shuttle bus to the nearby beach town of Blankenberge, where a train could be caught for the reasonably short trip to Bruges. We opted for one of the official trips with a coach taking us to Bruges and a guided tour of this wonderful city.

Our coach dropped us off at a large car park, and the guide chatted to us about all things Belgian as we walked into the old city. After a brief description of the tour, we were split into groups and put onto small boats for a delightful ride around the canals of the city. The canal system allows boats to go all around the city, and through parts of the picturesque back streets.

We had a knowledgeable guide on each boat to describe what we were seeing, and to talk about the history of the buildings, and garden areas.

This was a really rather special trip on a sunny Sunday morning in a very special place.

With the groups back on the land again, we were taken for a walk through the city with narrow lanes, bridges over the canal, and fantastic buildings. Bruges is regularly described as coming from a Medieval Fairy Tale, and yes, I can understand the similarity.

Our tour then had free time to explore at our own pace, and a chance to sample the ice-cream and find a souvenir of a simple but memorable morning in this Belgian city.

With our tour over, we relaxed on Aurora for much of the afternoon, and also explored a little more of this very beautiful ship.

In the evening, Captain Ian Walters welcomed us all back on board, and Aurora set off for the homeward journey to Southampton. The evening entertainment featured Allan Stewart who is a singer, impressionist and comedian. We saw him on the various ships on several occasions since then. There was also a show from the Aurora Theatre Company called '*Oh Boy*' with lots of rock and roll songs and dancing.

The next morning we woke up in Southampton, and after breakfast in the Orangery Buffet we grabbed our bags again and said goodbye to Aurora.

We were already hooked on this ship, and it wouldn't be long before we took the first of many much longer holidays on Aurora.

*Short Break Experience*

Looking back on the experience of that weekend break, we are glad to have been introduced to Aurora, but the concept of a short break didn't thrill us.

We did go on others, but we always looked for breaks that were four or five days long to allow time to get into the holiday mood, and enjoy the ship atmosphere a little more.

A good percentage of passengers on these short breaks are different to traditional cruisers, and although we love a good party, Deb and I like to have quiet time as well, and an opportunity to enjoy what we feel is the true feeling and atmosphere of a cruise.

## 2007 – Venetian Affair

Surprise, surprise, a year later and we were back in Southampton on 6th July for a return visit to the Adriatic. One of the reasons for booking this cruise was the chance to experience yet another new ship in the fleet. We were going to spend 16 nights on the almost brand-new Arcadia.

*Arcadia*

Built at the Italian shipyard of Fincantieri and coming into service with P&O in 2005, Arcadia was the newest ship we had ever sailed on. She was the second ship called Arcadia we experienced, and it was to be a wonderful holiday on a vessel that felt perfect for us.

A little bigger than the others we had been on, Arcadia was built as one of the Vista class, and could carry over 2000 passengers with far more balconies available than the other ships we had enjoyed.

The rumours were that the ship was originally destined for the Cunard fleet, with the planned name being Queen Victoria. Whatever the truth, she became a wonderful addition to P&O.

Externally Arcadia was of the classic ship shape, but on either side of the Atrium area there were glass lifts that went up and down on the outside of the ship. Passengers could go between decks while looking at the sea views, but for those who would prefer not to look at the sea, there were internal lifts as well.

Internally Arcadia was quite glitzy, and featured a theatre with two tier audience seating. She also had the traditional Crow's Nest at the front to allow the passengers to look at the sea around them, and sip a cup of coffee, or something a little alcoholic throughout the day. There were other entertainment lounges, and bars to meet everyone's expectations.

For those wanting to sit in peace, numerous quiet areas had comfortable seats, but they were all open spaces, and adjacent to the main internal corridor. This meant there was always a stream of passengers wandering by, which might have suited my interest in people-watching, but which constantly interrupted those moments when trying to concentrate on a book. There was no official cinema, but films were shown in a conference room, where rather uncomfortable chairs spoilt the experience.

There were two main dining rooms that were in the same area of the ship, but one on top of the other. If you had a table on the upper floor, you could look down to the other dining room below, and see what the next courses looked like. At the top of the ship was the buffet for the day and evening meals, and there was also a special dining room near the top of the Atrium for those more intimate special meals.

One final restaurant was high up on the ship near the funnel. It was the Orchid Room, and as the name suggests, featured a fusion of Asian food. It became a favourite place for a special meal, but eventually it was renamed as Sindhu, and the menu became almost entirely spicey Indian food that does not appeal to my taste buds, and certainly not to my stomach.

On deck there were two swimming pools. The main pool in the centre of the ship has a retractable roof, while the other is at the rear with a vast area around it to sit and enjoy the sunshine. There was also a Spa area with a small pool with much warmer water to relax in. Sadly, this was one of the first ships where the Spa had to be paid for, and was certainly not cheap.

There was plenty of places to lie in the sunshine, and as we often enjoyed a chance to be away from crowds, we discovered a wonderful area on deck at funnel level where few people ventured. It required a climb up some steps to get there, and this put many people off peaceful periods of sun worship. We didn't spend all our days horizontal, and tradition was maintained for passengers wishing to have a stroll, with full wrap around Promenade Deck. This appears to be a very British idea, and missing from many of the modern American designed ships.

Although not something that passengers noticed, Arcadia had one major difference to the ships we had experienced so far, and that was the propulsion system.

Rather than the usual electric motors spinning huge rotating shafts connected to propellers that push the ship through the ocean, Arcadia had what are called 'Azipods'. There were two of these units on either side at the stern mounted where propellers normally sat. Each unit has an electric motor that drives a propeller, so removing the drive shafts. The Azipods could each be turned through 360° allowing very flexible control of direction, as well as speed. This propulsion system meant there was no need for a rudder to steer the ship. As far as passengers were concerned, the Azipod drive system made no difference. The ship was driven quite smoothly, and there was still a wake from the rear of the ship to stare at.

*Our 2007 Cruise*

So, back to our cruise in July 2007.

It was one of the few cruises that continued to have a slightly romantic title. It was called a 'Venetian Affair, and our captain was Ian Walters who guided us out of Southampton on Friday 6th July. As usual our departure included a band below us on the quayside, and glasses of champagne quickly relaxed us into our 16-night return visit to the Adriatic Sea.

After a calm and sunny trip south on Saturday and Sunday, we woke in the port of Cadiz on the Monday morning. There was just a morning in port here, that allowed Deb and I a chance to stretch our legs with a walk around the city. Arcadia set off again just after 1:00 in the afternoon, and began a two-day dash across the Western Mediterranean, before turning northwards to the Adriatic for our next stop at the Croatian port of Dubrovnik.

This was to be a tender port this time, but strong winds and a large swell sadly made the visit too hazardous. It was a very disappointing announcement from Captain Walters on the Thursday morning. At least we had seen this amazing place before, but for others on the cruise, this was the major highlight.

Unfortunately, the weather does sometimes upset the plans on a cruise. This was the first real bad moment in eight years, and there would be several more over the years to come.

Arcadia slowed down, and headed towards Venice. The wind may have upset our plans, but didn't affect our enjoyment of the sunshine and warmth on our unplanned extra sea day.

*Venice*

Early in the morning of Friday 13th July Arcadia was making her approach to the glorious city of Venice for our second visit to one of the most wonderful cities in the world. Today we were on an organised tour which began with a tourist launch taking us on a relaxing trip along the Giudecca Canal.

Our first experience of the day was a ride in a gondola which we shared with two other couples. It was a lovely moment, but rather crowded, so not very comfortable. We promised ourselves that when we came back to Venice again, we would have a gondola to ourselves.

Then it was back on the launch to go quite a way from the centre of Venice to the Island of Murano. It has a history of high-quality glass production, and there are several factories still existing. We visited one of these factories and watched a fascinating display of glass blowing, and the sculpting of a small horse. Impressed by what we saw, there was the usual chance to buy a souvenir in the shops, and an ice-cream outside in the sunshine.

After a ride back towards the city, we stopped on the Island of St Giorgio across the canal from St Mark's Square. Perhaps not the most visited of the sights in the city, but it was rather beautiful. All that was left on the tour was the return ride to our ship, and the remainder of our day in Venice.

We left Venice late in the afternoon and after watching the sights of the city from our balcony, we treated ourselves to a very special meal in the superb restaurant called 'Arcadian Rhodes'. The menu was created by Gary Rhodes, and the food was sensational, enhanced by the incredible level of service. There was a supplement to pay, but in those days, the charge for an evening in the select dining venues was no more than £5 each. The meal was made even more special with a bottle of champagne (real) that Deb had won in the 'Weakest Link' style gameshow the previous evening.

That evening was one of the special moments of the cruise. Deb still has the Arcadian Rhodes apron that she bought on the ship as a reminder.

*Korcula*

Overnight our ship sailed south-east across the Adriatic for a morning arrival on the picturesque Croatian island of Korcula. It was the first time on this small island which is just a few miles south of Split. It is less than 30 miles long, and a little under 5 miles across, and has a population of 15,000 people. We were there when it was quite a new tourist destination, but it now attracts thousands of sun seekers each year.

Arcadia was anchored in a sheltered bay with beautiful scenery to stare at as we waited for our tender to shore.

Being quite a small island, the choice of tours was quite limited, but we sat back in our comfortable coach which took us from the town of Korcula along the main road running the length of the island to the town of Vela Luka. Here we had free time in the glorious warm sunshine to explore, and buy souvenirs. On the way back we stopped at a vineyard, where we were given a demonstration of traditional brewing techniques before being treated to some of the wine, and a selection of local snacks. The family who owned the vineyard were really lovely to talk to, and were extremely generous with the wine and food.

Back at Korcula town we thanked our guide and said goodbye to her. Like most of our tour group, we then made our way to a row of market stalls with lots of friendly locals trying to tempt us to buy their very good value souvenirs. The smiles on the faces of the locals were wonderful, and we did our best to help the economy of the island.

Totally satisfied with a lovely morning, we waited for a tender to take us back home to Arcadia. The afternoon was a chance to relax in the sunshine before our ship set off again for another new destination on the Greek island of Corfu.

*Corfu*

It was a hot and sunny Sunday morning, and the passengers of Arcadia woke up on the Greek island of Corfu, in the city that shares its name with the island.

As I took a peep out of the cabin window, I saw another cruise ship parked across the wharf from us. It was called the Ocean Village, and I instantly recognised it as the second ship we ever sailed on, when she was called Arcadia. So from our balcony cabin on the very new Arcadia, we were looking across the concrete wharf to the previous Arcadia. I don't suppose many people made the connection, or even knew the connection, but she had been a lovely ship on which we had thoroughly enjoyed our 2001 holiday.

Deb and I went to breakfast, and by the time we returned to the cabin, the Ocean Village passengers were beginning their tours. One group were on a cycling trip, and the 20 or more bicycles had their riders kitted out with helmets, and were being given instructions and details of their tour. After a noisy group test of their bells, they set off to enjoy the morning.

We had decided to have a leisurely morning, and got ourselves ready to catch a shuttle to the city centre, and simply explore this new place for a couple of hours.

Corfu is significantly larger than the island of Korcula, and far better organised to extract money from tourists. Around the harbour area there were plenty of cafes and small shops, and taxi drivers were doing their best to attract our custom. Deb and I jumped on the free shuttle bus, and soon we were dropped off close to a fort, and handed maps to help us find our way around.

Across the road from where the shuttle dropped us, was a large green area which is sometimes used for cricket matches. We strolled across the grass to a row of cafes and bars, where locals and tourists alike were enjoying a cup of coffee at the tables and chairs. The warm Greek sunshine seemed to be making everyone happy, and there was laughter and smiles everywhere we looked.

This was not what we were after, so we continued along what appeared to be a wide marble paved street which was dazzling us. Our map had suggested we would find some tourist shops a little further on. We turned left down a shaded lane, and found ourselves in a long street market, with small shops selling souvenirs, food, drinks, and most importantly for us that moment, ice-cream. I think we looked around for about an hour and came away with some little packages to remind us of Corfu.

It was oh so hot, and we were drained. The thought of cool air conditioning was more interesting than staying here any longer.

We would come back to Corfu again and explore the fort area, but for now we returned to the New Arcadia, and watched the comings and goings on the Old Arcadia, until we set off again towards our next destination on the Italian island of Sicily.

*Messina – Sicily*

On Monday 16th July, Arcadia arrived in the Sicilian port of Messina, which is the third largest city on the island. It is on the northern coast of Sicily, looking out over the Straits of Messina towards the toe of the Italian mainland.

We landed here in 2005 when we simply went for a walk, but this time we had a morning tour booked which focussed on the hillside village of Taormina.

Tours booked from the ship are never cheap, but are usually a good way of getting to see popular places. This was one of the better trips we took, and after the 30 or so mile coach ride from Messina we left the cool air conditioning and felt the heat of Italian summer.

Our guide was very good, and led us through the quiet streets of Taormina to begin our tour. There were a lot of tourists in this quite small town, and there were occasionally a few log jams with numerous guides describing the scenes, but delays were always short, and our group was always directed to some shade while waiting.

As we got to the far end of the town from our starting point, the guide took us to the Ancient Greek Theatre with the typical terraces of stone seating rising up from the stage area. Apparently, although created by the Greeks, there is a lot of later Roman influence in the building style. The guide explained this in some detail, but to be honest I went away still unable to recognise the difference between Greek and Roman theatres...

... typical tourist I suppose

Forgetting the technical bits, the view out beyond the stage was a stunning panorama of the eastern coast of the island. In fact, the view all around this theatre was spectacular, including the daunting sight of Mount Etna (in a quiet state), and a magical little monastery village perched high up on a craggy hill.

To round off the morning, we walked back through the town at our own pace, with a chance to buy a souvenir, and an ice-cream of course. Then we had refreshing air conditioning on the coach ride back to the ship.

As evening approached, Captain Walters welcomed us all back, and Arcadia set off westwards across the Mediterranean Sea towards our final stop of the cruise at Palma on the island of Majorca.

*Entertainment*

We now had another day at sea as Arcadia sailed through calm seas. Deb and I concentrated on enjoying what the ship had to offer during the daytime and the evenings on this rather lovely vessel.

The Cruise Director was a lady called Sally Sagoe.

Apparently, she was in Eastenders for a while, and she certainly made the most of this moment of fame whenever she could. Luckily that was not very often, as she didn't appear very often during the cruise. By now we have begun to notice that the cruise directors were spending more and more time in their office dealing with the administration, compared to our experiences on earlier cruises where they were involved in the actual entertainment.

As the years passed by, we rarely saw the man or woman in charge. The majority of these people were employed because of their experience in the entertainment business, but rarely had a chance to use their skills. They sadly became a manager, and relied on the rest of the entertainment team to keep the passengers occupied.

Sally Sagoe's team of youngsters worked their socks off every day and evening.

During the daytime, they looked after the regular deck games where winners won small prizes, or nowadays golden stickers. The most regular games are shuffleboard (a larger scale version of shove halfpenny) and target quoits. Many ships also have golf nets, and nowadays even golf simulators. Usually there are morning and afternoon sessions of these activities, with the entertainment teams looking after the action, recording the scores, and acting as referees for the occasional over excited disputes.

Deb and I rarely got involved in these games, but on this cruise, I discovered another traditional cruise ship game which was cricket.

This is played in the netted tennis court that all the ships seem to have, and as well as a number of fit young men, there were a very good number of older men pushing arthritic joints beyond their usual limits. Although not very often, a few ladies took part as well.

I will try and briefly describe how the game is played.

Rather than trying to produce the normal cricket action, the wickets are put at one end of the tennis court, and the bowler delivers the ball from the other end. There are usually two teams, and one batsman at a time is given the chance to score runs against the opposing team who are bowling, and fielding. As the batsman hits the ball forwards, he scores runs by getting the ball past the lines that make up the court. The first line is one run, the second two, and the third three. If the ball reaches the net at the far end of the court they get four runs, or six if it gets there without bouncing.

The batsman typically has two overs (12 balls) to score runs, and each member of the opposing team has two overs to bowl. If they manage to bowl the batsman out, or if someone catches the ball after a shot, the fielding team get five runs on their score, but the batsman continues for his (or her) allotted overs.

After each member of the batting team has had their chance, the teams swap over.

It should be pointed out that anyone can play, irrespective of age or ability. The teams are usually picked by one person per team being given the role as captain, and they choose someone in turn to be on their team. This is a bit of a lottery at the early stages of the cruise when abilities are unknown, but it isn't long before the same small number of passengers, with the least talent, or the most artificial joints, are waiting to the end to be picked.

I thoroughly enjoyed these sea day competitive exercise sessions, and continued with them on all the cruises whenever I could.

In the evenings the entertainment boys and girls hosted various sessions in the lounges with quizzes, pub games, and the usual 60s and 70s themed night. They also hosted game shows, and on this cruise, one was based on the ITV's Family Fortunes show, and another was similar to the BBC's Weakest Link. Deb took part in that one, and this was where she won that bottle of real champagne, that we enjoyed with our meal in Arcadian Rhodes.

The main entertainment venues on Arcadia were the Palladium Theatre, the Globe Show lounge, plus the Rising Sun pub, which was just across the corridor from the Casino. The cinema was known as the Screening Room close to Café Vivo where I first realised that we could have free cakes with our coffee, and they were delicious.

I will spend a little time describing the Palladium Theatre which was absolutely spectacular. It has three tiers of seats and multiple entrance or exits. We fell in love with the balcony level where the view of the stage was perfect. There were also two side pod boxes overlooking the stage for anyone wanting to have a slightly special experience. We didn't think the view was very good from these seats.

The Arcadia Theatre Company put on five shows during our cruise, and as well as musical reviews and dancing for various genre, they had a spectacular finale show called 'Le Cirque Arcadia'. This acrobatic spectacle made the most of a stage that could have ropes and trapeze as well as movable scenery and props. We were totally amazed by this show, and I have never seen anything quite like it since. With the introduction of the standardised Headliner Theatre Team a year or two later, such shows were never possible.

One very different feature of that Arcadian Theatre Company, was that for the final few minutes before a show commenced, the singers and dancers would come out from backstage, and sit with passengers for a chat. They would be in their opening costumes and happily talk to us and have a laugh. When they heard the announcement that the show was to begin, the boys and girls said cheerio and dashed backstage.

For lovers of vocalist there were solo performances from Tracey Quinn, and Shaun Perry. We didn't bother with them, but did go and see a duo called 'Smart Move'. This pair of men were really rather good, and we saw them again on other cruises.

As well as the usual abundance of vocalists, there were two comedy-based cabaret acts. One was from Vince Hill, whose act is long forgotten, and I have never seen or heard of him again. There was also a late-night adult shows from a pair called Junior Simpson and Simon Blight. The act was definitely for adults, and featured uncomfortable amounts of swearing, and very blue material. I am not a prude, but they were on the edge of being offensive.

At least I have seen and heard of Junior Simpson since then with numerous appearances on the television.

Classical music was supplied by a pianist called Daniel Hill, and he performed on numerous occasions through the cruise.

Another pianist was Bobby Crush who described himself as having appeared in many West End shows. I have heard his name since that cruise, but have never been enthused to go and listen to him.

Finally there was a guest speaker who made quite an impact while on board. It was a footballer called Neil (Razor) Ruddock, and was really rather good, and as well as his official performances, he gave numerous impromptu moments in the bar while he showed his ability to drink a lot of beer.

*Homewards*

The final stop of the cruise was another visit to Palma on the island of Majorca. Deb and I took a ride on a 'hop on, hop off' bus and at least saw a few more of the highlights of Palma beyond the central shopping area.

That just left a couple more days of Mediterranean sunshine to enjoy, but we soon woke up in Southampton.

This was the only cruise we had in 2007, but it had visited some new, and some rather special destinations, and Arcadia had left a sweet spot in our hearts.

# 2008 – Two More Cruises

This was my 40th year at work, and although I had enjoyed most of that time, the job was now becoming frustratingly mundane. Without a doubt it was no longer a career, but just a job that paid sufficient to keep Deb and I in a comfortable life style. Going to work also meant making enough money to allow us to go on regular cruises, and 2008 would see us going on two sea-going holidays.

*Spring Getaway on Oceana*

A bargain had been spotted, and in April we boarded Oceana for a short 7-day cruise. The cruise would take us down the Atlantic coast of France, Spain and Portugal. There would be yet another return to Lisbon, as well as the Spanish port of Vigo. The only new scheduled destination was La Rochelle in France.

This was simply an opportunity to spend more time on a ship, and whilst we were more than happy to look around Lisbon again, the other two ports didn't fill us with excited anticipation.

The cruise was described as an *'Iberian Sojourn',* and on Friday 11th April Deb and I were some of the first to get on the ship and were soon unpacking. This cruise was to be unusual, as we were in an inside cabin. The captain was Julian Burgess (new to us) and the Cruise Director was Hughie Taylor who had been on our first ever cruise on board Oriana.

The weather wasn't good as we sailed away from Southampton with quite chilly early Spring temperatures and very little sign of any sunshine. We did the usual first night things, and after introductions around the dinner table to four new temporary friends, we strolled around the ship and had a drink in a bar. The entertainment programme wasn't very exciting so after our drink, we took to our beds quite early.

## Vigo and Lisbon

After a bumpy ride across the Bay of Biscay, we arrived at the Spanish city of Vigo on the second day.

This city is situated in the north west of the country, in the region of Galicia, and is almost as close as you can get to the border with Portugal. It has a history of being the target for a number of invasions including failed attempts by Francis Drake, and the Turks.

Vigo is the second largest city in Galicia behind La Corunna, and has a population of around 300,000, The economy is based on the Citroen car factory, plus being home to one of the world's busiest fishing fleets.

As I suggested earlier, this cruise was all about a break from work, and purchasing tours were not high on our list of priorities. We ignored the organised introduction to Vigo and the panoramic drives around the countryside to explore mountain villages. Not even the wine tasting trip tempted us. Instead, we simply stretched our legs with a short walk around the shopping area, before returning to the comfort of Oceana.

Late in the afternoon Captain Burgess welcomed us al back, and we set off for an overnight trip to Lisbon.

This was our fourth visit to the capital city of Lisbon, and we spent a couple of hours wandering the beautiful narrow streets with buildings covered in ceramic tiles, and street cafes tempting us to sample the cinnamon flavoured coffee and the local sweet delicacy of custard tarts.

We had already adopted Lisbon as one of our favourite destinations, and have rarely ever looked to explore beyond the city.

La Rochelle

After leaving Lisbon, the cruise was half over, and Oceana headed northwards. There was a day at sea as our ship turned into the Bay of Biscay on route for the French port of La Rochelle.

This port is on the western coast of France about half way up the Bay of Biscay, and it was a cool and cloudy day when we arrived there. We were quickly tied up, and there were no obvious issues as passengers disembarked and set off on their tours. Then, with no explanation, the passengers were being stopped from leaving the ship. After a few minutes of confusion, the captain announced that there was some industrial action going on in the port.

The authorities had warned the ship that there might be some trouble, but this had escalated, and there was a threat of blockading the port to stop us leaving. No foot passengers had been allowed to leave the ship, and the tour coaches were quickly telephoned and making their way back to the ship. As soon as everyone was back on-board, Oceana quickly released the ropes and made a hasty escape.

By the middle of the morning, our ship was heading west out of the bay. The captain apologised for the change of plans, and announced that we would be making an unscheduled stop at the port of Brest the next day. The tour's group quickly arranged some last-minute excursions for this Breton port and they were soon available for passengers to book.

This had been a different sort of morning with a bit of excitement and intrigue. We have never been back to the port of La Rochelle, so I have no idea of what we might have seen and done.

Brest

This city on the westernmost lump of France is located in the Brittany Region and has a population of around 140,000 people. It is less than 200 miles south of the Cornish village of Looe, and often referred to as having connections to the ancient Celtic areas of Britain. It is very much a military port and its location meant the city was heavily bombed during the 2nd World War by Allied aircraft.

Brest remains as a busy port which directly or indirectly provides a huge percentage of the local economy. As well as being home to a fishing fleet, the port is large enough to welcome some of the world's largest ships.

So, Thursday morning we woke up in Brest where we would be docked until lunchtime. Because of the short notice of our arrival, there was little time to organise tours, but we decided to splash out and booked our only trip of the cruise. Our tour was called 'Breton Delights' and after breakfast we were soon on our coach, and setting off into the countryside.

Our first stop was at the village, or small town, of Argol. I vaguely remember looking at some ruins of a castle or a fort, but the primary reason for our visit was a cider museum. The owner beamed with happiness to have an unexpected group of Brits to look around his small museum, and did his best to explain the process of turning apples into a very tasty cider. He struggled with his schoolboy English, and we responded with our similarly confusing schoolboy French. Fortunately his enthusiasm, plus the addition of flamboyant gestures, usually succeeded in giving us enough of an idea of what he was describing. We became quite enthusiastic when it came to the tasting session, and the language barrier quickly disappeared.

Suitably happy with the fun of the visit, and slightly lightheaded, we moved on to another village called Lacronan. This was a sleepy place with hardly anyone around, but it was beautiful. Our guide showed us some of the notable buildings before we spent an hour just strolling around, looking in the shops, having a coffee, and of course, an ice-cream.

Then it was back to Brest to return to Oceana for lunch.

There was hardly time after eating to catch a last look at Brest, before Captain Burgess set off around Cape Finisterre and up the Channel towards Southampton. The cruise was over, and although the problem in La Rochelle was rather frustrating, we enjoyed our week away.

Our batteries were recharged, and I returned to work and looked forward to the next cruise.

*Aurora – 'Ancient Wonders'*

Later in 2008, Deb and I were in Southampton again, and ready to get on-board Aurora for a summer cruise to the Eastern Mediterranean.

This was our second time on this ship, but now it was for much longer than a weekend break. Our adventure would see us returning to some of the ports from our first ever cruise, and it would be the moment we began to see this ship as being rather special.

It was Friday 18th July 2008, and Aurora was captained by Ian Hutley. The cruise was going to be spread over 16 nights, and was a bit of a nostalgia trip taking us back to Istanbul, Athens, and the island of Mytilene which we visited on our very first cruise. Along with repeat visits to Malaga and Naples, we also explored a couple of new ports with Dikili in Turkey, and Almeria in Spain.

Sailing between these quite widespread destinations meant some long periods at sea, and without actually becoming aware, we were starting to fall in love with this ship.

After just a few days, Deb and I had searched out the perfect places to sit and read, and the quietest spots to lie on deck in the warm Mediterranean sunshine. There were three swimming pools, and one had a sliding roof that was used if the weather was cold. Close to this vast conservatory with its *'Crystal'* pool was another called the *'Riviera'*, that was open to the elements with fresh air. The third pool, *'Terrace'* was at the rear of the ship on Deck 8, and partially surrounded by the horseshoe tiers, that created amazing places to sit or lie in the sunshine and stare at the ever-changing sea scape.

Our cabin had a balcony, so when we needed time away from the other passengers, Deb and I could relax in our private space with the air-conditioned coolness close by if the Mediterranean heat became too much.

The main eating venues were the Medina and Alexandra restaurants, plus the Orangery buffet where we had most of our breakfasts, but there was also one other place to eat, and that was Café Bordeaux.

This Bistro style café gave 24 hours service of snacks or more substantial meals at lunchtime and evenings. Deb and I fell in love with this venue, and we regularly had lunch there, and the occasional evening meal as a change from our assigned dinner table in the Medina restaurant. Café Bordeaux's atmosphere was more relaxed, and the waiters had time to show their characters. They quickly got to know us, chatting and joking while we waited for our food.

In the evening there was another venue for a special meal, and that was when a part of the Orangery buffet was turned into a select dining restaurant with dimmed lighting, table cloths, and waiters serving us delicious and well-prepared food from a rather special menu.

In case we somehow managed to get peckish during the day, Aurora even had a Pizza snack bar beside the open-air swimming pool. To be honest, we rarely had to resort to the snacks as the food was wonderful, and our tummies never really felt hungry.

Entertainment was provided in various venues. There was the superb Curzon theatre where we watched the ship's troupe of dancers and singers, plus various visiting cabaret acts. This was all coordinated by the Cruise Director who was called Leon de St Croix. We would see him many times over the coming years.

As a little aside to the actual cruise, this was the year when the song and dance troupe became known as the '*Headliners*'. This heralded a virtually identical group of talented boys and girls on all of the P&O ships, performing the same lavish shows.

At the other end of Deck 7 from the theatre, was Carmen's, that was another large venue for cabarets, game shows, or dancing in the evening, plus talks and other events during the day. On this cruise there was a professional dance couple who taught the basics. They were called Keith and Judy Clifton, and they had a talented son and daughter who became regular professional dancers on Strictly Come Dancing for a number of years. At that time we loved to watch the dancing, and joined in with Barn Dances, but had no idea of how to waltz, cha-cha, or rhumba. That would be addressed over the following couple of years.

Between the theatre and Carmen's on deck 7, there was the popular Sports Bar called Champions, plus the library that stood next to Vanderbilt's where you could play cards, or board games, plus taking part in various quizzes throughout the day. Just beyond that was the Atrium area with Charlie's Bar for cocktails and champagne that was outside of the Curzon Bar. We quickly favoured the Curzon Bar for a drink on formal nights, or for our regular nightcaps.

Up one deck was Raffles, that served coffee and delicious chocolates throughout the day, and that became another regular place to sit and enjoy life. Along the corridor from there was the superb cinema (The Playhouse) that had comfortable seats to watch films when the entertainment elsewhere didn't appeal.

To complete the Deck 8 venues there was Café Bordeaux, and then the children's area. Although very much for the children, there was access from here through a door to the rear deck of the ship, with a big lounging area around the third of Aurora's swimming pools.

## Malaga and Athens

The cruise itself was wonderful. It was a mix of revisiting some amazing places, plus a few new destinations to top up our ever-growing list of *'places we have seen'*.

After a long sail down from Southampton to the Mediterranean, we had a chance to stretch our legs in Malaga. From there we headed east for the next stop at the Greek port of Piraeus. We had a tour here that began with a coach trip into Athens for our second look around this historic city.

The tour began with a panoramic drive around the highlights, with stops at the ancient Olympic stadium, and the Acropolis. The coach then returned us to the city centre for a chance to wander on our own in the Plaka area to do a little touristy shopping. Around midday the group met up again to have lunch in a Taverna where, they served a traditional meal and we ate from wooden platters using basic wooden spoons and forks. It was an unusual experience and most people enjoyed it, but the usual bunch of whingers found plenty to moan about.

## Dikili, Athens, and Mytilene

Aurora sailed on from Greece, and we moved into Turkish waters with a visit to a new destination at the town of Dikili in the Province of Izmir. This is quite a small coastal town with no facilities to allow Aurora to make landfall, so it involved a tender ride ashore. Deb and I weren't very adventurous and simply took a stroll along the waterfront looking in the shop windows.

Like many other passengers, we were saving ourselves for the following day when we would be visiting the cruise highlight port of Istanbul.

In the magical city of Istanbul, we booked onto a tour that gave us a scenic coach ride around the highlights to remind us of our wonderful visit in 2000. Our guide then showed us around the amazing Topkapi Palace where we had plenty of time to explore. No visit to Istanbul can be complete without a stroll through the Grand Bazaar, where we attempted to haggle with the traders over prices of souvenirs without much success.

It was only a single day visit to this city, but it brought back more of the special memories that were planted into our minds on that very first cruise.

From Turkey Aurora took us to the Greek island of Mytilene where more memories were stirred. Unlike the busy bustling streets of Istanbul, here the pace of life was so much slower and relaxing. After coffee in the sunshine, we bought some more souvenirs before rounding off our morning visit with an ice-cream. It was a simple morning, but Deb and I smiled a lot, and we thanked those looking down on us, for the thrills and joy that cruising had brought us.

Aurora set off westwards now as the journey home began, but there were still two more ports to enjoy.

Naples
---

Next we had a return visit to Naples, and we had a day long tour booked. It began with an early morning hydrofoil ferry ride to the beautiful island of Capri. As we left the port of Naples on our ferry, we were enveloped in a thick mist, and our trip across the bay wasn't the most interesting, but as the island came into view, the sun broke through the mist, and the remainder of the day bathed us in hot sunshine from a clear blue sky.

Once on the island, our guide loaded us onto a minibus and he enlightened and amused us for the day as we gained a flavour of Capri. The main memory was of going up the cliffside of the island in a cable car consisting of little more than a plastic seat, with a chain to stop me sliding out while my legs dangled in mid-air. I would never have volunteered for this experience had it not been for the guide telling me it never went more than a couple of metres from the ground...

... **LIAR**!!

OK so I was rewarded with wonderful views down over the island plus the deep blue seas in the Bay of Naples.

After another frightening ride down the hillside, we took our much more secure seats on the minibus for the ride down the steep bendy roads to the lower areas of the island. The road is quite winding, and we began to naturally sway. Our movements became seriously exaggerated when the driver put on Dean Martin songs including *'That's Amore'*. As well as swinging our arms and swaying in our seat, many of us sang along.  We were soon ready to eat, and we had a delicious Italian lunch with plenty of wine in a small Taverna.

After lunch it was free time to wander through the gardens, and then the shopping areas.

... Goodness this island is expensive, and we bought little more than an ice-cream and a drink.

The afternoon was very, very hot, and we were quite glad when the time came for the return ferry to Naples, and the air-conditioned delights of Aurora.

<u>Almeria (Spain)</u>

Westwards again, and our final stop was at the Spanish port of Almeria.

This was the first time we had been here, and we were in no mood to do anything active after some wonderful, but tiring moments over the previous days. We simply went for a stroll around the busy city streets, and stocked up on bits and pieces for the rest of the cruise home.

We then had several days to explore more of Aurora, and to soak up the sunshine before getting back home. By the time we woke up in Southampton, Deb and I had fallen in love with this ship. It ticked all the right boxes, and although we couldn't possibly know it at the time, we would eventually spend almost 12 months on this ship over the coming decade.

## How has booking a cruise changed?

Back in 2000, we booked our cruise at the high-street Lunn Poly travel agents. That was how it was done. There was no avalanche of glossy brochures dropping through the letter box, and while the internet was available, it was slow and not widely used.

Those glossy brochures were restricted to the shelves of travel agents.

Of course, two decades ago there were lots of different travel agents to choose from. The sales assistants focussed most of their time on tempting their customers to perhaps take a weekend break in London, or a package holiday to the Mediterranean sunshine and beaches. A smaller number of their customers might have been looking for the pure luxury of a fortnight on an Indian Ocean Island paradise, but at the turn of the century, there were relatively few people considering the world of cruising.

On that sunny Friday afternoon, Deb and I chose Stafford's Lunn Poly travel shop because they were the first one on our route as we walked from the car park into the town centre, but there were a lot of other places that could have won our custom that day. There were other national companies such as Thomson Holidays, Thomas Cooke, the Coop, Cosmos, plus several others all within five minutes of Lunn Poly, and like virtually all towns, we could have opted for a smaller independent agent. Many of the companies were different outlets of a main company, and Lunn Poly for instance was a part of Thomson Holidays.

Another difference in those days was that a family's summer holiday tended to be booked in the preceding Spring, and it was often for the same few short weeks of the summer school holidays. Competition wasn't very obvious, and prices were rarely flexible, so advertised brochure prices were what was paid. Any discount was down to how much of the agent's margin could be offered to regular customers, and maybe the big travel agent companies could give more discount than smaller companies who commanded less purchasing power.

Anyway, we were unaware of possibly getting discount when we booked our first cruise. We paid the full brochure price, and thought that this was the only option. The price for that 17-night cruise equated to approximately £125 per night each.

The first real change to booking holidays came with a technological solution added to television services. In 1974 the BBC began to use a teletext service called CEEFAX. Initially it allowed small amounts of information to be slowly created on the television screen displaying programme guides, sports results, or share prices. But as the decades passed, technology improved, and it became more flexible, and forward-thinking companies (such as travel agents) began to offer their products with a phone number to ring.

Most of those telephone numbers belonged to those same high street travel agents, but now independent agents could also reach customers sitting in front of their televisions. The benefit was that it could have been a single telephone line in a small cheap to rent office with very few overheads, and hence they were able to offer greater levels of discounts.

CEEFAX never appealed to me, but I admit to taking the occasional peek to look at the prices to see what bargains might be possible.

Then the biggest, and most exciting technology leap forward became available.

It was hardly more than a couple of summers after our first cruise when the Internet became fast enough, to become the next revolution in ways of shopping for holidays.

The internet gave customers a chance of seeing pictures and descriptions of multiple sorts of holidays without a trip into the town centre. It also enabled holiday companies to provide instant access to information that could enhance their adverts. Those simple glossy photographs in a brochure changed to being scores of pictures showing far greater detail of what was on offer.

On the downside, there were a lot of dodgy companies, and even some honest ones stretched their discount too far, and after a successful beginning, went bust.

Deb and I became a victim of one company working too near the edge. We booked a cruise with a very, very, good price, but we had a phone call a few weeks later from P&O to say the company had ceased trading. Luckily P&O honoured the deal and we still had our very cheap holiday, but that ended our love affair with cheap Internet deals from small companies.

As we moved into the 21$^{st}$ Century, the cruise industry in Britain was booming with new ships, which offered far bigger passenger capacity. More passengers meant greater efficiency; hence prices were reducing, and new customers were being encouraged to try cruising.

Following the success of our first cruise, we returned to that same travel agent again for a couple of years, but now we asked for discounts before buying our cruises. It meant that our next few cruise ship holidays were actually cheaper than our first adventure. We set ourselves a budget of £100 each per night as the benchmark for our holidays, and that price continued to be achievable for many years.

Brochure prices became nothing more than a starting point. Discounts were significant and our £100 benchmark sometimes became sufficient to have a balcony rather than the outside cabin that we had started with.

Of course, P&O also had their own call centres where you could book a cruise, but they could not (or would not) offer the same level of discounting compared to those available from the travel agents, or through internet deals.

With greater passenger capacity, the cruise companies wanted to sell more holidays, and this meant trying to tempt customers to book cruises for more than the current year.

Brochures began to advertise the cruises for 12 months ahead, or even longer. The incentive from P&O was to discount fares with no change to the standards and service, if you booked an '*Early Saver*' bargain. Sadly, this sometime created unusual situations where the initial price ended up being more expensive than a later brochure price, but at that time, P&O's customer focus was exceptional, and they promised that those who booked early were never disadvantaged.

The next marketing incentive to come along was '*On Board Credit*'. This enabled cruise companies to reduce the level of discounting while adding credit to the on-board account, giving the passengers money to spend while on the ships. The sums of credit varied according to the length of the cruise, or the standard of cabin booked. The levels of 'on board credit' were quite small initially but over the years it started to become serious with hundreds of pounds per person available on the standard two-week holiday. Customers were happily accepting less discounted prices for the cruise, as it was being offset by the on-board spending money.

Remarkably, some 15 years on from our first cruise we were able to find bargains that still hovered around the £100 per night for a balcony cabin, plus on-board credit to cover a lot of our bar bills and the cost of tours.

Of course, the time came when the cruise industry generosity ran out, and the first change was when P&O severely reduced the profit margins for travel agents and specialist cruise companies. This meant that it became almost impossible to get discount on the brochure prices. Whereas 10 to 15% off the price had been possible, now there was none, and the only incentives on offer were perhaps a bottle of champagne or a night in a hotel in Southampton before the cruise. It meant the price was the same everywhere and for the first time we had to increase our budget above the £100 each per night.

Ships still needed to sail full to be cost effective, so although P&O had more or less stopped discounts on its brochure price, they introduced a new deal called *'Saver Fares'*. These generally appeared around three months before a cruise sailed, and there were far too many unsold cabins. Obviously, these bargains were rare on the most popular cruises, but when the deals came along, they offered 30% or 40% reductions for those people willing (and able) to snap up a cruise at quite short notice. The drawback of these bargains was that passengers could only choose a grade of cabin, and had to wait until almost the last minute to find out where they would be sleeping. They also came with no on-board credit, no free parking, and no choice of dining times. The restrictions became even greater when 'Saver Fare' passengers had to pay for the shuttle buses that take passengers from the ship to a city centre.

Saver Fares really did offer superb deals. Loyal P&O cruisers, with flexible lifestyle arrangements, lapped up the chance to get back on a ship, and at these prices they could afford to take extra cruises each year. The bargains also attracted even more new customers, who suddenly discovered that cruising was within their budgets.

P&O were also happy because their ships were sailing with the majority of their cabins occupied.

On a more negative note, those Saver Fares also caused, and continue to cause, a lot of annoyance to loyal cruisers who often book their holidays at the main brochure price (currently known as a *'Select Fare'*) 12 months or more in advance. They now suddenly found that instead of benefitting by booking early, an identical cabin was potentially ridiculously cheaper for those who waited until three months before cruising dates ...

... and P&O no longer offered to compensate the early bookers who were out of pocket, compared to last minute deal hunters.

The on-board credit became less generous, although occasionally there are special offers for booking during a limited date range. This has caused yet more frustration, as one day Peter might pay full price and have £200 on board credit, while the next day John gets 30% off the price and £300 on board credit.

The array of possible fare options, plus special deals, has made booking a cruise something of a lottery. It is difficult to decide if we should book early to get a cabin of our choice with all the usual services, or wait and snap up a bargain without the frills.

During 2015/2016, P&O softened their approach to Travel Agents again, and they once more had some flexibility on offering discounts. The percentages were small compared to what we first experienced, with 5% appearing to be the best on offer, and then only to repeat customers. The online forums suggest that some passengers were bettering this, but I suspect the profit margins available were being seriously squeezed to allow this.

For comparison, the price for our usual balcony cabin on an 18-night cruise in June 2016, was £5140 after travel agent discount. The deal included £750 of on-board credit so the true cost equated to £122 each per night. This price was the full brochure price for a 'Select Fare', so better deals were possible for late bookings on 'Saver Fares'.

We failed to achieve our £100 a night target. But this was for a balcony, and in reality it was not very much more than we spent 16 years ago for an outside cabin on Oriana. This price stability sounds quite amazing, but something had to give, and it was becoming rather obvious to us that the standard of service on the ships was falling, and one by one, the little treats that we used to get, had disappeared.

Of course, we were from a group of passengers that was now in a minority of the huge customer base that P&O was selling holidays to. Most of these people were quite new to cruising, and had no experience of what the 'product' used to be. The package that P&O was offering was fantastic, and the cruise industry was continually expanding to meet demands.

Once referred to as 'Loyal P&O Customers', the hundreds of generally older cruisers were suddenly feeling less wanted. Some aspects of the cruising experience offered by P&O felt a little brash, and certainly less customer focussed.

# 10th Year of Cruising

The realisation dawned that 2009 was to be the tenth year that we had been cruising. The initial excitement was still the same, and during the preceding autumn and winter evenings we regularly watched videos of our maritime adventures over a glass of wine.

As was becoming the norm, we had two cruises booked for this year.

*Short Break on Oriana*

The first was a short four-day April break on Oriana that initially took us north for a return visit to Zeebrugge, and then south to the French port of Cherbourg. While in Zeebrugge we took a shuttle bus to the nearby sea-side town of Blankenburg for a walk in the unexpectedly warm Spring sunshine. This was just for a couple of very pleasant hours, and featured a visit to a bakery for freshly made waffles.

<u>Cherbourg</u>

Cherbourg was a new port for us. Situated on the Normandy coast, it is a busy ferry port and home to some of the French navy. The port has a memorable moment in maritime history as being the last place that Titanic docked at on April 10$^{th}$ 1912 before beginning its ill-fated Atlantic crossing. It had left Southampton the same day, and stopped to pick up more passengers at Cherbourg. From there it made one last stop just off the shore at Cobh in southern Ireland where the last bags of mail and passengers were tendered from the small harbour. Four days later it hit the ice-berg and sank.

Anyway, nearly 100 years on, we were having a very much less dramatic experience, and I remember little about the port of Cherbourg on our visit. We were booked on an early morning tour that took us around the Normandy countryside of the Contentin Peninsular. Our coach drove us through the Saire Valley, and our trip visited La Pernelle, St Vaast La Huegue, and Barfleur.

It was a pleasant panoramic look around the area, plus strolls around the quiet villages, but looking at the very few photographs of the day, I cannot recall very much.

Our short break wasn't booked to fulfil any ambitions, this was a very cheap last-minute deal that gave us a break away from home. We didn't regret going on the cruise, but it did confirm that four days wasn't long enough to really switch off from work, and settle into a cruise. It needs longer.

*The Mediterranean Again*

A little under three months later, we were back in Southampton for our main holiday of the year. This time it was for 17 days on Arcadia, and the highlight would be our third visit to Venice.

Tuesday 30th June, and Captain Ian Walters hooted farewell to Southampton and our next adventure had begun.

After two days and three nights at sea we awoke to the sounds of docking, and the bright and sunny view from our balcony was the port of Almeria in southern Spain. We had stopped there on a previous cruise, but never went further than the city's shops, but this time we had a half day tour booked to visit the hill-top town of Mojacar (pronounced 'Mahakka')

Almeria and Mojacar

We were on one of a very large fleet of tour busses waiting on the quayside below our balcony. There was quite a long coach ride to begin our trip, and we quickly moved through the early morning city traffic of Almeria towards the countryside.

Almeria lies on the southern coast of Spain in the region of Andalusia. It is a little over 100 miles east of Malaga, and perhaps 10 or so miles before the coastline of Spain turns towards the north. It has a population approaching 200,000 although swells considerably during the summer because of its popularity as a holiday resort. As well as attracting cruise ships, the port of Almeria also has busy ferry routes to North Africa.

Our guide gave us the usual introductions to the city and surrounding countryside of Almeria. The coach headed north eastwards, and soon the green and commercial views turned to an almost desert like scene with imposing hills in the distance. There are hardly any buildings, and we were told that this area was where many of the Spaghetti western films were created by the likes of Sergio Leone, and the music of Ennio Morricone in the mid-1960s. It obvious to us that this made a perfect location to make cowboy films, and I thought back to iconic movies such as *'A Fistful of Dollars'*, *'The Good the Bad and the Ugly'*, *'The Man with no name'*, *'A Few Dollars More'*, starring Clint Eastwood, and Lee Van Cleef. Some of the tours from the ship were heading for an old filming location in the middle of this desert landscape to savour the experience of a mocked-up cowboy town.

The hills we saw in the distance were getting bigger, and soon we spotted one hill with a town seemingly clinging to the top. Our route was now upwards, and the road became narrower as we approached the stunning town of Mojacar. The coach eventually arrived at a parking spot, and we were released into the searing heat of southern Spain. Our guide gathered us up, and we set off on foot for a short walk to the town centre. There was no room here for the multitude of daily tourist coaches to stay, and our driver soon turned back towards Almeria until it was time to come and collect us.

Our first experience was to have a cooling drink and a cake in a hotel. It was also the vital toilet break before properly beginning the tour of this peaceful town. Suitably refreshed and relieved, the guide gathered us up and took us outside into the town square, where she found a small patch of shade to describe her walking tour. She was from Britain but a few years earlier had moved to the warm sunshine of southern Spain. I doubt she was rarely out of work in her role as a guide for the thousands of British tourists each year, and certainly impressed us with her knowledge of Mojacar, and her familiarity of what a group of aging Brits needed from a tour.

Her introduction to the town was short but sweet and she explained that the first part of the morning would be a walk around the lower part of the town, where the streets were reasonably flat. Later there would be an option to move up to the upper areas where our walking ability would be tested, but if that was not to our liking, we could simply wander around the small shops close to the square until it was time to go back to the coach.

After checking that we were all clear with what was happening, we set off down the first of several typical narrows Spanish streets with whitewashed walls adorned with terra cotta pots of flowers. The town of Mojacar has a population of around 9000, and no one rushes as they go about their daily lives. There were occasional groups of the more senior men sitting under olive trees discussing the woes of the world, and numerous ladies with baskets or bags of groceries who walked on the shaded side of the streets. The local people were used to tourists, and smiled at us as we passed by. Some disappeared into a doorway or through a gate, and there was usually a cat or dog that stirred sufficiently to welcome home their owners, before returning to their dreams.

Every now and again we would come to small squares that sometimes had a café. It was early and the only activity we saw at them was a waitress setting up the parasols and chairs for the up-and-coming lunchtime rush (perhaps). Our guide gave us facts and snippets of history about the town and nearby countryside, but she often allowed us quiet moments to absorb the deliciously quiet and relaxing atmosphere.

A few corners more, and we found ourselves back at the main square. It was decision time, and most of us agreed to follow our guide to the upper level. Deb and I had no issues with the initial climb and the small effort was worth it. Now we had views of houses that were a little more spaced out compared to the streets below. There was little shade up there, and our time was limited by the guide to ensure we didn't suffer. As well as seeing the houses from a different perspective with roof tiles, water tanks, and air conditioning units, we could also look out over the desert-like plain below.

Back at the square again, we had free time to look around the shops for a souvenir, plus a cup of wonderful coffee in a café with views out over the side of the hill. There were small doughnuts to go with the coffee, and local sparrows knew what to expect, and tamely came right up onto our table to share the sweet cakes with us.

As instructed, our group appeared from all kinds of shady spots at the agreed time, and we followed our guide back down the hill to wait for the coach to reappear. It was late, and the heat was sapping us but although there were a few moans, we soon relaxed on our air-conditioned coach for the journey back to Almeria. The guide gave us a few last thoughts about Mojacar to ponder on, and many of us took the opportunity to consider her words more carefully by closing our eyes.

It had been one of those special tours that left a particularly sweet spot in my memory, and certainly made many of us jealous of the stressless life style we had witnessed.

Back on Arcadia we had some lunch before relaxing on our balcony watching the comings and goings of coaches below us, and the cars and vans gathering in the adjacent ferry terminal before their evening crossing to North Africa. Our beautiful ship set off before their journey began. We cruised eastwards now across the Mediterranean to move into the waters of the Adriatic with the next stop in Croatia.

Dubrovnik

This was our second visit to Dubrovnik in Croatia, and our plans for the day had been made weeks ago, and almost as soon as we could get off Arcadia, we were on a shuttlebus heading for the old town.

Once we had got off the shuttlebus, Deb and I quickly joined the hordes of visitors heading towards the enormous gateway into the old town. This castle like town is surrounded by a wall that is both wide and high, and for extra protection a moat was dug beyond the wall, and some of this still exists. Once inside we remembered the atmosphere of our first visit in 2003. In front of us was a large circular stone-built construction that looks like a monument with seating all around it. I assume it was originally the town's well, but now allows visitors a place to sit and rest, and today there was a musician playing a traditional stringed instrument screeching out a haunting melody that could be heard for some distance.

The old town of Dubrovnik is a very special place with a recent cruel wartime history that tugs on the heartstring of visitors, but this is mixed with a beauty that also makes visitors smile.

Once we had sufficiently absorbed enough of the atmosphere, we made our way to a booth and bought tickets to allow us to climb up onto the top of the wall where we were looking forward to walking around above the roofline of the town.

It took us well over an hour to stroll alongside hundreds of others with the same plans as us. It was sensational to look down on the houses and gardens to one side, and then the rocks and sea on the other.

I honestly think this should be on the bucket list of any person with an imagination beyond beaches and full English Breakfasts.

Deb and I rounded off the walk with a ground level wander around the harbour area plus an ice-cream to cool our dehydrated throats. The streets were packed by now, and the sun's heat had sapped our energy. It was time to return to our ship and put our feet up after the quite exhausting, but rewarding walk.

That morning we had walked in an anti-clockwise direction around the wall, but we had already decided that if we came back here again, we would repeat the wall walk in the other direction.

Our floating home was quiet, and after lunch we made the most of the almost deserted decks to lie in the sunshine with cool drinks.

As the afternoon headed towards evening, the ship filled again with passengers discussing their experiences in this wonderful place. Soon Captain Walters announced that Arcadia was ready to set off again for a slow and steady night crossing to yet another *'not to be missed'* destination, and the city of Venice.

Venice

Our third visit to Venice, and we were quickly off the ship and on our way into the centre of the city. We were on a mission. Today Deb and I were going to hire a gondola and relax on our own as the gondolier in his blue striped shirt gently steered us through the canals. Since our last visit we had both been taking evening classes in Italian, and when confronted by the gondoliers attempting to gain our trade, I was able to respond to him in my still very amateurish Italian.

Our early morning adventure along the waterways was expensive, but delightful. The peace of Venice before the city came to life was a lovely experience. The only sounds were the lapping of the water, the occasional splashing of the oar, and warning cries of "**Olah**" from our gondolier as he came to a bend in the canal, plus sometimes an "**Olah**" response coming from the other direction.

The highlight of the 45-minute ride was turning from the smaller side canals into the main waterway of the Grand Canal, and the sight of the Rialto Bridge. The water traffic was very busy even early in the morning and the bridge had seemingly hundreds of visitors looking down on the Venetian version of traffic madness.

Our gondola ride was soon over, and we strolled along the many alleys and squares that criss-cross the city. We had an ice-cream of course, but this time I ordered it in Italian…

… and we received what we expected.

The plan for the day had been completed, and after absorbing much more of the beauty and magic of Venice, we returned to Arcadia.

That evening we set off again, and treated ourselves to a bottle of champagne on the balcony as our floating hotel gently sailed by the city, and towards the Adriatic Sea. This was most definitely becoming a favourite place, and with more to see, it wouldn't be very long before we'd be coming back to Venice again.

Split - Croatia

Overnight we had a smooth voyage, and the next morning we arrived at a new port. We were back in Croatia again, but this time it was at the city of Split.

This city is in the south of Croatia, and the second largest city in the country, after the capital Zagreb. It has a population of around 180,000.

Its history dates back to the 3rd Century BC when it was a Greek settlement. Split has seemingly been fought over by its neighbours, with Romans, Venetians, Germans and Austro-Hungarians making their presence felt. More recently it was a part of the vast Yugoslavian nation, but after the turmoil of the 1990's Balkan wars, the huge Yugoslavia was divided into several smaller countries, and Split became a major city in Croatia.

On Wednesday 8th July, Deb and I woke up to the sounds of Arcadia docking at Split's quite large and modern cruise terminal. Checking what was around us, the centre of the city was just a few minutes' walk from our berth, and first impressions were that Split was a clean and well looked after place.

We had an organised tour in the morning, so once breakfast was out of the way, we gathered our bits together and joined the hundreds of passengers preparing to begin their adventures.

Our splendidly air-conditioned coach protected us from the hot bright sunshine, and our guide quickly explained the morning's itinerary before we set off. To begin, the coach took us through the busy streets of the city before moving into the countryside. The first stop was only about 5km from the city centre at the ruined remains of the Roman city of Salona, which dates back to the 2nd Century AD, and was the capital of the Roman Province of Dalmatia.

As is always the case with ancient ruins, it can be very difficult to visualise what it once looked like, but our guide did her best to conjure up pictures in my mind. It was once quite an important settlement, with an amphitheatre, and temple. One rather obvious reminder of the history was a graveyard with an abundance of very ornate stones. We witnessed some of the research work going on here with tombs being investigated.

To make a change from the ruins, there was a villa that was very much still in use. We didn't go inside except to use the toilets, but we did wander around a beautiful garden for several minutes, then it was time to get on the coach and cool down before driving back towards Split.

The next part of our tour was a walk around the older part of the city. As we walked along narrow lanes leading to the remains of the Diocletian's Palace, there was a local band playing music that was certainly entertaining the young, but too loudly to allow our guide a chance to talk about what we were seeing.

One popular visitor highlight was a tall statue of a monk. There was a long queue of people waiting to get close enough to follow a local custom of rubbing the statue's toe, while making a wish...

... who were we to refuse a local tradition?

Onwards again, and we finished our morning with a look at the caves under the palace. It was like a small town down there, and although some of the diggings were revealing remains of ancient dwellings and markets, there were also up to date stalls and shops down there was well.

Back in the dazzling sunlight, we said goodbye to our guide, bought a few souvenirs, and enjoyed a delicious ice-cream. The heat and brightness of the marble paths and buildings was overpowering, so we were soon back on Arcadia for lunch.

Refreshed and cool again, Deb and I enjoyed the afternoon on the ship before Captain Walters revved up the engines late in the afternoon and said goodbye to Croatia.

Corfu – Greek Island

After another calm night at sea while Arcadia sailed southwards, our view from the balcony was the sun-bathed island of Corfu. This was our second visit, and the morning plan was to go and explore the Old Fortress.

There was no rush, so while the passengers on early tours set off towards their coaches, we had a relaxed breakfast, before leisurely gathering our tourist bits and pieces. With the rush over we jumped on a shuttle bus, which offloaded its already hot passengers out into the roasting sunshine. We already knew the bus would take us to a parking spot adjacent to the Old Fortress, and soon we were heading towards the large rocky hill on which the fortress stood.

It is the first thing many visitors see as they arrive by ferry, as it stands high above the old town and its harbour. It was built by the Venetians, and stood strong against attacks as long ago as 1537. Now it is a passive tourist attraction for many who want to check out the view from the top.

But beware, this is no gentle stroll.

Hot and thirsty, Deb and I finally reached the top, after staggering up a series of steep roads, followed by climbing steps carved in the rocks, as well as a tunnel. The view was stunning, and momentarily our tiredness was forgotten as we stared out across the harbour, and the typically Greek buildings and rooftops below us. We quickly realised the need to find some shade and get a drink. It took perhaps another 20 minutes of exposure to the searing heat before we found the shaded tourist shopping street we remembered from our first visit. After a coffee, and an ice-cream our energy levels were revived and a little souvenir shopping was possible before we called a halt to the exposure to Corfu's heat.

So, our visit to Corfu hadn't been overly exciting, but once cooled down in our cabin, we looked back on the morning, and were satisfied with what we had done.

It was time for Arcadia to move on again, the next day would herald another new destination for us.

Zakynthos – Greek Island

Friday 10th July, and our wakeup call was the sound of anchors being dropped as Arcadia settled herself in the bay of the Greek Island of Zakynthos. Like Corfu, this is another of the some 600 Greek islands that attract thousands of tourists annually to enjoy the almost guaranteed sunshine, and golden sandy beaches.

The official population of Zakynthos is around 40,000 people, but for the majority of the year it will have significantly more visitors from all over Europe and beyond, to swell this number.

Today we were anchored, and passengers would have the delight of tendering to shore.

Deb and I were keeping life simple. We had no tour booked, and no plans beyond a trip to shore, and then a walk around the town. Sadly, I remember very little of the island, and there are very few photographs to trigger any memories.

Perhaps a bit of a waste, but we were happy.

Homewards

This had been a very lucky cruise in terms of weather, and our journey westwards allowed us to make the most of warm sunshine on a beautiful ship.

Before leaving the Mediterranean Sea to sail north towards Southampton, we had one final stop at Gibraltar. After numerous visits here, we simply took a walk to stretch our legs, look into the shops, and have a coffee.

However, our walk this time did extend our knowledge of Gibraltar a little.

Deb and I strolled all the way along Main Street and came to another gateway. To one side there was the 'Trafalgar Cemetery' almost hidden in a little glade a few steps down from the road.

We spent perhaps 20 minutes there, just wandering around and looking at the names and stories on the headstones. It was peaceful down there under the trees, and some very ornate headstones told little snippets of history about the victims of the battle in 1805.

For once, our visit to Gibraltar left us with a few thoughts about the significance of this place, rather than the prices of duty-free cigarettes and booze.

Back on Arcadia, it was time to wave goodbye to this supposed little bit of Britain, and soon we noticed the sea begin to change to a more grey Atlantic Ocean rather than the blueness of the Mediterranean.

After two days at sea when the temperature dropped, and the water became lumpier, we woke in the bustling city of Southampton. Maybe we hadn't done too much on this cruise, but it had been wonderful. We had made the most of Arcadia and found the best places to relax in the sunshine, knew far more about its bars and lounges, and discovered her nooks and crannies. She was a truly superb ship...

... to be honest, all the ships we had been on were superb

Now, where shall we go next?

## Becoming Cruisers

We had been sailing for ten years now, and slowly, and imperceptibly, the cruising experience was beginning to change for us.

Without obvious signs or symptoms, Deb and I had lost the *'kids in a sweet shop'* magic about going on a cruise, but we were far from losing the thrill and excitement…

… it was just different

Before our first adventure, I questioned if we were the right sort of people to be going on a cruise. Well, after disappearing through the huge opening in the hull of Oriana into the seemingly magical world of a beautiful cruise ship, we most certainly felt confused, and probably appeared a little uneasy, during the first few days. It wasn't that we were not enjoying the experience, it was because we could never have known what to expect.

I remember a couple we met called Bill and Betty, who sort of adopted us on the first or second night of the cruise. After two or three days, Betty said we had changed, and it was true. We had relaxed, and had begun to accept the almost fairy-tale experience. Deb and I had settled into life on board, and the magical experiences that initially confused us, now became a dreamy normality. And as we grew more comfortable, further new exciting discoveries were embraced.

Yes, we **were** the right sort of people to be going on a cruise.

During the first few years, a major aspect of our excitement was seeing so many new places, savouring new cultures, learning about centuries of European history, and staring at amazing architecture. As we sailed between some of the major cities around the Mediterranean and the Atlantic Islands, we lapped up the glorious sunshine, enjoyed wonderful entertainment, and met lovely people. Now the time had come when our cruises were regularly going back to the same countries and ports as we had already visited, but that didn't take away any of the excitement; we were simply enjoying the cruise in different ways.

When we arrived at a familiar port, it was still exciting, but our plans were different. They involved experiencing new things, and tours regularly featured more aspects of local culture, with visits to farms, or perhaps family run vineyards. Our two or three hours in the countryside often treated us to demonstrations of traditional customs or dances, while sampling local food and drink.

At other ports Deb and I simply shied away from any of the organised tours, and after a short stroll around the shops, or exploring the backstreets, we would try out the local coffee, or ice-creams, before returning to our floating home to happily spend the remainder of the day on the more peaceful ship. It was an opportunity to throw away any reminders of work, and simply enjoy the relaxing sunshine or to read a book.

On sea days we found ourselves joining in with far more of the organised ship's activities. There were daily talks from guest speakers, or we amused ourselves by learning to do something new in an activity class. One of these classes taught passengers the fundamentals of dancing, and we began to learn a few steps. This was enhanced when we returned home and we enrolled in more formal dance lessons. Evenings in the ship's ballroom were no longer restricted to jealously watching couples moving smoothly around the room, as we became far more active and showed off our new found skills of a Waltz, Cha Cha, Rumba, or Quickstep.

Of course, a major attraction of a cruise for most passengers is the chance to lay in the sunshine. While the majority would head for the areas around the swimming pool, we sought out different places where we might occasionally escape the crowds, if that was our choice for the day. Most ships have somewhere to soak up the golden glows where the bulk of the passengers avoid. They were away from the most popular poolside spots, and maybe up stairways where the less able could not access easily.

On some days when these more secluded spots were affected by the wind, we were just as happy to mix with the other passengers around the sheltered pools. It was rare for anyone to disturb us, and we ignored the coming and going around us while relaxing in the warmth and soaking up the sunshine. Sometimes I amused myself by tuning in to a nearby conversation and listened to what people had done, where they were going next, or quite regularly, what they were moaning about today.

Many of the passengers planned their days to begin by finding a spot around the pool, and stay there until the end of the afternoon with short breaks for lunch and occasional visits to the buffet for cakes. Deb and I could rarely last longer than an hour in the sunshine, and we were often just as happy with a cooler shady spot, or even indoors in one of the wonderful air-conditioned lounges. There were daily puzzles to complete, and an endless supply of books to peacefully read, but when it suited us, it became natural to speak to complete strangers sitting nearby, and many would become friends for a fortnight and join us for a drink and a chat.

There were lots of moments when we found ourselves just looking at the changing colour of the sea, or standing at the stern silently watching the ship's wake. On so many evenings we spent ages staring in awe at the changing hues of sunsets, or dreamily looking at the moon casting its magical fingers of silver across the sea.

Cruising suited us. If we wanted daytime peace and quiet, there were plenty of places to keep ourselves quietly to ourselves. But if our moods demanded something more sociable, there were always classes to join in with, a game where we could be a little competitive, and there was rarely too long a gap in the programme without a quiz.

In the evenings we'd tuck away our casual shorts and tee shirts, and dress to the suggested standards for the night. On most evenings, the dress code was casual, with men wearing tidy trousers and shirts and the ladies in skirts and blouses, or light summer dresses. Of course, with P&O's traditions, there were a small number of nights when a more formal dress code was expected. Men dug out their tuxedo from the wardrobe, and put on the crisply ironed white shirts and bow ties, while the ladies had cocktail dresses or full-length gowns to make the ship dazzle.

A lot of newer passengers struggle with this form of 'dressing up', but to Deb and I, and to thousands of other cruisers, it is all part of the experience that we love.

As the years have passed by, we see more and more requests, and even quite forceful demands, for the formal dress code to be ceased, but we hope the companies like P&O, Cunard, and many others hang on to this custom. There is always the option to dress casually on formal nights, but certain dining rooms and entertainment venues are restricted to those adhering to the dress code.

Alternatively, the passengers who wish to have the flexibility to remain casually dressed, have many other cruise lines who will gladly give them more casual cruising holidays.

Back at home, our friends would often ask if we got bored on a cruise, and they couldn't believe just how happy we were. For some reason many people feel content to sit all day on a beach for a fortnight, but the thought of being restricted to a ship fills them with horror. Our experience is that the cruise ships offer all the same treats of sunshine and warmth, but have much more entertainment and activities available to also give our minds a change (and a rest) from the day-to-day aspects of work.

As we looked at the brochures (or the internet) to plan our next adventures, we consciously began to look for longer cruises which allowed more days at sea, and perhaps more distant ports. There were still lots of different areas of Europe that could be reached by cruise ships, and also different ships to try out. But we were just as happy to go back to familiar ports that we had been thrilled by, and explore a different part of a city, or the nearby countryside.

Deb and I were completely hooked on this style of holiday.

We had become cruisers, and after ten years of cruising, Deb and I were still revelling in holidays afloat with P&O, but we were very aware that the cruise industry was changing in a direction we weren't keen on.

# Changes to the P&O Fleet (2008 to 2016)

In 2008 the P&O fleet had a major new addition with the arrival of Ventura. This was an enormous ship carrying over 3000 passengers, increasing the P&O (UK) capacity to more than 11,000 in its six ships. Ventura was one of the *'Grand'* class of ships that were appearing all over the world, and many people (like us) realised that the days of a traditional shape with a pointy end at the front and a rounded stern were numbered. Ventura looks beautiful from the front, and is beautiful inside, but the rear end is just a shapeless slab of cabins.

Sadly, it was the beginning of a new chapter of the cruise industry. The wonderful sleek lines of traditional cruise ships were being replaced by a vast block of identical apartments bolted onto a hull. Their size, and more importantly their passenger capacity, make them financially far more effective, and the days of smaller cruise ships are over except for the high end of the market companies, at the top end of the price range.

Two years after the appearance of Ventura, P&O welcomed another *'Grand'* class ship called Azura. The fleet in 2010 was now up to seven ships with potentially over 13,000 passengers being wined and dined in the P&O white hulled vessels with their Ochre coloured funnels.

Deb and I looked at the brochures, and decided to ignore these new ships, and continue in the size of ship we had become comfortable with.

In 2011 there was a change in the fleet's small ships, with Artemis saying farewell to P&O to become the Artania with a German cruise company. She was replaced by the Royal Princess, which was renamed as Adonia to fly the P&O flag. Even smaller than Artemis the Adonia carried around 700 passengers, and took over the role of thrilling those people who like the more traditional cruising experience on small ships, which could visit smaller ports.

For several years, P&O had been moving some of its fleet to the Caribbean during the winter months, offering fly cruises in the warmth. Winter also meant that two of the other ships continued a P&O tradition of worldwide travel, and went on exotic major 100-day circumnavigations of the globe. That left just a couple of ships continuing to offer cruises in and out of the UK during the less attractive sailing season.

When summer returned, so did all of the ships. The P&O fleet came back to their Southampton base, to cruise around Europe. But to keep pace with the competition, the company decided it was time to base a ship in the Mediterranean for the summer season. Ventura was the first to be used for summer fly cruises with Venice and Genoa as her temporary base ports. This was an attempt to gain passengers who prefer their cruises to start and end in the warmth, and to avoid multiple sea days getting to and from the Mediterranean. P&O were now competing against the other giants of European cruise lines such as MSC, and Royal Caribbean who offer fly cruises. The other six ships of the UK fleet continued to sail in and out of Southampton.

A year later in 2015, the Oceana became the Mediterranean fly cruise ship, but that year also saw a more important fleet alteration with the arrival of yet another new ship.

This was the MV Britannia.

She cost in excess of £450 million to build, and offered a passenger capacity of over 4000. Launched by Queen Elizabeth II she also heralded the new P&O livery colours with a blue funnel and a large coloured emblem on either side of the bow resembling the union flag.

The change of colour scheme was slowly rolled out across the fleet and was not universally appreciated, but certainly announced that P&O ships are British.

So, P&O's UK fleet was now eight ships with a combined passenger capacity of around 20,000 people. There was little Adonia, then medium sized Oriana, Oceana, Aurora and Arcadia, plus the gigantic Ventura, Azura and Britannia.

In early 2016, plans were announced for a temporary loss of Adonia. The parent company (Carnival) decided to introduce a new experimental style of cruising (called 'Fathom) designed to attract passengers with a social conscience. The concept was that the ship would go to various locations and offer the chance to become involved in voluntary work on a Caribbean Island perhaps, or Amazonian communities.

In the meantime, P&O did not have a replacement small ship, so many seasoned cruisers expressed their disappointment with this gap in the fleet. They watched to see how successful the 'Fathom Cruises' proved to be, and many suspected Adonia would never return to the fleet.

## 2010 - Going North, and Going Big

By early 2010, my job was depressing me. After spending over thirty years at the sharp end of Satellite Communications and Digital Television technology, my role had changed into training mainly concerned with an antiquated telephone network. My days were all about training recruits on how to fit a telephone, and diagnose faults on copper wire connections.

I was bored with it.

The job involved spending more and more time away from home, with regular weeks delivering training courses in Yorkshire, Croydon and Scotland. Most of my weekends at home with Deb finished early, by packing suitcases on a Sunday morning and setting off in the car after lunch to a hotel, before arriving home late on a Friday evening after long journeys in busy traffic.

Plans for retirement were already made, and although not announced to my managers, my mental calendar had the end of 2011 pencilled in. Most of my lunchtime hours at my desk were spent working through scenarios of how much my pension would be if I quit early. The remainder of my spare time, regularly turned to my new hobby. I had begun to write a book about that very first cruise back in the year 2000.

To be honest, my new found passion for chronicling my memories wasn't always restricted to lunchtimes

Away from work, Deb and I made the most of a regular income and booked cruises to get us away from work, and allow our minds to be refreshed.

We continued to prefer the ships we had already been on, but after seeing a lot of bargain offers, and against our better judgements, Deb and I booked a cruise on the monstrous Ventura for early May.

Our decision to try out Ventura was finally swayed for two other reasons.

First of all, it was the destination, with the cruise going in a different direction for us, heading north towards the Fjords of Norway.

Secondly, on the night before the cruise, the amazing Riverdance show was being performed in Southampton's Mayflower Theatre. I am an utter nutcase for this show, and have seen it multiple times. By now we were regularly staying in a Southampton hotel on the night before a cruise, so we would be able to go and watch the show.

On Friday 7th May 2010, we drove to our overnight hotel near the dockside terminal in Southampton where Ventura would be waiting for us the next morning. Once settled in, we went into the city centre to have a meal, and then went on to the theatre. The show was marvellous, and after strolling back to the hotel, we had a glass of wine to round off the day, and to celebrate the beginning of another cruise holiday.

The next morning, we explored the shops before making our way to the terminal where Ventura was waiting for us. We tried very hard to keep an open mind about this ship, and really hoped our negative thoughts about her would be dispelled once onboard. Ignoring the external impression that she looked like a block of apartments, our first views were quite positive about the inside of the ship. It was still very new, and certainly had glitz and sparkle, and there was plenty of room as we walked along the long main corridors that wound its way like a street, with cafes and lounges on either side.

Our cabin had plenty of room to relax in for the seven days of the cruise, and there was a bonus of a balcony.

… perhaps we had been wrong about this ship.

On the first evening we explored the ship, and internally she really was bigger than we had encountered before. Although there were several different venues to eat, the number of lounges, bars and entertainment rooms were virtually the same as the other ships, but they were bigger to accommodate the number of passengers.

As on the other ships we had been on, Ventura's main entertainment venues were a theatre at the front and a large cabaret lounge at the rear, but we did encounter one rather negative aspect of a bigger ship when we decided to watch both of the evening shows. We quickly discovered that there was quite a long trek to get out of the crowded theatre, and walk along a corridor for the length of the ship to the cabaret lounge. Rather more annoying, was the fact that at the same moment as some 800 people were walking from front to back, another 800 were going in the other direction on the single internal walkway.

However, the venues were comfortable, and the shows were rather good.

To round off our first night on Ventura, we found a bar for a drink, before getting an early night.

The next morning as we set off towards the buffet for breakfast, there was a cheery **"Good Morning"** from someone coming out of a nearby cabin. The voice was vaguely familiar, and when we turned to respond, we realised it was ex-politician Edwina Curry. She was on the ship to give a series of very interesting and candid talks during the cruise.

Later that morning we found a quiet spot near to the glass roofed swimming pool, and she appeared again asking if she could tuck herself away in a corner behind us, so as to be less conspicuous.

Without doubt her talks were a major positive element of the cruise entertainment, and I even managed to give her some political news that she used in her final show. It was the day after the general election, and as Deb and I were leaving the cabin there was a news item to say that David Cameron had just driven into Buckingham Palace for a meeting with the Queen. As we passed Edwina Curry outside of the theatre, I told her the news, and it delighted her, and certainly gave her a chance to show her continued support for the Tory Party, as it meant David Cameron was now the Prime Minister.

*The Cruise Itself*

Late in the afternoon, Captain Alastair Clark revved up the engines and reversed Ventura out into Southampton waters. Our 14th cruise was about to begin.

The English Channel and the North Sea were very kind to us, and it was a smooth trip to our first destination at Bergen in southern Norway. This was a new port for us, but we hadn't booked an organised tour, and just went for a walk around this charming city.

Our morning began by watching the minor chaos of getting a huge number of passengers off the ship to get to their coaches. Ventura was still quite new, and P&O were learning new ways to speed up the disembarking process. Deb and I were quite happy to wait for the crowds to disperse before we made our exit to the quayside, where a shuttle bus took us to the city centre.

Bergen

Bergen is a coastal city on the south western lump of Norway. It has a population of around 270,000 people, which is quite large by Norwegian standards, and is the second most populated city in the country after Oslo.

It began as a trading city, with a history dating back to the 11th Century when it was founded by King Olev Kyrre. Its name then was Bjørgvyn, which means 'The Green meadow among the mountains'. As the name suggests, the city of Bergen is surrounded by mountains, but that is typical of most places in this country.

As well as the obvious tall newer office buildings, the city also has an abundance of older buildings around the quay area, called the Bryggen. It is a World Heritage Site, reminding locals and tourists of a traditional way of life, and a reminder of Norwegian houses of the past.

Deb and I spent most of our time in the Bryggen area as we stretched our legs. It was quite cold, and there were flurries of snow to welcome us to Norway. We also explored the fish market area which had numerous stalls, which weren't restricted to fish, to attract Ventura's passengers. Woollen hats, scarves, and gloves tempted many, but the most popular souvenir purchased that day was a Troll. This unofficial National Object came in various sizes, and stall holders offered several folk tales to enhance their sales.

There were several sights to tempt us to explore more, and many passengers went on the Fløiban Funicular railway up the Fløyen Mountain, for a sensational panoramic view of the city and nearby countryside. Others took a trip on a boat to see the nearby Sognefjord, while some of the less active visited the Edward Grieg House which the composer once lived in.

Our first impressions of Norway were quite positive, but Deb and I were cold, and after buying a new hat, we set off back to the ship.

## 11th May Olden

Overnight we had sailed further north and while we were asleep, Ventura entered the 'Nordfjorden'. Waking rather later than usual, we had missed the more spectacular views of the Fjord, but there were still plenty of Nature's magical creations on show.

By the time we were at breakfast, our journey brought us to the next call on our cruise at the port of Olden. Unlike the busy city of Bergen, this was just a village of less than 500 people. Olden is situated at the southern extremes of the Nordfjorden, where the Oldedalen Valley begins.

Soon most of Ventura's 3000 passengers were spilling out of the ship to invade this quiet village before exploring the spectacular scenery. Deb and I were on a trip to the Briksdal Glacier to get up close and personal with an amazing piece of Nature.

Our tour involved a short coach ride down the Oldedalen valley before beginning a quite long walk further along the valley beside the river. Our walk was sometimes flat, but at other times we were following well-trodden paths and steps through craggy outcrops of rock as we approached the source of the river at the Briksdal Glacier.

As a slight disappointment, winter was hanging on longer than usual in Norway, and the normally busy and powerful ice and snow melt river was little more than a gentle stream. There were still some waterfalls to look at, but rather than being noisy and spectacular, they were quite placid. Deb and I were still impressed with the landscape that had been created over hundreds of years by the power and destruction of a major glacier.

Our guide was knowledgeable and began the walk by describing the scene and answering questions, but after a while he became tired of his group's gentle arthritic pace, and took off on his own. At least there was no way of getting lost, and soon we caught him up at the stunning business end of the glacier where the blue tinged ice melted into a huge lake.

Various groups of tourists stood around in awe of this amazing sight, and some took to canoes on the lake, while others clambered up the ice wall. Most of Ventura's passengers were content to stare at, and photograph the vista. It was made even more special as there were passing snow showers to remind ourselves of the Norwegian climate.

Suitably visually thrilled, our guide rounded us up for the return trek. After perhaps 30 to 45 minutes we were back at the hotel where our coach was parked, but before heading to the ship, we had a treat of hot chocolate and scrumptious cakes inside the beautiful hotel. Traditional Norwegian cakes are rather special, and we all enjoyed the free snacks, but anyone with thoughts of purchasing second helpings soon realised just how expensive this country is.

Back on Ventura we remarked on how special this day had been, but looking out at the little village below our balcony, Deb and I couldn't help wondering what the local people think of the regular arrivals of the mammoth cruise ships invading their lives.

As Captain Clark steered Ventura away from Olden, we began a leisurely trip along the Nordfjorden. Most of the passengers stared out from the balconies, or hung over the ship's rails to look at the incredible sight. Ventura is a large ship, but it felt as if we were on a little toy boat as we craned our necks upwards to absorb the overpowering views of steep craggy cliffs towering above us. At lower levels there were areas of trees, but above them were just individual ones clinging to the cliff faces. Higher still and there were no trees at all.

There were occasional drifts of snow on any flatter surfaces, and then there were waterfalls that seemed to come out of nowhere spewing thousands of gallons of water down over the cliffs.

The light soon began to fade, and it was becoming cold. Dinner was calling us, and we left the stunning views of the Fjord to the hardiest passengers, as we had a warming shower before going to the restaurant.

Late in the evening our floating home left the Nordfjordan, to begin the journey home. Ventura sailed southwards towards another Fjord called the Sognefjord, and a morning arrival at our next port.

## Wednesday 12th May, Flamm

At the eastern end of the gigantic Sognefjord, we came to the village of Flamm. This one has an even smaller population than Olden with about 350 people at that time. Our car park for the day was to the side of a bay with little houses in clusters around the tranquil scene.

We had another tour here with a rather special train journey.

Just after 10:00 we strolled the short distance from the ship to the railway station where a group of us had tickets for a trip on the Flamm Railway. This 20 km journey winds its way up the mountains from Flamm along a single-track line to the station of Myrdal.

The line is open throughout the year so the journey changes with the seasons from the freezing snow of winter through to the sunny greenery of summer. It is always picturesque and a pleasure for the hordes of cruise ship passengers that arrive at Flamm each year.

I said it was a single track, but there is a section roughly half way where there a second line allows the down train to pass the up train. At this point there is a chance for passengers to get off the train to look at one of the beautiful waterfalls that allow the snow melt to tumble down the mountain side. From the memories of that day I believe there was a cave behind the waterfall which our guide talked about as being a fairy grotto.

… or maybe it was just something my mind has made up.

Anyway, as the down train passed by us, we set off upwards again to Myrdal where we got out and found ourselves in a snow-covered station. Our train carried on further from here to a station which linked up with the mainline services. It would pick us up again when it came back downward towards Flamm.

As a part of the tour, we had a snack in a hotel where we enjoyed a delicious local delicacy. It was a waffle with jam and cream plus a cup of coffee, and it was wonderful. After refreshments our gang of British cruise ship passengers went outside to wander around, and generally enjoy the snow. The sun was shining, and it didn't feel too cold, and some of us played like children…

… for a while anyway.

The views were spectacular, and cameras had a chance to capture nature's magic. Soon the train reappeared, and little more than an hour later we were back at sea-level and boarding Ventura again.

That evening, our ship slipped quietly away along the spectacular Sognefjord with towering cliffs on either side and more waterfalls, sending the melted snow into the still fjord below. While we went and enjoyed our dinner, Captain Clark set a course towards the final stop in Norway at the city of Stavanger.

## More about Ventura

By now me and Deb had spent ten years cruising. We had become accustomed to a way of life that was quite genteel with most people behaving themselves in a polite way. The holiday style was very much about relaxation, and good food, mixed with traditional entertainment that wouldn't offend or annoy passengers. There were lounges to have noisy fun, but also quiet areas to sit back, chat, or read your books.

Ventura was the first ship P&O used which was based more on the Carnival Cruises style of American holiday. It was very much more of an open plan layout where to walk from end to end meant passing through dining areas, shops, and entertainment venues. It was seemingly designed to enable, and even encourage, a noisier, alcohol fuelled atmosphere. There was hardly a spot you could sit without being able to hear music, and hardly a moment when someone wasn't trying to sell you a drink...

... and that was both inside, and out on the open decks.

We sort of settled into the atmosphere, and we generally enjoyed the cruise, but the ship just wasn't right for us.

It was a moment when we realised that the traditional style of cruise holiday we had been introduced to, was a thing of the past, and the future was moving towards creating a non-stop

Friday evening pub crawl. The new customer base that was discovering cruising in Britain and probably all over the world was going to love this ship. Life belonged to a new generation where many people had been brought up on a far higher amount of alcohol and noisy nightclub entertainment.

If this was the way ahead, we were not sure if cruising was right for us – well with P&O anyway.

Thursday 13th May, Stavanger

It was the last stop of the cruise in the city of Stavanger situated in the south-west of Norway, and almost on the same latitude as mainland Scotland.

Ventura was berthed in the middle of the city within easy walking distance of the centre, and we had chosen to go on a walking tour, that featured a stop for coffee. We had been warned about the price of refreshments in Norway, and carefully chose tours with drinks and snacks included.

I'm not sure what we did and saw on the city stroll, as I have no recollection of it. Perhaps by now we had just about had enough of Ventura, and were thinking more about getting home.

… and we have never been back on Ventura again.

*July 2010 and time for some Sunshine*

It was just over two months on from our cruise north on Ventura, and on Sunday 18th July 2010 we were back in Southampton again, to board Arcadia to get some sunshine. This was to be our main holiday for the year with a fortnight on the more comfortable Arcadia for a trip to the Mediterranean. Captain Ian Walters was in charge and late in the afternoon he powered up Arcadia's engines and glided down Southampton waters towards the warmth of the Mediterranean Sea. I have very few clear memories of those 14 days, but looking at the pictures I took, it appears our voyage started in the sunshine, and that continued throughout the cruise.

After two full days at sea, our first stop was at Cadiz, where for a change, we had a walking tour. Our guide described what we were passing as we strolled through the back streets. Our destination was a Trattoria bar where we had a snack of several Tapas dishes plus wine and Sangria. As the food and drink made us content, we were also entertained by some traditional Flamenco music and dancing.

With alcohol breaking down the inhibitions, several of the women in our group were given shawls to wrap around themselves while they attempted to stamp their feet and whirl around to the guitar music...

... and of course the men enthusiastically applauded their efforts.

It wasn't long before we had returned to the ship and were dozing off the alcohol in the sunshine back on-board Arcadia.

Late in the afternoon the ship set off from Cadiz and by the next morning we had entered the Mediterranean Sea, for another sea-day before arriving at our next port.

Without a doubt, our cruising habits were changing. More than a decade on, we had visited most of the popular ports around the Mediterranean, and looked around many of the highlight cities within reasonable distance of those ports. While we still adored cruising, and continued to be thrilled by experiencing the sunshine, warmth, and new cultures, we wanted something different.

Quite often when we re-visited a port, our day might just be a stroll to pay homage to the memories of the place, and a look in the shop windows, perhaps buy a small souvenir, or sample the local coffee and ice-creams.

Before the cruises we looked at the list of excursions and often ignored panoramic tours, and visits to Cathedrals or vast numbers of architectural gems. Instead our eyes were drawn to visiting farms where we could see how traditional life and cultures had been continued, and the choice of tour was often swung by a chance to sample local food, wine and cakes. For the next three days we were revisiting ports where we had no tours booked.

On the 23$^{rd}$ July we drew open our curtains, and from the balcony we could see the quite familiar sights of Barcelona.

Here as with our visit to Marseille the next day, we just took a shuttle into the city centres for a stroll, looked in the shop windows, while soaking up the sights, smells, and the way of life. If in doubt, there was always a cup of coffee on offer, or the sweet delights of the ice-cream.

We were never out for very long as the lure of a sunny spot on the ship was our priority on this cruise.

After Marseille Arcadia made the short journey along the French coast to the Italian mainland. On 25th July we were moored offshore from the pretty little town of Santa Margherita which is about 40 km from Genoa in the north west of Italy. Here we were a little more active, and took a short ferry ride to the beautiful town of Portofino. During the morning we relived some things we saw on our first visit here in 2001. Incidentally, on that cruise we were sailing on the previous Arcadia.

Portofino is for the rich, and although it was wonderful to walk along the cliffs and stare down at the blue waters, this was not our sort of place, and once satisfied that our memories had been refreshed, we hopped on another ferry and were soon back on our temporary floating home.

Our next stop was the highlight port of the cruise at Civitavecchia where hundreds of the passengers would be joining coaches for a day in Rome. Instead of Rome, we opted for a quiet tour around the area of Tuscania and a visit to an Olive Farm, plus a traditional local snack.

There were no dramatic cathedrals or churches, no dancing or singing, no hard sell of local pottery, it was just a few hours of beautiful countryside, a farming family proudly showing us their way of life, plus local people going about their day-to-day business. It was so different to the hustle and bustle of Rome that we had experienced in the past, and there was no stress of keeping up with the guide, crossing busy roads, and avoiding street pedlars or pick-pockets.

From Civitavecchia, Arcadia left mainland Italy and headed westwards to the Island of Sardinia and the port of Palau. We had visited this Italian island three times before, but this was our first time in Palau.

It was Tuesday 27$^{th}$ July, and this was my birthday. The day started with a tender boat trip to shore, and with nothing on the tour list to tempt us, Deb and I set about exploring the shops, and squares, and pretty pastel-coloured buildings.

We were content with what we saw, and more importantly happy with our morning out.

In the evening as Arcadia continued its gentle trip in the smooth Mediterranean, we had a meal in the Arcadian Rhodes, the superb select dining venue created by the celebrity chef Gary Rhodes. The cover charge wasn't very much and well worth it to savour the delicious food, and wonderful service. There was even a bottle of champagne which Deb had won in a gameshow.

Like several of the days on this cruise, our day had not been about seeing special places, or experiencing new things, but it was still a magical day like so many others we have had on a cruise.

Arcadia purred westwards across the Mediterranean with another sea day before arriving in Gibraltar on 29th July.

Strangely, although we had avoided booking tours at most of the ports, today we were going out on one. The decision had been made to avoid simply going for a walk from the ship to Main Street, as we really have done that so many times. So, as hundreds of passengers set off to the cut price booze and cigarettes outlets, we joined a minibus for a tour called 'Fortress Gibraltar'.

It was still one of the busy traffic moments, so our trip began with quite a slow congested drive through the town before getting on the quieter road south towards Europa Point. This was simply a pleasant drive and a chance to stare out across the Straits and the high numbers of ships going in both directions on this stretch of maritime motorway.

Photographs taken, we returned to the town and spent the rest of a very enjoyable morning looking around the tunnels that had been created under the rock during the second world war. It was amazing just how many tunnels had been created with garrison accommodation, ammunition dumps, and a hospital. Except for ammunition, most things were left as the military units left in the late 1940s, and it was quite poignant to spot names scratched or chalked into the rock, of the soldiers who had lived and worked there.

Every few minutes we would pop out from the sparsely lit tunnels into the sunshine of a lookout position, or where a gun had been mounted. The views were spectacular of the town below, and in one direction was the airport with planes preparing for journeys, but quite a strange view was looking down on the cemetery with rows and rows of headstones.

Late in the afternoon, our temporary home set sail again with a noisy deck party on the rear deck, playing loud patriotic music accompanied by even louder dodgy singing. Deb and I are not fans of sail away parties, especially those proclaiming our Britishness. In the early days of our cruising, we had been to a few, but the events have become just another excuse to sell alcohol.

It was time for Arcadia to leave the Mediterranean Sea and begin the northerly courses home towards Southampton. Over the next two days, the sunshine lost a lot of its warmth, and the sea began to remind us of its strength. Then early on Sunday 1st August we woke to the familiar clanking sounds and dockside transport, as our baggage was offloaded, and supplies began to arrive for the next cruise.

It had been a simple, but lovely cruise, and confirmed our thoughts that Arcadia was a totally nicer ship to be on compared to our experience of Ventura. We likened that ship to a floating version of a land-based resort, rather than a traditional cruise holiday.

It was time to look at the brochures again, and stick to our favoured ships.

Of course, we already had one really special cruise planned and booked. That was the 99-day World Cruise that would be whisking us around the globe in January 2012.

## 2011 - Our Lives were Changing

This was going to be a very special year.

Yes, we had a cruise booked for the end of May on Aurora, but this year there were rather more important, and exciting things on our mind. As the winter turned into spring, our thoughts were turning more and more to retirement.

This year I would be 60, and eligible to take early retirement from BT with my company pension. I had been with the company for 43 years, and while I had enjoyed many wonderful years, the last decade had been frustratingly boring, and my body was beginning to show noticeable signs of arthritis. Deb and I had spent many Saturday evenings discussing our futures over a bottle of wine, and a decision was made. Deb would quit her job in the autumn, and although I could have retired after my birthday in the July, I would work on until virtually the last moment of the year to maximise my earnings.

There were a couple of reasons for delaying my retirement.

To celebrate our retirement, we had booked a world cruise leaving the UK in January 2012, and there were a lot of extra things that would need to be paid for, so those additional four or five months' salary would cover them.

Secondly, I was keeping quiet about the date I would be leaving in the hopes that BT would offer me a package to leave the company. The company was downsizing and almost everybody was being offered a generous lumpsum and enhanced pension, if we left before reaching the traditional retirement age of 65. Around the office where I was working, perhaps 50% of the people I worked with had already taken an offer, or would soon be offered one.

Most people knew about our plans for a world cruise, but the dates were being kept quiet. At my salary level, I was almost certain to be made an offer, and I was voicing my interest to the management on a regular basis. If the offer came along, it would make our lives far more comfortable, and would certainly pay for our circumnavigation of the globe.

Our world cruise had been booked for several months, and as it got closer, our preparations became more intense. One of the major challenges was finding travel insurance. For the previous eleven years of cruising, we had taken out insurance from various companies, and the policies were quite inexpensive. Things were different now, with a 99-night cruise going to a serious number of destinations, of which some were not favoured by insurance companies. In my usual way, I checked with different companies on line, but few seemed keen on our mega-journey.

Eventually it came down to two different companies, but I didn't have 100% confidence in booking the insurance on line. I rang the companies, and had quite amusing, and time consuming, phone calls with agents. The basics were identical to policies in the past, but when it came to duration, and countries being visited, the conversations became a little complicated. One problem was that I didn't always know where some of the destinations were, and I had to refer to worldwide google maps to match ports with countries.

Once the itinerary was sorted out, it came to the quotes. By the time I had the second quote, I managed to suppress the gasp of financial distress, but that insurance was going to be very expensive. There was no way of ignoring the insurance, and after a few days to stop my hands from shaking, the premium of more than £700 was paid.

Another quite unusual problem was what to do with Twiggy, our much-loved cat. The idea of putting her into kennels for over three months, was horrendous, and we wondered if we could find someone to look after her.

Then at Easter, Twiggy took matters into her own paws.

Out of the blue she became ill, and after a visit to the vet it was diagnosed as a kidney issue. Less than a week later, and after various attempts at easing her pain, Deb took her into the vet for the last time, and Twiggy was put to sleep in her arms.

Bless you Twiggy, and thanks for all the lovely moments you gave us.

## 2011 Summer Cruise

Early in the summer of this year, there was a break in the preparations for that world cruise. It was time to go on our summer holiday.

On Saturday 21$^{st}$ May, we woke up in the Holiday Inn hotel in Southampton. By this stage of our cruising experiences, we were booking a package at this hotel that gave us an overnight stay before the actual cruise, plus car parking, and taxi trips to and from the terminal. This made our holiday less stressed, and a much simpler process on cruise departure morning.

Anyway, after a less than healthy breakfast, we had our customary stroll around the West Quay shopping centre, where we often bought that *'**Oh dear we've forgotten to bring**….'* items. There was also plenty of time for a cup of coffee, before returning to the hotel to await our taxi for the short drive to the cruise terminal where Aurora was waiting for us.

Early as usual, we joined the short queue in the 'Priority' lane to make the most of our loyalty status with P&O. Then while I sat with the hand luggage on the seats, Deb went to the free magazines rack for a handful of holiday reading. Almost immediately, the *'bing bong'* announcement said that we could now board the ship. This was our 16$^{th}$ cruise, and Aurora was fast becoming our favourite, and very familiar ship.

We also had the bonus thought, that in seven months' time, we would be back on Aurora again for that world cruise adventure.

Our summer cruise began with three sea days as we sailed down the Atlantic coast of Europe, and turned into the Mediterranean. Our first port was on Wednesday 26th May at the island of Majorca and the city of Palma. After bumping around in the ship for three days, it was pleasant to take a shuttle into the centre and stroll around the shops and sights. It was a warm and sunny day, and it felt so good to be back on holiday in the Mediterranean, after a long British winter.

From Majorca, Captain David Pembridge sailed east across the beautiful waters for a day before docking in the port of Catania on the Italian island of Sicily. It was time for a tour, and after breakfast we prepared ourselves for a trip titled 'Etna Lava and Wine'.

It was a rather pleasant morning out in the sunshine as we explored a little bit more of Sicily. We started with a coach ride to the town of Zefferana where our guide showed us around the quite small town with a pretty church near to a park, with its glorious fountain that sparkled in the sunshine. Back on the coach we moved a little further up the slopes of Mount Etna which still regularly announces its volcanic power to the world, but not that day.

The guide took us on another walk to where a previous lava flow ended. It showed the destruction caused by the lava that swept away everything in front of it. The local people have built a shrine at the point the lava stopped as a thanks for being saved.

A little way from there we came to a farm that had started to recover from the volcanic destruction, by breaking down the lava into workable soil, and planting grape vines. We were shown the newest plants and then others approaching bearing fruit, and finally the established plants that were producing the year's crop.

The farmer's daughter than showed us around the production sheds, with vats, bottling plants, and packaging in full swing. As established cruisers, we smiled at what we saw, knowing there would soon be a chance to taste the wine. Sure enough, we were soon seated at benches sampling several glasses of the wine produced, and accompanied by local delicacies of bread, cheese and olive oil.

What a simple, but wonderful morning.

Back on Aurora, we enjoyed the afternoon in the sunshine as our alcoholic jumbled heads recovered.

*Checking Out Aurora*

Deb and I did our best to explore as much as possible of Aurora on this cruise. In a few months' time she would become our home for nearly 100 days. The balcony cabin we were in, was identical to what we had booked for the world trip, so we looked long and hard at storage space, and potential wall space to hang a map plus the mass of paperwork that a cruise generates.

We realised that the wardrobe and drawer space would easily be overloaded with the clothes we'd be bringing. So, one morning we went and had a chat with the future cruise officer, and asked what the price would be if we changed to a larger balcony cabin for the cruise in January. We managed to keep straight faces when the quote came back that it would be another £6000.

... never mind, we'd have to keep some of our clothes in the suitcases under the beds.

Around Aurora we investigated every bar, and lounge, plus all the various places to sit. This was our third cruise on the ship, and we already had a number of favoured spots to simply sit and read, but new places were discovered, and more comfortable sofas and chairs were tested.

Outside we checked out all the sun worshipping spots to give us more choices to suit our moods. Sometimes a place by the outdoor pools was perfect, but on other occasions a quieter bit of deck was needed.

*The remainder of the Cruise*

There was also a lot of time simply enjoying the ship and the cruise. From Sicily we sailed north to the Greek island of Cephalonia in the Ionian Sea. This was the only time we have visited this island, but Deb and I set off for a simple wander along the waterside to look at the shops.

Around a corner we came upon a land train, so we paid a few Euros and had a ride around the town. It was rather fun, with the driver blowing his whistle and clanging his bell to announce the train was coming. At one point we passed by a group of noisy people with placards and banners complaining about something, but we never found out what their protest was about.

From Cephalonia we sailed further north to Dubrovnik where we had the planned anti-clockwise walk around the old city walls, and explored the rather pricey souvenirs in the shops below.

The next stop on this delightfully warm cruise was Venice, and our day consisted of a gentle stroll around this delightful city. We treated ourselves to a very expensive cup of coffee in a café on the canal side within a few metres of the Rialto Bridge. Somehow the cost was worth the experience of becoming the subject of the photographs being taken by the visitors. Our morning in this magical city ended with a pizza lunch in a café set back an alley or two from St Mark's Square...

... Delicious!

From Venice we began the journey homewards with a call at the Croatian island of Korkula. We had been here before, and knew a tour would be a way of getting to know a little bit more of the culture. Our trip was titled a 'Korkula Village Experience' featuring a Pasta making demonstration, plus wine tasting and a traditional lunch. The morning was rounded off with half an hour to explore the souvenir stalls in the market.

After two days at sea, we had our final stop at the rather familiar city of Cadiz. We are very comfortable here and strolled to the shops, and sat in the shade with a cup of coffee watching the tourists.

Now it was time to head north to Southampton. The sea became bumpy, the temperature dropped, and sunshine less appealing. There were two days at sea to explore and check out the last few details of Aurora before we arrived home on Monday 6th June.

The fortnight away had been a wonderful break from work for us, and really helped with our planning and preparation for the adventure to come in seven months.

# Final Preparations for the World Cruise and Retirement

Back home from our cruise on Aurora, Deb and I didn't have to look at the brochures to find the next cruise. It was already chosen, and before we knew it, we would be paying the balance for it.

In the meantime, there were more aspects of that three-month cruise that had to be addressed. I think my next major task was to sort out travel arrangements between home and Southampton. There was no way we could leave the car in a hotel car park for that sort of duration.

We considered making use of the P&O organised coach system, but the nearest pick up and drop off point to us in Staffordshire was some 30 miles away. Another option considered was to book a taxi which wasn't working out to be overly expensive. There were also companies around the docks that offered long duration secure parking, and they worked out cheaper than a taxi ride. Unfortunately, at that time a lot of these parking companies were getting bad press because of rogues. Finally we looked at the idea of hiring a car for the journeys, and that was probably the least expensive, and least stressful option.

So, having already committed to well over £20,000 for the cruise itself, plus some £700 for travel insurance, we now added another £300 to our adventure's cost.

... and we knew there was a lot more to do yet.

A little bit less expensive few hours of organisation that needed to be done, was to sort out visas. We were lucky that there were no major obstacle countries on our journey, but India was certainly a time waster. They needed documentation to be organised with photos, and sent off for ratification, plus a chunk of money of course. Elsewhere we had to get entry permission for the USA and Australia, but most other countries would be addressed on board the ship as we visited them.

While the cruise was using up a lot of our attention, there was a little matter of retirement to sort out. Deb had already told her employers that she would be leaving at the end of summer, although they pleaded with her to simply take a career break for the cruise and come back. She was not convinced, and retirement, meant retirement. I was continually being asked by my management if I would be retiring, and when, but I lied a little by saying I wasn't sure yet.

To be honest, by then I had worked out how much annual leave I would be entitled to by the end of the year, then factored that in to a planned final retirement date at the beginning of December. I would be taking the three weeks annual leave in November, so I began to ensure I was not being scheduled to run any courses during that period.

With these plans organised, we realised that with retirement, we could get rid of one of our cars before we went on the cruise, so I spent some time at our garage discussing ideas.

Eventually after deciding on using a hire car to go back and forth for the cruise, we came up with a cunning plan.

The first car would be sold to the garage as soon as our retirement began. Then on the day we left for Southampton to begin the cruise, I would drive the remaining car to the garage and hand it over to them. I would then walk to the hire car depot and pick up the hire car. When we returned three months later, the garage would have a brand-new car waiting for us to buy.

Yes, there were some quite radical actions organised for this cruise.

As summer was in full swing, another major outlay came along, that was not connected to cruising. We bought a flat in nearby Cannock and this would be our son's new home. It was initially planned to be an investment for our retirement, but our son was never forced to pay the going rate to live there, it was a solution to make sure he was housed and secure for the future.

I have forgotten to mention, that Deb and I were really very excited by now.

The end of summer also meant it was time to pay the balance for the cruise. We were able now to see if our estimates while planning the adventure were close to the reality. Of course we had spent more than we initially considered, but this was going to be a very special holiday of a lifetime.

As weeks passed we bought various new clothes, ordered a stock of prescription medicines, and covered our spare bed with deodorants, shampoos, conditioners, plasters, mosquito spray, magic creams, a huge map of the world, spare batteries, torches, a small kitchen sink, and a new set of suitcases to put things in.

There was just one more major thing that needed organisation.

The house insurance company needed to be informed about the house being empty for such a long time. Amazingly, they accepted the risk as long as we adhered to some rules. This meant ensuring that no major repairs were anticipated while we were away, keeping the heating on a low setting at all times, and organise regular visits by someone who could be trusted to inspect the house. Even more surprisingly, they didn't ask for any increase in the premium.

There was also a very special moment in 2011.

As Autumn approached, I was finally happy with my very first book, (**'A Cornishman Goes Cruising'**) and it was self-published to the world. I received my first royalties in October, and felt so very proud. When years and years ago, I began writing this quite short book, it was just a bit of fun, and I never thought it would ever be available for other people to read. But now it was out there, advertised on Amazon, and people were buying it. Of course thoughts were forming in my head that this world cruise might be the subject of a second book.

To help with book sales, I decided to create a blog to advertise my book, but it also became the diary of that cruise around the world. Titled '**Around the World without Wings**' the blog became quite popular with the cruising fraternity. I continued posting on that blog until 2016, and it was viewed at least 500,000 times. Not bad for a cruising blog. The entries about the world cruise became the basis of the second of my books, and shared the blog title. I feel this was the best book I have written, and sales have certainly exceeded the others.

In October I finally told my manager that I would be retiring in the first week of December, and that I would be on leave for most of November. I never did receive an incentive cheque, but to make it even worse, as I was signing the resignation paperwork, a couple of my colleagues in the office were smiling with delight at having been given their payoffs.

Undeterred, my daytimes through November were spent tidying up the garden, and repairing odd niggly bits and pieces around the house. In the evenings Deb and I read through the holiday documentation, and studied the tours on offer as we would progress around the globe.

Those tours were so exciting, and to be sure of not missing out on some of the most exclusive, we booked them in advance. The bank balance took another hit, but we knew there was virtually nothing left to buy now.

During the first week of December, I returned to work for the final couple of days. My desk was cleared, and I took away a pretty good stock of second-hand pens, pencils and stationery that has kept us supplied with most things ever since. I had worked for BT for 43 years, and even though the last decade hadn't been stimulating, I had enjoyed my career. There were lots of wonderful memories and I met some amazing people. The last day was both exciting and sad as I said my goodbyes, and let people know what would be happening in just four weeks. My farewell gift from my workmates was a kindle reader, and it became invaluable on the world cruise, and I'm still using it a more than a decade later.

As I picked up my brief case for the final time, shook hands with my manager, and handed over my identification card, I left the office with a huge smile on my face, but just a few tears in my eyes.

It was time to move into the next phase of my life.

# Around the World Without Wings

On the 3rd January 2012, Deb and I set off from our home in Staffordshire to sail around the world.

The cruise began with a night in the Holiday Inn hotel in Southampton before boarding the ship the next morning. The next three months rate as being the third most amazing '**wow**' moment in my life after the experience of getting married to my wonderful Deb, and the arrival of our children, Andrew and Lynsey.

I have a serious fear of flying, and having been forced to fly to and From America with my work in the early 1980s, I vowed I would never go on a plane again. So, these next three months were going to give me experiences of visiting countries I thought would never be possible. Without a doubt my life changed on that world cruise, and so many things on a bucket list of life's adventures were fulfilled.

At around midday on the 4th January we boarded the Aurora at the Mayflower cruise terminal in Southampton. Deb and I were among some 800 passengers that would be sailing completely around the world, covering some 33,000 nautical miles, crossing the three major oceans, visiting 35 ports in 26 different countries.

This was not a holiday; it was an adventure.

I should explain that although our adventure was described as a 'World Cruise', it was actually split into five sections (or sectors) with a major port to end each one. These sectors could be booked as separate cruises, so alongside the 800 of us completing a full circumnavigation of the globe, another 1000 or so people who would be just staying for one or two of these sectors. This meant we saw different people around the ship every three or four weeks, and temporary friendships were forged as we progressed around the world.

Having written over 110,000 words about this adventure, it is impossible to precis those three months into something short enough for this book. I will however try to give you a flavour of my most memorable recollections of more than six months of planning, three months of the actual magic, and a decade since with so much still bright and sharp in my mind.

A world cruise is not something a lot of people undertake. Let's be honest, one of the major obstacles is the cost, but being away from home for over three months also puts a lot of dreamers off. Although the thought of a world cruise might be appealing, it probably doesn't appeal to the modern cruisers who enjoy a fortnight of partying on a floating hotel, and visiting glitzy cities in the sunshine almost every day. Crossing an ocean is not quick, so there are long periods when the view from your balcony, or from the side of the ship, is simply water. You might not even see another ship for days let alone a port. I overheard a comment from a somewhat frustrated lady passenger as we approached our first Caribbean Island, "*If I had known there would be this many sea days on the cruise, I'd never have booked it*".

I can only assume she never really studied the brochure.

Deb and I were already comfortable with sea days, and we both spent hours simply watching the ever-changing water go by. From the often-angry sea of the North Atlantic, we soon came to the more predictable southern waters as we neared the equator. The colour changed from greys to splendid blues reflected by the clear skies above us. Jumpers and trousers were exchanged for shorts and the thinnest T shirts in our wardrobe.

There were thrills as we made arrivals at new ports in new countries. The sheer amazement of steel and glass cities such as San Francisco, Auckland, and (of course) Sydney, were matched by the simplicity of a Pacific Island thousands of miles from their neighbour with local people beaming at us for visiting their homelands.

And yes, the people were different as we progressed westwards. Most were pleased to see us, and excitedly came out to greet us. I saw so many different cultures from typically business-like lifestyles of cities, to laid back islanders, ever smiling people of south eastern Asia, and the mysterious less open people of the Middle East.

On board the ship, those of us going completely around the world were treated so well by the crew, and we became friends meeting up for morning coffee, evening glasses of wine over a quiz, or while practicing our amateurish dancing skills. Perhaps we were viewed with suspicion by those just sampling a sector, and a regular question was about a reluctance by us to be partying each night. The answer was simply that this wasn't a holiday, it was a voyage of discovery...

... and we wanted to have a working liver when we got home

While I tapped away at the keyboard writing these last few paragraphs, more flashbacks of those weeks have crawled out of the distant nooks and crannies of my mind. I can still visualise faces of our dining table mates and the hard-working waiters, plus people who regularly sat near us at quizzes, or during the shows. I still feel the warmth of the sea on the Pacific Islands, and the joy of walking among tropical fish. I even remember snippets of conversations, perhaps about the occasional bad moment where a port had to be missed, or talking about a less than exciting cabaret show, but mainly I remember the joy at each new experience, the smiles, the laughter, and the sheer thrill as my mind was expanded by that adventure.

That is as much as I am going to write about that cruise. For anyone that might be interested in taking such an adventure, or just curious about how we spent those three months, the book (Around the World without Wings) is still available.

I regularly think back to those three months in 2012, and smile with delight at the places we visited, the different cultures we sampled, and the wonderful people who shared our voyage.

Yes, there were some not so good times as well. We missed one or two ports, there were periods of bad weather, and there were even drug smugglers using the ship. But those bad times have been hidden in the vast mountain of good times.

The only problem was that as soon as we got home, our thoughts turned to how we could afford to repeat the experience.

# The Remainder of 2012

Even after spending the first three months of 2012 away on our world cruise, we were soon itching to get back on a ship again, but 2012 had another very special moment.

It was the Summer Olympics held in London.

Some of my earliest memories of life were listening to sport on the radio, that then came to life with television. Sadly, I never became any good at sport, but loved to try it out, or simply watch it. The Summer Olympics were a very special moment every four years, and I would be glued to the television for hours.

This year it was going to happen less than 200 miles away from us.

I volunteered to be a 'Gamesmaker' and went to Coventry one morning to be interviewed. I was successful and offered the chance to work at the Olympic Pool. Then the bombshell was dropped when we were told we would have to organise and pay for our own accommodation in London.

Now retired, my pension was good, but not excessive, our savings were earmarked for our future, so my opportunity to actually be at an Olympic Games had to be turned down.

Our daughter, Lynsey, had similar ambitions and just like me, was offered the chance to work at the Swimming Pool. She accepted this lifetime dream, and we helped her just a little. It was my chance to ensure she has something to tell her children one day.

It was my birthday on the day that the games commenced, and when the Opening Ceremony began that evening, I had tears in my eyes to see what was happening so near to us. I was delighted that there was so much sport to watch on the television, but for the first week I concentrated on looking at the swimming, perhaps hoping to spot Lynsey, but also hoping that we would win some medals.

In the weeks leading up to the Olympics, I was so disappointed at not actually getting to the games, that my attention was easily drawn to offers in the newspaper for cruises. After discussion with Deb, the decision was made that perhaps getting away during the Olympics might be a good idea. The offers were really very good, and we found a number of possible cruises to consider.

So, on the evening of what was to become known as Super Saturday of the Olympics, we were in our usual hotel in Southampton ready to set off again on Aurora the next day. We watched the TV and saw Britain winning a magnificent haul of medals. I hoped it was a good omen for the remainder of the Olympics, and also our cruise.

The cruise we chose turned out to be one of the cruises that Deb and I especially enjoyed. It was on a very familiar ship, but the destinations, plus the friends we made, brought so much more to the experience.

# Baltic Cruise on Aurora – August 2012

With millions of people closely following the Olympics, there was a minor glut of unsold cruise ship cabins for the sporting weeks. It didn't take us long to be attracted to the vast number of adverts for some quite spectacular offers. Glancing on the Internet at some of the bargain cruises, we discovered a couple of alternatives that appealed to us. Both were going at virtually the same time to the Baltic region where we had never been before. One was on the Oriana whilst the other was on Aurora. After some discussions we decided the offers were too tempting, and chose to return to Aurora and remind ourselves of the ship that had become our temporary home on the World Cruise.

So, on the 4$^{th}$ August Deb and I packed the car and drove to Southampton and stayed overnight at the Holiday Inn. As well as the familiar hotel we also went for an early evening meal at the usual Italian restaurant, before going to the Mayflower Theatre to watch the 'We Will Rock You' show. This was something neither of us really expected to enjoy, but by the end we were up on our feet clapping along with the several hundred other people in the audience, and shouting out for the encore version of 'Bohemian Rhapsody'.

One memorable moment of humour occurred before the show started. As we sat in anticipation, we overheard the family group behind us discussing the show. The father figure asked his wife and two teenage children if they knew what **'hits'** the band Queen had recorded. Expecting some form of list to be recited, Deb turned to me in shock when there was total silence. None of them had any idea of Queen songs which was seriously disturbing when the stage curtain had the name of the show projected onto it, that I assumed would have been a bit of a giveaway.

When near the end of the show, 99.99% of the audience stood, clapped, and waved their arms in unison to "**We will - We will - Rock You**", I peeked behind me to see this family unit sitting in some confusion at the scene around them.

... perhaps they chose the wrong show

When we came out with the memorable music ringing in our ears and smiles on our faces, we returned to the hotel and had a quick nightcap before going to bed. It had been a wonderful evening.

The next morning (5th August) our pre-cruise routine began with suitcases being returned to the car before walking around the shopping precinct of Southampton. We had a cup of coffee, then finished our shopping by buying chocolate and a bottle of champagne for the cabin fridge. By 11.30 we had returned to the hotel, and were jumping into the car for the short drive to the Mayflower terminal, and the good ship Aurora.

This was our first experience of being at a loyalty level in the Peninsular Club, that gave us priority boarding, and a reasonably exclusive luncheon in the Carmen's show bar. We did our best to be polite, but soon gave in to the free champagne (ish) to get us in the mood for our twelve-day holiday.

Soon our cabin was ready, so we made our way down the usual confusing maze of corridors...

... Is it left at the bottom of the stairs, or right?

For this relatively short break cruise, we had booked a simple outside cabin low down in the ship. We decided the trip was more important than having a private place to sit outside, and with very few sea days, plus the weather not expected to be very good, our choice was perfectly adequate. It was initially a little strange looking out of the window at almost quayside level compared to recent holidays, where we stared down from balconies seemingly the height of a cliff above the ground, but we soon got used to it.

Suitcases were found outside the cabin door and quickly unpacked. Next we strolled around the familiar decks and lounges, but it was soon time for the muster station drill and safety chat. That went quite quickly with only a few freaky people insisting on wearing the lifejackets for the complete session...

... and not a single whistle was blown.

It was time now for sail away and we went up on deck to savour another free Peninsular treat glass of champagne

Things had changed since our world cruise, and for the first time there was no band to play the jolly seafaring tunes on the quayside as we waited to cast off. The captain announced we were ready and after a quick hoot of the horn, a tug helped us leave the dock and we glided down the Solent. This was the third time we turned left at the Isle of Wight, making our way east along the Channel and then north for our trip to the Baltic Sea. Our cruise would be visiting several Scandinavian and Baltic cities, including a highlight stop overnight in St. Petersburg.

Time for dinner, and our table was for eight with a nice mix of mainly experienced cruisers, although not all regular customers of P&O. We were quickly drawn into conversation about previous trips, and that unfortunately opened the flood gates for us with too many stories about the world cruise to tell. I am sure we didn't make the best of impression initially, but they did ask the question. To be fair one of the other couples was rather enthusiastic about expressing their preference for Thomson cruise ships, and over the days to come, we learnt that apparently, the choice of food is wider, the entertainment is better and the crew are far friendlier. We were not convinced and will stick to the P&O experiences.

For the rest of that first evening we relaxed and visited one or two of the venues without any pressing thoughts about doing anything. The Crow's Nest was quiet, and so was the pub style Champions bar. Even the casino appeared deserted. There was formal dancing in Carmens but I was still suffering from a problem that began on the global circumnavigation, that I thought (at the time) was a hernia, so dancing was out of bounds on this cruise. Everything looked and felt so familiar and when we had a goodnight drink in Andersons a waiter recognised us from the winter adventure, and as the bar was quiet, he came and chatted to us. The wonderful waiters are always keen to chat, and sometimes I feel they really want to have a conversation, but so much of their time is about just being polite and saying the expected things rather than opening up and having a true discussion. When in the past we have managed to have a decent conversation with them it is fascinating to hear their views on the ships, and favourite destinations, or what their home is like, or just to talk about their families.

We are usually very tired on the first night of a cruise and this was to be no exception. Hence after a cup of hot chocolate in Café Bordeaux, where we chatted to another familiar face, it was time for bed.

*Sea Day*

We woke up early on the 6th August and although it was not a day for sunbathing, it was dry and the North Sea was reasonably calm.

After breakfast in the buffet was digested, we were ready to face the world and decided to enjoy the warmth of the covered Crystal pool while we read our books listened to music. There was plenty of time to 'people watch' and look out for anyone we recognised, or to spot those with ill-fitting wigs perhaps, or other 'stand out in a crowd' people.

In terms of the organised activities, we spent a lot of the day listening to the port talks as this trip was visiting so many places that were new to us. We hadn't booked many tours so this was a chance to make last minute decisions as to how we spent our days in port. We also went to see the dance instruction, not because we intended to join in, but because the instructors (Alan and Ginny) were the couple that were on the ship for the first half of the world cruise. We had danced most evenings with this pair who encouraged everyone to join in, as their personalities lit up the ballroom each night.

This was the only day at sea before our first stop, so the evening was in formal dress code and started with the 'Welcome on board' cocktail party, including a chance to meet Captain Neil Turnbull once again. After being in his company for nearly three months on our previous adventure he recognised us as we shook hands and had our picture taken. We were one of the first in the queue arriving at the Crow's Nest allowing us a clear area to look around and spot a likely officer to chat to. It was a good choice as we made a beeline towards an officer flashing several stripes on his shoulder. His name was Erik and he had Kate, his wife, with him (as a passenger) and we became friends for the cruise. We all had a healthy appetite for a drink and the stewards kept us topped up at this and the other receptions when we met up. Well into our second glass of fizz it was time for the captain to make his formal welcome to us all, and to make one of his, quite familiar, little speeches that still amused us and we laughed and clapped our appreciation on cue.

Time for dinner and a little more chat about the merits of P&O compared to Thomson ships, and also those of other companies that our fellow tablemates had sampled.

The evening entertainment in the Curzon theatre was comedian 'David Copperfield' with a show that we saw on the world cruise, but we still laughed our heads off throughout the forty-five minutes, and I think most other people also had a good time. After that we allowed our aching chuckle muscles a chance to relax by looking in on the ball in Carmens and then having a drink in the Crow's Nest listening to one of the resident bands. They were a bit too jazz biased for our tastes but quiet enough to chat to each other and reminisce about this ship and the amazing adventures we had had on her.

It was time for bed.

*Copenhagen*

The next morning we were approaching Copenhagen and ahead of us was Oriana, the sister ship of Aurora. We were both on a similar cruise and ended up in the same dock on several occasions. Oriana got to her berthing point before us and we sailed by, to a spot much closer to the city. Our plans for the day did not include a guided tour as we had been assured that we could see many of the tourist attractions by just having a walk.

As we got off we saw Erik's wife (Kate) on the quayside. She was theoretically having a free cruise but she had to pay her way by chatting to passengers at cocktail parties (that will be us then) and also as P&O's representative on some of the tours. That was her role today and she greeted us as we passed by wishing us the best for the day.

From our docking point we wandered along the waterside park area (known as the Langelinie) toward some of the main areas of the city. The first thing we came to was some shops and a café as well as a booth selling open top bus and boat tours. We were tempted but resisted it and stuck to our walk.

After a few minutes stroll we came to a noisy crowd of Italian tourists peering into the water with cameras working overtime. They were capturing the simple magic of the 'Little Mermaid' statue, and after they eventually moved on, we got a clear view of the tiny statue on its little rocky island. It is smaller than I expected but still as good as described. Of course, there are several little stalls nearby selling replicas of the statue, along with ice-creams and other Danish sweet things. We resisted buying anything at this point believing that it could well be cheaper elsewhere.

As we walked by grassy parks and playground areas, there were numerous statues and monuments, and one series of gigantic bronze men impressed us. Their identity was a mystery, but we took photos in the hopes of identifying them when we got home.

Another park had the huge Gefion Fountain depicting a woman driving an oxen pulled chariot. Water gushed away from her and trickled down steps to a square in front of the St Albans

Anglican Church. This was another tourist trap and the Italians, Japanese, and Europeans with all kinds of different languages stood around and enjoyed the views.

We had reached the central area now and our final highlight was the beautiful Amalienborg Palace with an arched entrance into the palace courtyard area. The main feature was another huge statue of a regal figure on horseback, perched on a marble plinth riding towards the green domed roof of one of the palace buildings.

Now we wanted an ice-cream but the queues were horrendous so we looked around and watched the 'changing of the guard' ceremony before turning back towards the ship. We looked at all the statues and monuments again and finally got our ice-cream, plus a souvenir fridge magnet. Now we realised that Denmark is expensive.

At the dockside with just a little way to go before the ship, it started to rain. In fact it poured, and we took shelter in the shops. Several of them sold traditional pattern woollen jumpers, hats, and other clothes that didn't appeal to us, especially at their prices. Other shops had Scandinavian figures and more hats as well as the usual worldwide available fridge magnets, key rings, thimbles and so on. We were not tempted to spend anymore, and as soon as the rain stopped, we walked the last few metres to Aurora and lunch.

Copenhagen is a beautiful clean city with lots of spectacular and historical buildings to see. We had seen enough to give us a taste of the place, so didn't get off again. I think an open top bus ride, or a boat trip along the waterway would have been equally as interesting, and probably more informative than our walk, but we were sticking to a plan of saving money for those places we most wanted to see in more detail. It also gave us an excuse to come back again one day.

We continued our relaxation on the ship for the afternoon and joined in with the Individual Quiz before going to dinner. In the theatre it was the Headliners team presenting one of their shows, and although we had seen it before it was an enjoyable way to pass the time. In Carmens there was a 60s & 70s themed party where we spent a few minutes at over a glass or two of wine. We were sinking back into a very familiar and sweet routine that we had enjoyed for so many weeks during the winter. Without a doubt we enjoyed the ship almost as much as visiting new places, but there is always a bit of excitement about waking up in a country that is new to us, and this cruise had several more to come yet.

*Sea Day and a Peninsular Club Lunch*

After we left Copenhagen we began the 670 nautical mile hop from Denmark to Sweden. During the night we passed north of the island of 'Zealand' before passing through the 'Belt Straits'. We were told that while we slept, the ship sailed under the 'Great Belt Bridge' and finally made our entry into the Baltic Sea.

Throughout the next day we sailed north-eastwards along the southern coast of Sweden. The weather was pleasant with temperatures in the high teens but with quite a strong following wind. We enjoyed the comfort of Aurora and relaxed with our books and our music as well as listening to further port talks.

As faithful P&O customers we had reached the dizzy heights of the Peninsular Level of the loyalty scheme that entitled us to a few perks. Today we enjoyed a splendid lunch for the small band of passengers who were in this club. So, as lunchtime approached, we dressed in smart casual clothes and made our way to the Alexandria Restaurant.

When we entered, we were escorted to our table by a waiter in his crisp white waistcoat. Every table had a host officer, and we were pleasantly surprised to see that our host was Eric with his wife. We laughed at the coincidence but it meant we were already first name friends and could relax straight into the free booze. There were three other couples with us on the table, two were married couples of a similar age to ourselves, and then a young lad who was with his grandmother.

… what a pity the lad was too young to share our wine!!!

There was plenty of alcohol with a champagne welcome drink followed by endless refills of a good red or white wine. The food and service were superb with a menu that was markedly superior to the normal one.

The captain and the loyalty club officials made little speeches, and we had a table photograph with Captain Neil Turnbull. That photo (like so many others) is now in the folder that Deb created for each cruise with photographs, menus for all the meals, daily news sheets, and details of the trips. What started off as a couple of folders on a shelf turned into a couple of shelves of folders spanning two decades. It became so bulky that Deb scanned all the documents, and they are now stored electronically. The folders and paperwork have long since gone, but the electronic material has been invaluable as I researched our cruising history over 20 years of adventures.

The rest of that day was a little alcohol blurred but there were quizzes to torment the mind before another dinner.

... yes, more food.

The evening's highlight entertainment was a show from the 'Headliners' based on Abba, plus a cabaret from a male vocalist that we ignored.

The night ended with hot chocolate in Café Bordeaux again, and another early night in readiness for a morning tour when we arrived in Stockholm.

*Stockholm in Sweden*

During the night Aurora reached the Aland Sea, and early in the morning two local pilots boarded the vessel to guide the ship on her 54 nautical mile passage through the archipelago towards Stockholm.

We were berthed by 8:30 in Stockholm which is the capital of Sweden and has a population of nearly 900,000 people. It is very much the economic, political, and cultural centre of the country. Most people around Europe will think of Abba when they come to Sweden, and Stockholm was where they formed.

We were off on a water cruise around the city, and after breakfast we made the short walk along the dockside, to the rather smaller boat that was waiting for us just a few metres in front of Aurora. What a pleasant surprise to find Kate was the P&O representative for the tour, but apart from making sure no-one fell overboard, she would not have much to do.

The waterfront of Stockholm allows the visitor a very relaxing couple of hours while looking at many of the landmarks of this city. The Swedish like to display their sense of humour and one of the first things we saw was a crane on the dockside painted like a giraffe with the jib as its head and neck. We passed one of the museums that many visitors head for known as the Vasa Museum, and it is the home of a warship (The Vasa) that sank on its maiden voyage. Rather strangely the ship's masts are so tall that they poke out of the museum's roof.

Our guide gave us a commentary throughout the ride as there were plenty of splendid architecturally spectacular buildings to photograph. The National Museum nestled amongst huge waterfront hotels, and then on the other side were tranquil parks and gardens for the workers of the city to grab a quiet moment during their lunch-breaks. Our gaze was directed towards the imposing Royal Palace and also the famous City Hall where the various Nobel Prizes are awarded.

Our little boat then went through a lock, known as the 'Slussen', that is in the centre of the city and separates the Baltic Sea from the Lake Malaren. This vast lake is still a part of Stockholm, and is surrounded by many of the more residential areas of the city, including some forward-thinking ecological architecture to save energy.

The couple of hours were quite special and at the end we were told how to get to the city centre for a chance to walk around the landmarks.

That allowed us to see the Royal Palace in more detail, and we arrived just as a group of blue suited soldiers on horseback and armed with rifles, walked stately along the road towards the palace to change the guards... good timing!

It was a long time since breakfast so we went into a park and bought a cappuccino and a piece of carrot cake each. The café was run by a jovial Caribbean gentleman whose humour made the price of the snack feel a little more acceptable, but £15 for coffee and cake reminded us of the Scandinavian expensiveness. Very refreshed (at that price we had to be) we continued our walk and found a busy park right in the middle of the shopping centre. The shop windows were glanced at, but buying anything was quickly forgotten. The park was free and there were lots of things to occupy young people including a huge screen showing the Olympics.

We had almost forgotten the Olympics after four days away from Britain, but this reminded us of the fantastic time our daughter was having while volunteering as a Games Maker. She spent the first week of the games at the Aquatic Centre and will never forget an experience of a lifetime.

We were tired and it was time to make our way back to Aurora.

The early evening sail-away coincided with a change in the weather, with a shower as we made our way back out into the archipelago again. The rain didn't put us off looking at the sights including a huge fountain with water pouring out of a large metal arch known as God the Father on the Arch of Heaven.... very poetic.

Before we went to dinner we saw a few of the little islands as we slowly made our way out into more open water, on the overnight journey to Estonia and the city of Tallinn.

*Estonia and Tallinn*

Friday, and we woke up to our arrival into Tallinn the capital of Estonia. This was our third port and the third capital city we were visiting...

... this was quite a cruise

We had a tour booked, and it was something quite different. Instead of going to one place, or to look at a particular aspect of a city, we were going on what was described as 'Free Time at Three Stops'. What this meant was that we would be taken first to the Upper Town area and left to wander for a set time. Then we would be driven to the Lower Town area for another period of time, and finally there was a visit to a museum and waterside area to complete our tour.

It sounded a good idea and probably allowed us to see more than just going on a single themed tour. Off we went with our guide giving us all the usual facts and figures about Tallinn and Estonia, before suggesting some things to go and see at our first stop.

The Upper Town is known locally as the 'Toompark', and it is the older area of the city with architectural delights to savour. After a couple of minutes' walk from the coach we arrived at the glorious Alexander Nevsky Cathedral with its beautiful façade, and onion shaped domes that are so typical of Eastern Europe. It stood on one side of a square and faced the Estonian Parliament building that was just as spectacular.

There were narrow roads packed with tourists from all over the world and we moved together from one beautiful little church to another, passing pretty but unassuming houses or other buildings, with signs or unusual plaques displaying the occupant's business or their famous history. There were also places marked that had a good view and photo opportunity, to look down on the Lower town area and see the rooftops and tall towers, that we would be walking between later on.

... they do seem to like towers in Estonia

Forty-five minutes later, and we were sitting down on the coach for another quick chat from the guide, about what we had seen and some more tips for us to consider at our next stop. From the quiet tranquillity of the Upper Town, we drove into the more commercial area of the city, and it was obvious that the atmosphere was noisier, and things moved faster.

A short walk along a narrow street took us away from the noise of traffic, and we came to a small market. Now we were able to look up at the building and towers we saw from above just twenty minutes earlier. It was busy again, but now it was mostly local people going about their daily activities. Music was attracting our attention from somewhere, and turning a corner we came to a large square overlooked by the town hall, and a much larger market area including a stage with the source of that traditional Estonian music. Actually the music changed between folk based and more pop style genres while we walked around the market stalls.

The produce here was a mixture of day-to-day food and household needs, plus quite high-quality artisan or craft-based souvenirs. Of course there was food as well and we sampled a few things, but could not agree on something as a more substantial snack. After several unsuccessful explorations of the lanes leading away from the square, we found a bakery and bought a couple of local pastry items... delicious.

Part two of our tour was over and eventually all the passengers returned to the coach carrying just a little bit more in our bags than when we arrived. As the coach moved away the guide gave her final introduction to what we were about to visit. The drive this time took us out of the commercial area and it felt like we were leaving the city with buildings changing from pretty and homely to starker and military looking blocks. This was a totally different side of Tallinn and the short journey took us to a dockside with a museum of wartime naval ships and other maritime craft. Just across the road and behind some trees was a now disused prison block that was not mentioned very much, but had a sinister political past.

The museum was rather special, and other displays were housed in an old ship building warehouse that had been modernised, to show visitors a little bit of the country's history of ships and sea life. There was also a café come restaurant where we had a lovely cup of coffee. Outside on the dockside there were several small navy ships and a historical steam ship. Across the water we could also see Aurora, and worryingly there was a row of old cannons on the quay that were all pointing towards our floating home.

About three hours after we had set off, our coach was on the way back to the ship, and I believe we had all enjoyed this slightly different way of seeing a new place.

It was a formal evening and there was a 'Black and White Ball' later. Dancing was still out of the question because of my dodgy leg that I hurt during the world cruise six months earlier, but we still popped into Carmen's to see the dancers and feel the atmosphere. The cabaret was a magician called Matthew McGurk and although we had seen him before we enjoyed his show.

The ship was buzzing with anticipation during the evening as Aurora was steaming towards Russia and the city of St Petersburg where we would be arriving tomorrow. For many of us this would be our first visit to this famous city and the culture of Russia.

*St Petersburg - Russia*

Saturday 11th August and early in the morning Aurora was berthed in the city of St Petersburg, and we were in Russia. This is the fourth country in five days and I have to say that a Baltic cruise is certainly rather interesting.

Oriana was in port as well meaning that upwards of 3500 British passengers were about to venture into a city renowned for its fantastic architecture and museums. We are also going to sample one of the most serious border control procedures in the world. We had been warned about it and knew that everyone (and I mean everyone) would be checked individually each time we entered the terminal building and every time we returned as well. To achieve this, the terminal building has a vast row of booths with traffic lights to control the queues, as each passenger is stared at while passports and entry documents are carefully inspected. The booths work in two directions, and as volumes of people return to the ship, some of the booths change to allow these tourists to be checked out of Russia rather than letting people in. If you are unfortunate enough to be in the queue when the booth changes direction, there is no apology, just a wagging hand directing you to another queue.

We had been told very clearly not to complain, argue, gesticulate, and even look upset as the authorities have no sympathy and could become even more difficult if provoked.

Our visit to St Petersburg was for two days and we'd squeezed in three tours. The first one was to the 'Peterhof Palace' a few miles away from the harbour. Tour tickets, passports, and multiple documents ready, we bounced down the gangplank and walked carefully along the prescribed pathway to the terminal building, and joined the queue as directed by an unsmiling, silent, Russian woman. There is only one other place where I have seen immigration control personnel so unfriendly, and that was in San Francisco. How amazing that two of the largest countries in the world have the same insecurity complex when it comes to visitors.

Anyway, the ordeal was quickly over and we followed the waving hands along the pathway to our coaches and reasonably soon we were on the road. The guide introduced herself and the driver, and quickly went over the plans for the morning before pointing out the buildings that we were passing. In the dockside area the buildings were not pretty, and in fact they were stark concrete towers of apartments with no character, and appeared to have been ready for demolition decades ago. This was bringing us the reality of the Russian society, where the vast proportion of its citizens are poor and have little to smile about.

On our way to Peterhof the journey went through the more attractive areas of St Petersburg, and soon we were passing spectacular buildings such as The Cathedral of Christ's Resurrection known locally as 'The Church of the Spilled Blood', with shiny golden Onion domes that were to become a common, but still beautiful, sight over the next couple of days. We also crossed the 'Griboedov Canal' and the 'River Neva', as well as passing the 'Kazan Cathedral', 'St Isaac's Cathedral', and the 'Yusupov Palace' where Rasputin met his end.

The buildings became less noteworthy as we left the main city area and drove out into the countryside. The guide gave us a history lesson about the Siege of St Petersburg and as we travelled along a long straight barren road, she brought the misery to life with unbelievable stories of hardship suffered by the people. Eventually we stopped for a comfort break at a restored village known as 'Amaranta Shuvalovka', that depicts a typical peasant village of the Tsarist era. Log cabins told the story of everyday life but we were not there for the views, we were there for the toilet, and then an extended chance to go into the souvenir shop. The Russians may not be over friendly but they do want our money.

Back on the coach we made the last few miles of the journey to the 'Peterhof Palace' with more instructions about how we were to behave:

... any large bags would be taken from us and put into a store

... soft overshoes will be provided to protect the fragile floors

... stay in our groups and don't get left behind

But our visit was worth the annoying procedures and rules.

The palace is beautiful with the huge main creamy, yellowy coloured building, standing in manicured grounds with fountains and statues between sculptured hedges and trees in all directions. To one side was another smaller building with golden onion domed roof, and this was just the front of the palace. The insides were even more spectacular, and finally the gardens at the rear rounded off a truly wonderful visit.

As promised the entry into the museum was tortuous, with more sinister Russian women ensuring we did as we were told, and only went where we instructed, wearing only what we should. Once again the wait was worth it with ornate stairs and sculptures, sensational ceilings, vast wall murals, large and small paintings that can only be imagined.

... and I mean imagined, because photography was rarely allowed and the only way of getting a memory was to buy the postcards.

When we got outside into the main gardens it was the first time we had been allowed the freedom to walk unguided since our arrival in Russia. First there was a vast grassy bank with hundreds of people waiting at the top and on the long flight of steps on either side of a central series of fountains and waterway. At 11:00 precisely, loud music started and the fountains were switched on for a magnificent display of water ballet that would continue for the rest of the day. Once we had savoured the display for long enough, we wandered through the park and came across other water features including some that are humorous, catching the unwary visitor out by soaking them with unexpected jets of water. The children absolutely loved it.

There were statues of course and many reflecting the history of the area including more than one of the revered Peter the Great. In the wooded area a band was playing with each person playing different length brass horns that required stands to hold them up. Further still and we came to a small building that was the retreat of Catherine the Great…

… what a place this is!

At the very bottom of the park we came to the sea and looked out across the Gulf of Finland, with a view towards the built-up centre of St Petersburg. This was where we caught a hydrofoil for the speedy return to the dockside we had started from three hours earlier. It had been a superb tour and the history and architecture had been breath-taking.

Now we had to face the queues to return to Aurora through the immigration hall with its booths controlled by the ever-present Russian witches. Once again it was more efficient than expected and we were quickly back on the quayside with our paperwork stamped accordingly. It was time for lunch followed by a little rest as we had another tour later.

After grabbing a snack in Café Bordeaux at the end of the afternoon we showered and dressed a little less casually, as we were going to the theatre to watch a Russian Folk Dancing show. The routine was well known by now and we got to the terminal building early, to make our way past the inquiring eyes in the booths again, as our paperwork was scrutinised once more. It was actually slightly quicker now as we had already been stamped on our morning tour, so this time it was just a confirmation that we were who we said we were.

On the coach our guide introduced herself and explained what we were going to see. On the way into the centre of St Petersburg she pointed out the landmarks again and then decided that we had enough time for an unscheduled stop to look at St Nicholas's Cathedral. This was another stunning church in blue with almost white pillars, plus the obligatory gold onion dome.

... actually five of them

Back on the coach again we assumed the next stop would be the theatre but the guide gave us another stop at a tourist souvenir shop. This was surprisingly good as it started with a tasting session of vodka. The shop was good and not overly expensive and Deb quickly bought a tourist guide book for the city in English. Our only problem limiting our purchases was that they wanted Euros or Dollars and we came with a wallet full of Roubles. We did buy several items here once we had convinced them that we wanted to use local currency.

At last we were at the theatre and slightly later than expected, so we had to go straight in and find seats. We had little choice by now and decided to take up a couple of seats in the empty front row. Some other passengers behind us suspected we might be chosen for audience participation, but we had no fears.

The show was superb. There was music with typical Russian instruments, there was singing which sounded good, but we had no idea what it was about. The dancing did not let us down, with lots of different styles from pretty little women making gentle moves through to full in your face Cossack mania. The show lasted some two hours with a break in the middle where we had a glass of champagne. We met up with Erik and Kate (yet again) and as very few people seemed interested in the champagne, we emptied a few more glasses.

At the end of the show Deb and I agreed that this had been a very special day and well worth putting up with the overzealous border security. Deb did win a small battle at the booths on the way back to the ship. She got to the head of the queue when the duty witch declared that it should change direction and we were directed to another queue. Deb sighed rather loudly and lifted her hand in frustration, and the young man in the booth responded and let her through. His supervisor (Head Witch) was livid and gave him a serious telling off, and I was pretty mad as well as I had to join a different queue, while Deb waited on the other side laughing at me.

The next morning, we had another tour in the morning going to the Hermitage Museum. There was no way we were coming all the way to St Petersburg without visiting this world-famous place. As our paperwork was inspected once more, and we found our coach we had a little time to watch the activity around us. It was quite disconcerting to see so many men giving orders to the predominantly female guides, and realising where the power was. I was pretty certain I could see lumps under the jackets of these men, that looked suspiciously like the shape of revolvers. Anyway, we were quickly on our way past the Stalin-era apartment blocks, over the river and the canal, down the roads close to various Cathedrals and churches, and finally stopping at the Hermitage Museum that is also known as the 'Winter Palace'.

We had been warned, and we already knew that it would be busy, and the queue to get in was horrendous with visitors speaking in languages from all over the world. This really is a magnet for tourists. After several minutes of hustle, bustle, and shoving, our guide got the tickets and pushed us to the correct entrance, where we passed through a gate while being scrutinised by guard dog style women checking that we were not carrying bags that were too big, and that we had the correct tickets. Then we joined a queue that was our tour. You don't have the option to wander freely here, you just follow the line of people and do your best to stay close to your guide, so that her commentary can be heard on the earpieces provided.

The Hermitage is overpoweringly stunning. The building itself is externally beautiful, but inside as you enter up the huge main staircase to the first gallery, you are surrounded by so much gold leaf and marble and murals on the walls that it leaves your jaw drooping. Eventually your eyes succeed in looking upwards at the ceiling above, and that makes you gasp in awe at the artistic imagination of the Russian past. Then you start to snake through room after room of statues and other sculptures by Canova and Michelangelo before realising that you are walking on stunning floors that are inlaid with dreamy coloured marquetry wooden patterns, and then above are chandeliers dangling from panels that are works of art in their own right.

Now came the paintings, and I am no art lover, but I was quickly amazed to hear artists' names that I recognised and was seeing paintings that were worth fortunes. In a trance I walked by art by Leonardo da Vinci, Raphael, Rembrandt, Gaugin, Van Gogh, and Claude Monet. True lovers of the subject stood in awe of tiny masterpieces while Japanese clicked their cameras as if a plague of beetles had invaded the museum. That tour of just some of the Museum's rooms was painfully crowded and I felt claustrophobic, but I am so glad that the opportunity to visit another iconic destination had been possible.

Once passed the most crowded galleries we had a quieter walk past less famous, but still beautiful artwork before emerging into the cool of late summer in St Petersburg. There was a last chance of a photo or two outside the Winter Palace, and its square across the road from it with its arches and the Alexander Column. Then it was back on our coach and a return trip through the now quite familiar streets of the city, plus a last chance to try and spot even the slightest smile on the face of the border control officers.

During the afternoon on Aurora we lazed and reflected on a wonderful couple of days in a city that has so much history and tragedy associated with it. We discussed if we would ever come on another Baltic cruise, and agreed that we had only seen a tiny bit of what this city has to offer, so yes I think we will come on a similar cruise one day. Aurora left St Petersburg just after 5:00 in the evening and we had a very chatty meal with equally enthused dinner table mates. After that there was a Headline show called 'Stop in the Name of Love', that Deb enjoyed because of her love of Motown music. That was followed by a Motown themed quiz in Masquerades with a drink or two to round of a delightful couple of days in Russia. Tomorrow we would be in Finland and its capital city of Helsinki.

*Finland and Helsinki*

Monday 13th August and there were just four days left of our Baltic adventure as we woke up in Finland, and its capital city of Helsinki. This was the third country on this cruise, that we were visiting for the first time.

From the port talks and various peoples' recommendations we had decided not to have a tour but to do our own thing and go for a walk around the commercial area of this city. Another factor that influenced us was that we were quite exhausted from the excitement and splendour of St Petersburg and just needed to chill out.

Fortunately P&O laid on a shuttle bus from the dock area to the centre of Helsinki, and as the city started to come to life we found ourselves at a bus stop with one of the couples from our dinner table. The bus driver had directed us to go in one direction, but the useless map we had been supplied with made no sense at all, and we weren't sure where the helpful driver had actually directed us...

... we went that way anyhow

We were intending to go to the harbour area where there was a market and a little bit of 'life', but we soon discovered we had made an error. As we walked down the road, while trying to locate our position on the map, it was getting busier with lots of local people walking in different directions. The buildings became bigger, glitzier, and most definitely commercial, and we knew we had gone in totally the wrong direction and we were now in the shopping centre. The increase in people was because of a bus terminus, or possibly railway station, that we walked through and into a huge shopping mall which at least kept us amused and interested for thirty minutes including a cup of expensive coffee.

Now that we were almost in tune with the street map the four of us trotted off again towards the harbour area. After no more than half a dozen discussions about *"**is it left, or right?**"* or *"**do we have to cross here?**"* we saw tell-tale signs that we were getting to our goal.

... the boats and market stalls gave it away

We split up from our table mates now. We hadn't got on with them too well at the meals as they were the couple that regularly found fault with the food, or the menu, or the service, compared to their favoured Thomson Cruise ships. We had actually seen one of the little blue ships sailing the other way one afternoon and commented on it. Unfortunately, that initiated an interrogation. "**Which one was it?**"..."**How many life boats did it have?**"

... but we failed to identify the ship's name

On our own again Deb and I walked down the South Harbour Esplanade passing ornate buildings that turned out to be the Town hall, and the Swedish Embassy. We also admired a huge fountain of a naked lady staring around at the visitors. Before we ventured into the street market, we spotted an older small building that looked interesting and headed in its direction. Its previous use was as the Makasiini Terminal presumably for ferry traffic but which is now a covered market selling fruit, vegetables and cakes... and delicious looking cakes at that.

Easily tempted we stopped in a small café and had coffee and cake to check if they were as delicious to eat as they were to look at.

... yup superb!

From there we went to the main market area where Deb sampled some local hot food. One looked like whitebait and the other was fried elk bits. I was not tempted even when Deb gave her approval. Other stalls sold more obviously recognisable snacks but we were more interested in buying souvenirs and moved to the arts and craft area. Half an hour later we came away with our local purchases and our memories of another city to add to our list. As with all Scandinavian countries, it was clean, the people were polite, and everything was more expensive than most places we have visited throughout the world.

At least the sun was shining and it was a little warmer than it had been in Russia.

We returned to the city centre, found the bus stop to board the shuttle and were soon back on Aurora. It was warm enough to relax on deck during the afternoon and after briefly watching sail-away we went to humiliate ourselves at the daily individual quiz, before having a shower in preparation for dinner. That evening we ate in cafe Bordeaux and had a delicious meal with superb service and a very special atmosphere as our favourite ship's band 'Caravan' played music. This group of men have a repertoire of dance music that they normally play, but also they excel with songs from the 60s and 70s that most cruise ship passengers remember. We sang along a little, but applauded a lot and when we finally left with full tums and an alcohol fuelled happiness we waved at the band, and gave them a silent clap as a thank-you for the good times they have given us.

There was a show by the Headliners in the theatre again, and just time for a goodnight cup of hot chocolate before we made our way back to the cabin. There were two days at sea now to get to our last stop at Zeebrugge so we had a chance to savour the ship and enjoy what she had to offer.

*Zeebrugge and the final days*

There were two days at sea now as we moved away from the Baltic region and Scandinavia. The journey south towards the North Sea was uneventful, and with a smooth sea we enjoyed what Aurora and her entertainment team had to offer. There was an interview with the captain that we knew would be quite enjoyable, as we had seen a similar interview session with Captain Neil Turnbull on our world cruise. We didn't go to it this time and we also missed the Entertainment Team Variety show that makes the passengers chuckle. We did watch the Headliners' tribute to Queen and another show based on dance music from around the world. The magician reappeared as well as a male singer so the passengers' tastes were well catered for. We watched those that interested us and took part in quizzes to give our minds a little bit of exercise as well.

There was also the final 'Formal' night with a pre-dinner party, where the loyalty club managers thanked us with free drinks, and a raffle with quite a nice prize for one lucky couple... as usual it was not us.

On Thursday 16th August we completed the 1300 nautical mile journey from Helsinki to the Belgian port of Zeebrugge for our final stop before home. We had been there before and didn't bother with any of the tours to nearby Bruges or smaller villages. Instead we simply took the shuttle bus to the closest town of Blankenburge.

We had been there before as well but it was a chance to stretch our legs and buy some Belgian Waffles and chocolate plus the obligatory ice-cream. This little sea-side town is always busy with tourists and we watched families with buckets and spades (just like Britain) making their way to the beach. Our stop in the town was for little more than an hour and we were soon back on Aurora to finish off the unpleasant job of packing our suitcases.

The final dinner was superb as always and we had a good chat with our fellow table mates. Strangely the couple who had run down P&O from day one, and compared everything with Thomson ships, actually said they would come back to Aurora as it had been a very nice experience. We all have different opinions about ships and cruise lines but at the end of the day most of us are addicted to the cruise holiday experience and find enjoyment on nearly every trip.

That evening there was a female vocalist that I am sure was very good, but we ignored her like many tens of other female vocalists over our years of cruising. Instead we went to the Crow's Nest and met up with Erik and Kate for a final couple of hours of drinking and conversation. We had a good time and laughed our way around our experiences as we sailed down the last stretch of the North Sea and into the Channel. Final farewells were made and it would be nice to think we will meet up again someday on a ship sailing to faraway places and warm sunshine.

The next morning (Friday 17$^{th}$ August) we woke to the familiar sounds and sights of Southampton. During our twelve-day cruise we had sailed a total of 3407 nautical miles, visited six countries, and four capital cities. It had been a cruise with unbelievable architecture and historical sights to savour and I would certainly recommend it to anyone considering it. It is not a guaranteed hot and sunny destination but it does offer a lot of different ports and cultures in just a few days. I was sure we would be back in the Baltic region before too long, and a P&O ship the likely transport.

*Note*

*This cruise turned out to be our only adventure to the Baltic Region, but it still remains on our list of* **'We must go back'** *destinations.*

… and we have never seen the officer, or his wife, again.

# Time in the hands of the NHS

We were settling into a routine that retirement had allowed us. I had been determined to stay active, and my days were full of time in the garden and the allotment, as well as an increasing number of DIY projects around the house. Deb and I were also loving a late in life discovery of Ballroom and Latin dancing, that also meant a new circle of friends.

Sadly, there were a few changes that were not so positive. Perhaps it was due to the change of lifestyle, or just a natural aging process, but I was becoming less agile with numerous aches and pains.

I had suffered with an arthritic knee that had been causing me occasional *'ouch moments'* from as far back as the early 1990s, but that was now affecting me on an almost daily basis. Alongside the knee, I had also developed an ache, or pain, in my groin. This had appeared while on the World Cruise, and almost immediately on our return, I began a very long, frustrating, and painful period while the NHS tried to diagnose the cause, and to put it right. Initially my GP simply thought it was a muscle strain in my thigh, but when several weeks of *'rest'* didn't improve the situation, I was sent to the first of many hospital appointments.

By then, my GP's diagnosis had changed to me possibly having a hernia. After a six week wait for the hospital appointment, I had a scan of my groin area, and not long afterwards presented myself to the consultant surgeon. He looked at my scan and agreed that I did have a small hernia, but it couldn't be producing the levels of pain I was suffering from. He lay me on the couch, and after prodding for a while, he grabbed my leg and proceeded to waggle, wrench, and bend it in all directions.

His diagnosis was that I might have a problem with my joints, and referred me on to a second group of medical magicians, this time in the orthopaedic group.

By the end of October 2012 my knees and hips were being inspected by an orthopaedic surgeon in nearby Cannock hospital. The first job was to get some x-rays, and then I sat with the surgeon as he looked at my pictures. He began by saying my dodgy knee was quite badly affected by osteo-arthritis, but not serious enough to consider any treatment, but he quickly moved on to the hip and made a statement that totally dumfounded me.

I probably needed a new hip!

That was the beginning of several months of consultations, scans, injections, and even a small exploratory operation (called an arthroscopy) on my knee. In the middle of April 2013, things were getting serious, and the surgeon said it was time to go on the list to have a new hip.

That was when I dropped my own bombshell. Deb and I had decided to move house, but it was not going to be nearby in Staffordshire, we were moving to Herefordshire. We were already well into the process, with an imminent moving date, so any plans to have a hip replacement in Staffordshire were scrapped, and I said goodbye to the surgeons and consultants of Staffordshire.

I would have to start all over again once settled into our new home in Herefordshire.

## 2013 – A New home, and another Cruise

A little later than planned, we made our move from Stone in Staffordshire, to the small village of Kingstone in Herefordshire. It was May 2013 by then, and the aches and pains had to be forgotten for a few exhausting weeks while we unpacked boxes, got used to our new house, and continually moved furniture from one position to another.

As the unfamiliar house felt more like a home, our thoughts turned to a holiday, and we picked up a late bargain deal for a cruise. This adventure began on the 4th June, and was for 12 nights on Arcadia sailing to the sunshine of the Mediterranean.

Deb and I were always comfortable on the beautiful Arcadia, and this cruise allowed us to calm down, enjoy being pampered, and recharge our batteries after a hectic six months. There was only one new destination to add to our *'Been There Portfolio'* and that was the Spanish city of Valencia. Pre planning had been negligible, so our visit to Valencia simply involved a shuttle bus ride into the city centre, and a stroll around the shops where we bought a pair of ceramic tiles as a number plaque for our new house. The visit to the sun-baked city was rounded off by half an hour people watching while we had a coffee.

To be honest I remember very little about Valencia, and hardly anything else about the holiday, but by the time we arrived back home in Herefordshire, we were ready to continue personalising the new house.

Sadly, those ceramic tiles had been left in an overhead cupboard on Arcadia.

After the usual bureaucratic delays, we managed to register with a doctor, and I quickly raised the issue of my hip. It took the usual six weeks waiting to get an appointment with the local surgeon, who then refused to accept any information I passed onto him about my hospital visits in Staffordshire.

The process of diagnosis, x-rays, scans, and pain killing injections was going to begin all over again. It would be almost another frustrating 12 months before I finally had my hip replacement in June 2014.

This saga became another of my books called simply '*You Need a new Hip*'. It talks about the diagnosis, plus the various treatments, as well as the actual replacement operation. It then continues by describing the recovery and recuperation months that eventually culminated in forgetting I even had a new hip, with the pain almost a distant memory.

## 2014 - A Busy and Varied Year

This was a busy year, but most of my thoughts were about the operation to replace my hip.

As the days and weeks ticked down to the operation in June, Deb and I continued a never-ending task of turning our new house into a home. It was around this time that my mind began to agree with the thoughts of many retired people. How on earth did I ever find time to go to work. Of course, the impending operation on my hip was rarely out of my thoughts during the Spring, and the constant pain was making many of the DIY projects around the house very tiring, and it also limited the time I could spend on more green fingered magic in the garden.

In the relaxing evening moments, the idea of having a holiday were rarely very far from our thoughts. This was especially true as I knew the hip replacement would rule out a holiday in the summer. My eyes were always scanning adverts for a break. One day in March I spotted a last-minute bargain that was something different from what we had been used to.

It was a coach holiday for a couple of nights to the Isle of Wight for a Murder Mystery weekend.

The coach was comfortable enough, but the hotel was pretty basic. Although we had a few days relaxation, and a bit of fun, it certainly wasn't as good as a cruise, but at least we had a few minutes at sea on the ferry each way from Southampton.

We didn't feel the coach trip had been enough to satisfy our holiday needs, so it was back to the adverts again.

The house projects were exhausting both of us, and we were yearning for a rest and a bit of pampering. With the date for my hip operation pencilled in, we had a window for a short cruise and when I spotted a last-minute bargain, it didn't take us long to make up our minds.

So, on 30th April we boarded Arcadia and set off for our 19th cruise on the P&O ships. This time it was for 10 nights cruising down the Atlantic Coast of Spain and Portugal to visit four ports. There was only one new destination (Oporto in Portugal) but this was really all about getting away for a few days.

I'm not sure if this cruise was the moment our thoughts about P&O began to change, but it was definitely around this time when we were maybe noticing the influence of the American parent company was becoming apparent.

Popping back a couple of years when we were on the World cruise, one of the senior managers (Carol Marlow) sailed with the ship as far as the first stop. She spoke informally to many of the passengers, and at a presentation Carol talked about the regular question concerning changes in P&O since being taken over by Carnival Cruises.

Her views were all positive about protecting the traditions of P&O that were so important to the passengers. She described it as the special *'P and O ness'* that the company were promising to protect. There was a rousing round of applause...

... but two years later, I wasn't so sure that this was the case.

One thing that had definitely not changed significantly was the price of the cruises. Fourteen years on, and we were still able to get a good cabin at a cost that had hardly increased. In that same period P&O had moved on from one of the most expensive cruise lines in Britain, to one of the cheapest.

The company was continuing an expansion of its fleet, and from just three ships when we first sailed with P&O, it now boasted six vessels. Passenger capacity had increased threefold to around 15000. The popularity of the British cruising product was still increasing, and yet another new ship (Britannia) was being built. She would be bigger than all the others with around 3500 passengers, and there were more ships to come.

Our arrival into cruising was on a ship that looked beautiful with a pointed end at the front, and a rounded one to the back with curved tiers where passengers could stand and stare at the world as it passed by, and be stared back at by envious people on shore. As your eye moved up the side of the ship there were circular portholes at the bottom, then rectangular windows a little higher, and finally balconies.

They looked like a ship that a child (of that time) would draw.

Now the designers of ships cared little for pleasing lines, and the rear end was just a wall of almost identical cabins with balconies, and a similar wall of cabins to the side.

A child now drew a cruise ship that looked more like a skyscraper hotel.

Yes, these new ships had wonderful cabins with sumptuous facilities, superb dining rooms and lounges, and gave the new cruise passengers a similar '*Wow*' factor as Deb and I marvelled at in 2000.

... But it was a different sort of '*Wow*' factor.

What the latest designers couldn't create was the traditional atmosphere, with a choice of lounges where you could party, but then other places to sit in peace and quiet with luxurious furniture and fittings.

Sadly, the majority of the thousands of new customers going cruising were looking for a 24-hour party atmosphere, rather than the quiet spots that more traditional passengers sought.

Of course, the cruise companies needed to make a profit to keep shareholders happy, and that meant giving those new passengers the party atmosphere they craved for.

The product we fell in love with was changing, but we still enjoyed what was on offer. The conscious decision was made to look at the smaller but older ships, rather than the new floating hotels.

Our ten-night cruise on Arcadia was the perfect way to relax from the needs of a new house, and for us to forget about my hip replacement for a few days. The Portuguese port of Oporto was added to our list of places we had visited and we had a morning exploring the area, and sampling the delights of a Port Wine factory.

There was plenty of sunshine, calm seas, pleasant food and terrific entertainment.

With that holiday over, there was just five weeks before I went to the Hereford hospital to have my new hip fitted. Some of the remaining jobs in the new house became quite urgent, as was my time in the garden getting vegetables into the ground to give us some form of harvest.

I will not go into any detail about my hip operation as it is a long-drawn-out story. Suffice to say, it went well, but my recovery was so frustrating when so many things around me had to be temporarily put on hold. If you would like to know more about the actual operation, and the first few months of recovery, then it is covered by a short book called 'You Need a New Hip'.

As 2014 progressed, I was able to do more and more in the garden and around the house. The small amounts of vegetables that we managed to get in the ground were a treat, and we made a new circle of friends with our neighbours, plus those we met up with in the local pub.

The pain from the worn-out hip joint were a thing of the past, and as Autumn set in, the weather cooled, and Deb and I had the itch again to go on a cruise before Winter.

I scanned the adverts and offers again, and it wasn't long before we found a last-minute bargain for a short trip on Oriana that featured a day on the island of Guernsey, and another in Zeebrugge. Guernsey would be a new port for us, giving another notch on the suitcase handles of places we had been to. That cruise was only for five nights, but getting back on Oriana was really rather special.

Our love of cruising continued. We had been sailing on P&O ships now for 15 years with 21 cruises on six different ships. Without spending ages looking at all the itineraries, I cannot tell you how many ports we had been to, but we had sailed on the three major oceans, and visited countries in six different continents - we haven't been to Antarctica. Distance wise I am confident we had sailed more than 60,000 miles around the globe.

Our sights were firmly set on having another world cruise, and if it hadn't been for the hip replacement, we would have been setting off again in January 2015. That planned circumnavigation was scheduled to be on Arcadia, but the P&O customer teams listened to our medical issues, and had been very helpful, moving the booking on to January 2016.

In the meantime, Deb and I began to look for new adventures with cruises that went to different ports, and the possibility of trying out different cruise lines became a regular topic of the plans.

As we began to plan our holidays for 2015, the impending World Cruise in the following year was the main focus of our thoughts, but we needed to have something to look forward to in the months to come. There were very few options of new ports, so we eventually went for our favourite European destination of the Adriatic. It was a two-week cruise on Arcadia visiting Dubrovnik and Venice again, but at least there was one new destination with the island of Hvar in Croatia. Being a little careful with our money, we opted for a relatively new fare offer called an 'Early Saver'. This was saving us about £500 on the full brochure price.

Knowing there was a cruise pencilled in for the summer of 2015, including being at sea on our 40$^{th}$ Wedding Anniversary, Deb and I could relax in our new home for the winter.

# Fluid Pricing, and Our First Visit to Ireland

With my hip replacement almost forgotten, it was 2015 and we were settled in our new house in Herefordshire.

## P&O's Fluid Pricing

In March as Winter bade us goodbye, it was coming up to the time to pay the balance on the cruise we had booked on Arcadia sailing at the end of June. Being curious I glanced at the current price before ringing the travel agent to pay that balance, and was shocked to see that the original price was now seriously reduced, and was less than the supposed bargain 'Early Saver' we had booked.

I was very annoyed, and felt P&O were cheating by penalising passengers who booked early. I spoke with P&O and received a brush off from their customer support agents who quoted the small print that says they have the right to change prices without consulting the customer. Trading Standards agreed that this was not good practice, but could offer no real solution.

This was our first experience of P&O's Fluid Pricing policy.

The idea is quite clever, but very annoying. As the brochures for the coming year were published, the fare advertised was simply to get some interest. Very few people booked a cruise at those prices, with most knowing that bargains were available. Newspapers, or mail drops offered special offers such as the Early Saver Fare, or special enhanced on-board credit. As hundreds of hopeful holidaymakers telephoned the call centre, or logged on to the internet to get details, they had no idea that the verbal requests, or internet 'hits' on a cruise were being monitored, and as the number of people asking for details, or checking online reached a certain level, the price was increased.

As the popularity of a cruise diminished, the number of calls or online checks reduced, so fare prices were dropped to attract more interest. Instead of and Early Saver Fare, the adverts changed the offers to simply 'Saver Fares' or 'Getaway' deals suggesting they were selling off remaining cabins.

Of course, this way of selling only works if people who have purchased a cruise, don't go back and look at the prices again before the holiday begins. It didn't take long for seasoned cruisers to spot what was going on, and Facebook warned others of what to expect.

Unhappy about being 'ripped off' I quickly cancelled the cruise booking, which meant we lost our deposit. Then I immediately rebooked the same cruise at its new much lower price. We even managed to get a higher-grade cabin, and still saved enough to cover the lost deposit. Looking at Facebook this cancel and rebook process was quite a common practice, but the episode left me with yet another bad thought to be added to the list of doubts about P&O.

*Another Coach Break*

To ease the frustration of P&O's pricing fiasco, Deb and I looked around for a short break away from Herefordshire. Having had the experience of a coach holiday, we were not put off the concept, so we booked another, and this time it was going to Southern Ireland. It was a last-minute decision, and of course, it was a good deal.

On Sunday 19th April we had an early pick up in the centre of Hereford to begin our little holiday to the Republic of Ireland. The coach had multiple pickups on the way to the Ferry port of Holyhead in North Wales. This was quite a long journey, but I managed to stay comfortable on the coach and enjoyed watching the countryside from the unusually high up position. The ferry crossing was quite pleasant, and we arrived in Dublin at around 5:30 in the evening.

We then began a crazy 250 mile dash across Ireland to our hotel in the beautiful little area of Bantry Bay. There was just one short stop on the way, and it was after 10:00 by the time we arrived at the hotel. Sadly, the chef had already gone home, and after less than polite discussions with the management, we were given a bowl of soup and some bread rolls. To round the day off, there was no hot water, and we went to bed wondering if this really was a good idea.

It didn't surprise us, when there was still no hot water the next morning. It seemed the hotel had been closed for some time, and a plumbing issue meant some of the rooms had the water problem. At reception, the very apologetic staff gave Deb a key to a room that did have hot water where she could have a shower. The receptionist promised that the problem would be resolved by the time we came back from the day's trip out. At least the restaurant was ready for us, and we had a decent breakfast before going out on the first of the organised coach tours.

For our first excursion, we had a panoramic tour around the Beara Peninsular with glorious green hills and small mountains broken by peaceful bays with still water. We stopped for a snack in a small town called Castletown with coffee and scones to keep our stomachs happy. On the return journey we had a stop in a place called Glengarriff allowing us to explore little gift shops, and sit in the unexpectedly warm spring sunshine with an ice-cream.

Back at the hotel we turned on the tap in our room, and were greeted with piping hot water.

Before dinner Deb and I tried out the hotel's swimming pool, and the refreshing few minutes soothed my legs after the hours of sitting on the coach. Then it was time to eat, and there was plenty of well-prepared food on offer as we chatted to new friends over a glass or two of wine.

The holiday started a little badly, but it was now far better, and we were enjoying ourselves.

On day two our coach driver (Angus) took us to Blarney Castle where several of the more agile climbed the steps to the top to kiss the stone. I was not tempted, but Deb was game for the experience. From the castle we drove to Cork where we had free time to wander around the second biggest city in Ireland. The free time was too long, and we were very glad to board the coach for the return journey towards the hotel.

After dinner we walked down to Bantry for a delightful evening in a pub, to sample a glass or two of Guinness while we listened to a local folk group playing traditional songs.

Day three, and we opted out of another day in the coach. Instead, Deb and I walked down to the town again to explore more of Bantry and a chance to meet and talk to some of the friendly local people.

There was another lovely meal in the evening, plus a chance to enjoy the hotel staff trying to entertain us, but the idea of Karaoke was a step too far. We had an early night, and packed most of our bits and pieces before our homeward journey started in the morning.

The drive from Bantry to Dublin was far more relaxed with three stops in total including coffee and cakes. We were in Dublin by 2:30 and had a couple of hours to wander around the city. Deb and I went to Dublin Castle to learn a little about its history, and then spent some time and money in the gift shops.

There was then a drive through the Dublin rush hour traffic to our hotel near the ferry port where we would be going to the next morning. This hotel was adequate, but nothing like the friendly one in Bantry.

The homeward journey was another long day of travel. We set off before 7:00 in the morning and once on the ferry we settled down to a foggy crossing to Holyhead. At least we could sit in comfort on there, but before midday we were back on the coach.

The journey eventually ended with a taxi ride from Hereford where the coach dropped us off. It was gone 7:00 when we finally walked into our house in Kingstone.

The week away had been very enjoyable except for the long journeys each way. It certainly gave us an appetite to return to Ireland, but if we ever went by coach again, the journeys would have to be broken by a night in Ireland somewhere, rather than trying to go all the way in a single day.

*Adriatic Cruise Again*

Back from a generally very good few days away in Ireland, we settled down in Herefordshire, and I concentrated my efforts in the garden. I was beginning to realise that there was a lot of grass to cut, and a long conifer hedge to keep under control. My new hip was being thoroughly tested with several hours walking around behind the lawn mower, and several sessions of swinging a hedge trimmer around, including being at the top of a ladder.

Never mind, it wasn't long before we were back on-board Arcadia setting off across the Mediterranean.

It was another wonderful couple of weeks away on this lovely ship. The cruise followed a very familiar course with stops at Cadiz (Spain), and Messina (Sicily) before celebrating our 40<sup>th</sup> Wedding Anniversary on the Greek island of Corfu. Then it was a couple of our real favourites with Dubrovnik and Venice. The homeward journey included a first visit to the Croatian island of Hvar before a quick stop at Gibraltar where we didn't even get off the ship.

As we sailed up the Atlantic coast towards Southampton Deb and I were aware that our next cruise would be back on Arcadia for the World Cruise in less than six months.

*Another Change of Plans*

Well, it just wasn't to be.

First, I began to suffer from an ache in my side where the hip had been replaced. After the traditional few weeks of waiting to see a consultant, I was added to a surgeon's list to investigate why I was having ongoing hernia issues.

Secondly, and more concerning, Deb had a cancer scare, and that was more important than any holiday.

Fortunately, all was declared well with Deb, but in the meantime, we had contacted P&O to put off the World Cruise again before we had to pay the balance.

P&O were wonderful with us, and we were given another postponement for a year without any penalties. But this would be the final chance to reschedule for free.

So, any imminent plans for a January 2016 World Cruise were postponed for a year, and in 2017 we would be going away on Aurora to circumnavigate the planet again.

Without any worries about cancer, or fitting in the postponed world cruise, I could be flexible with a date for an operation to strengthen the muscles of my groin. I was assured that the plastic mesh to be inserted would prevent any reoccurrence of the hernia troubles. That was eventually scheduled for early in 2016, and I quickly recovered sufficiently to find an alternative holiday.

## 2016 – Fred Olsen Cruises

Saturday newspapers, well ours anyway, feature an abundance of holiday adverts, and the ones tempting me with cruises are like magnets. During the early months of 2016 as I pondered on what we might have been seeing and doing on the World Cruise, one of those adverts caught my eye for longer than usual. However, it wasn't for a P&O cruise, it was a last-minute bargain for a Fred Olsen ship. I think the destination somehow interested me, as it was a cruise going to Ireland, and the memories of the previous year's coach trip flooded back.

It was time to have a chat with Deb.

The cruise was just for a week, and was on a ship called the Balmoral, going to three ports, Belfast in Northern Ireland, plus Dublin and Cobh in the south. It didn't take us long to make up our minds, and we were soon handing over our money for a basic outside cabin. The idea was to have a short holiday, but also to try out the Fred Olsen product as an option for the future.

Fred Olsen Cruises are one of those rare family companies. Very much from Scandinavian roots, they are quite popular with the British cruise passenger base, with hundreds of loyal customers. Most of their ships were small, and many getting quite old. I think that if I had selected a different brochure from the top shelf in the Travel Agents, we might have booked a Fred Olsen cruise 16 years earlier. At that time they were cheaper than P&O, but with the Carnival Corporation influence,

P&O fare prices had remained fairly static while the competition had increased theirs, and Fred Olsen were now on a par, and even more expensive than we had been paying recently.

*Balmoral*

Balmoral was one of the bigger ships in the fleet with a capacity of around 1300 passengers. She was built in 1988 at the same Meyer Werft shipyard in Germany as P&O's Oriana and Aurora. For her first eight years she changed name back and forth between Crown Odyssey and Norwegian Crown. In 2007 the vessel was purchased by Fred Olsen, and as I write this chapter, is still with the company.

The ship had some major structural work before going into service with Fred Olsen. She was sliced into two halves, and an extra 30 metres section inserted into the middle. This increased the passenger capacity by around a hundred.

There are ten passenger decks, and we had booked an outside cabin which was slightly smaller than the P&O equivalent but perfectly adequate. Being Scandinavian, the food featured a lot of fish dishes that was not to my liking, but we always found something good to eat each night. The evening entertainment was similar to what we had been used to, but with a smaller number of singers and dancers, who shared their showtime duties with daytime activities.

It was 27th March when we boarded the ship at Southampton. Deb and I immediately explored the ship once we had unpacked. Obviously smaller, there was still a good range of bars and plenty of places to sit and relax. The crew were friendly, and first impressions were very good. The opening evening in the dining room went well, especially as we had purchased an inclusive drinks package. From dinner we went to see the first entertainment show with smiles on our faces.

Sadly our departure from Southampton coincided with the arrival of Storm Jasmine into the English Channel, and when we went to bed we found ourselves in some of the worst conditions we have encountered on a ship. Deb is quite comfortable with rough seas, but I suffer, and especially at the beginning of a cruise. I wasn't sick but the night didn't allow much sleep as I tried to stay on the bed.

The plan was for Balmoral to be sailing north towards the Irish Sea by morning, but we awoke to find ourselves still ploughing through the storm along the coast of Dorset. My day was all about finding somewhere in the middle of the ship to maintain my stomach and my dignity. I was not the only one, and comfortable seats away from windows were at a premium.

In the afternoon I joined a queue to get some sea-sickness relief from the doctor. Next in line to me were two young girls with a less than fashionable green hue. One of them kept her head very close to an ice bucket, while the other was madly in love with a waste paper bin. This really was quite a storm, and many passengers who believed themselves to be good sailors were struggling with the unpredictable zig-zag course of Balmoral as it was being tossed around.

I have always been aware of my sea-sickness, but for several years I had successfully used a little white pill called Avomine to control my wayward stomach. Sadly, in recent cruises I had discovered that this pill now made me hyperactive. As this was one of the most popular remedies on cruise ships, it now meant I had to have something different. The overworked ship's doctor prescribed a short sharp scratch in the bum with a different potion, and I came away with my bill, and hopes of some relief.

Within an hour or so I felt a bit better, and to be honest the sea was beginning to become a little friendlier as we rounded Land's End. Initially I thought that going to dinner would be too much to bear, but soon I was ready to join Deb and enjoy another delightful dinner, and even the accompanying free wine.

*Belfast*

The capital city of Northern Ireland is situated near the North Eastern tip of the country, some 300 miles north from Lands End and 20 or 30 miles west of Stranraer in Scotland. It is a major port standing on the River Lagan, and is the 12$^{th}$ biggest city in the UK with a population of around 340,000 people.

Our encounter with Storm Jasmine meant we were late for our arrival in Belfast, but eventually Balmoral was tied up alongside, and we could all enjoy an hour or two of *terra-firma* to walk on.

I had been to Belfast several years before when I was delivering training, so had some knowledge of landmarks, but my work didn't allow many opportunities for exploration. We had booked a very enjoyable coach tour of the city and had a stop in the centre to explore the area around the City Hall. From there we moved on to the newly opened Titanic Quarter in the dockland area of the city where the doomed vessel was built. We visited the superb exhibition hall and Deb was in her element as the history of the Titanic is one of her personal likes. There was a chance to have a cup of coffee there, as well as a look around the actual dock area where the ill-fated ship was launched from.

We both thoroughly enjoyed our afternoon in Belfast.

After a slightly shorter than planned visit to Northern Ireland, Balmoral tooted a farewell and we set of southwards for an overnight voyage of around 120 miles to our second stop of the cruise in Dublin. The wind had relaxed, the sea was friendlier, and the journey became far more comfortable as we began to truly enjoy the ship.

*Dublin*

This city is the largest on the island of Ireland with a population of over 1.1 million people. Our visit to Dublin included a night in port, so there was ample time to have some different tours.

Deb was really looking forward to this visit because of her passion for history. The visit would give her a chance to find out more about the Easter Uprising of 1912.

After the initial rush of early tours leaving the ship, we prepared ourselves for some exploring of Dublin on our own. A shuttle bus was available during our stay to take passengers back and forth with the centre of the city, and we were soon setting off from the busy port area. One of the first things I saw was quite a special moment for me. It was a major concert venue called The O2 that was previously called 'The Point'. It was the venue for the 1994 Eurovision Song Contest where 'Riverdance' was first introduced to the world. I fell in love with the sensational show based on that interval music and dance performance. I have been to watch it on numerous occasions, and have multiple CDs and DVDs of it.

... less memorable was that the winning song was from the Irish act of Paul Harrington and Charlie McGettigan who sang Rock 'n Roll Kids

With that personal thrill over, we completed the shuttle bus trip to the city centre, and armed with maps set off on our adventure. One of the ideas we had planned was to go to the GPO building where much of the Easter Uprising armed conflict took place in 1912. A new exhibition had just opened there, but the queues were far too long so we could just walk by the building. Instead we went to the Ambassador Theatre where there was another exhibition covering the history, and the outcome of the battle for Irish rule.

Our hour or so there was really quite special. We have access in England to one side of the story, but in Dublin we gained a far more comprehensive account of the reasons behind the conflict, much more about the people concerned, and masses of details of the fighting.

Perhaps this had been a little serious, so after leaving the exhibition we became more like typical English tourists and explored the street life of Dublin. We walked alongside the River Liffey, and then explored the busy shopping area. There were several different styles of music being played by single buskers or little groups of musicians. Souvenir shops were full of the traditional tourist items, and we bought a few things to remind us of a quite special morning.

We rounded off the trip with a snack in a French Bistro that overlooked the river. We were just a couple amongst the thousands of tourists, students, and normal local people enjoying this beautiful city.

Once back on Balmoral, we had a rest before getting ready to go out again for an evening meal in a local pub where we were to be entertained by an Irish Folk group. A coach took us a few miles out of the city to a fishing village called Howth and the Abbey Tavern. The meal was a traditional Irish Stew plus a few drinks including Guinness while we listened to the local music, and watched some local dancing. It was a superb evening, and I think most of us went to bed with contented alcoholic levels, and Irish songs in our heads.

Day 2 in Dublin and it was another organised tour for us. This time it was a Panoramic trip on a coach to look at the major buildings, and historical sites. It included a drive through

Pheonix Park, plus a drive past other major landmarks and tourist hot spots of the city. One place we drove slowly by was the Guinness Factory, and Deb remarked that we really ought to visit there one day. When we arrived back at the port area there wasn't a lot of time left before Balmoral throttled up the engines, and we set off southwards to our final stop of the cruise.

*Cobh*

The quite small port of Cobh (pronounced locally as 'Coff') is situated just outside the much larger port of Cork. It is little more than a harbour with a small town, but it is of serious historical interest to many. It was here that the Titanic anchored just a few metres offshore and took on her final passengers and supplies before setting off on her maiden voyage across the Atlantic Ocean.

We were able to now build on the stories and history of Belfast where the ship was built, and look around where the hundreds of passengers and crew that perished saw land for the final time.

Docked early as usual, we looked from Balmoral towards the harbourside. This is a small port, and after just a couple of minutes' stroll across the dockside, passengers can walk onto a train that will take them into the city of Cork. For those who wanted to stay nearby, there is a museum 50 metres away that looks at the history of emigration from the port, plus a lot about the ill-fated Titanic of course.

The landing place for cruise ships is virtually straight into the small sleepy town, and in ten minutes you can be wandering around the shops and watching the daily life of Cobh.

It was raining. Deb and I were in no hurry to get off or to get wet, but eventually we made a dash to the museum (free entrance) where we spent a lovely hour or so looking around the exhibitions. We also had a cup of coffee and a scone, and chatted to a few of the passengers, and some of the friendly local people. First impressions of Cobh were very positive.

After lunch on the ship we went ashore again. It was still raining, but hardly enough to be put off exploring a little more. This time we headed for the centre of the town, but our target was the old White Star Line ticket office where Titanic's passengers began their voyage back in 1912. The building is still there, and has been turned into an exhibition for people to learn more about the experience those passengers had. Deb has always been fascinated by the story of Titanic, and I was soon emersed into the history as we looked around and relived the hours as they bought their tickets, boarded the tender boats and set off towards the luxurious ship.

The town was called Queensferry at that time, and around midday on 11th April, 123 passengers were tendered out to Titanic along with a number of mail sacks. The ship soon set off west with 1308 passengers, and 898 crew. The ship (said to be unsinkable) hit an iceberg just before midnight on the 14th April, and sank a few hours later.

Around 1500 of the passengers and crew perished.

From Southern Ireland, Balmoral made her way back to Southampton, and before we knew it, we were home again in Herefordshire. Experimenting with a different cruise company had been a success. The product that Fred Olsen offered was superb, and it was a pleasant change to see so many of the crew actually smiling as they did their job.

Another silly little observation was that the girls working in the bar and restaurant had proper shoes to wear. On the P&O ships, it was quite obvious that the company did not supply the girls with anything but large heavy protective boots. Worse still, they didn't have the correct sizes and they had to clomp around awkwardly in the totally unsuitable footwear.

OK, so Balmoral was old, and not overly stable in the rough seas we encountered. But the cabins were good, the entertainment was good but on a smaller scale, and the food very pleasant – except for the abundance of fish. I was quite sure we would go back to Fred Olsen again if a cruise was going to an interesting destination.

## Life is not all about holidays

A little under three weeks after returning from our trip on Balmoral, there was a sad moment when Deb's mum (Jean) died. Jean had been in a care home for several years, and as the passing years slowed down her body, dementia was slowing down her mind.

In the end she caught pneumonia, and was forced to leave her care home where she was so happy, and go into hospital. We knew it was heading towards the end, but at least Deb and her brother had a few days to say goodbye.

Jean was cremated near us in Hereford, and most of the remaining family came to bid farewell, and chat about the good times we remembered.

Jean was the last of our parents to go on their final voyage, to be reunited with Deb's dad (Jim) who died on Boxing Day in 2010. My dad (Marshall) died after being knocked over by a car in 1965, and my mum (Mary) never stopped loving him until she joined him in 2001.

As I write this chapter of the book, it is September 2022 and virtually the whole nation is mourning as the Queen has just died. I was born when King George VI was on the throne, but I only have memories of Queen Elizabeth II as our monarch.

Death is a sober reminder that we are just temporary visitors to life. We are just drops of rain that last no more than a split second before being swallowed up by the planet to make way for the next. It is no good mourning for too long. Our brief moment of life shouldn't be wasted, and we should all try to make the most of what we do, and to leave wonderful memories that others might reflect on when we have gone.

## Back on Aurora

We had to cancel a cruise to concentrate on saying farewell to Jean, but as tears dried, and smiles returned, we looked for a chance of some summer sunshine again.

With Fred Olsen tried and tested, our thoughts were back with P&O.

Deb and I found a suitable summer cruise on Aurora that would take us back (yet again) to the Adriatic, featuring Dubrovnik and Venice.

Without a doubt, our favourite ship in the P&O fleet was now Aurora. We were so comfortable on her, and didn't need to go in search of favoured spots in the sunshine, or most comfortable seats in the bars for a glass of wine, or relaxing spots to read a book and maybe have a doze.

The destinations on this particular cruise were all ones we had visited before. Many were special to us, and we searched for different places to explore, or different tours to try. In Dubrovnik we had a simple walk, but then took a touristy boat ride on a pretend pirate ship. This took us out from the small harbour into the open sea, then around the small rocky Lokrum island. It gave us a view back towards the old town of Dubrovnik we had never been able to see before. The walls that we had walked on in the previous years looked immense and daunting, but we could see the hundreds of tourists walking on them, and imagine their smiles and pleasure looking out towards our little boat.

The next day we were in Venice with another overnight stay. On the first day we wandered around the city that appeared even busier than we remembered with large parties of Americans, Chinese, and Japanese tourists. The majority of them were insisting on posing for 'selfies' in front of spectacular scenes, rather than looking at them direct.

In the evening Deb and I went for a meal in a traditional trattoria with a pizza and a bottle of wine.

Following an overnight stay in port, we caught an early shuttle to St Mark's Square to fulfil our plans of visiting the Doge's Palace. On our previous visits, there were always queues to get in that snaked far around the square, but this time our arrival was timed perfectly to go straight inside.

The Doge's Palace was all about history, culture, furnishing, and grandeur from a different era. There was superb architecture to marvel at, and artwork from long-ago when the artists' aim was to reproduce a scene or a face, rather than the more modernistic attempts of creating an alternative version of reality. At one point we crossed over the canal below us, using a covered walkway that was the Bridge of Sighs. This was the route supposedly used by hundreds of people on their way to their execution. We looked out of the small windows, and saw the hundreds of tourists looking at the exterior of the bridge, and photographing our faces peering out.

After perhaps an hour in the delightful palace, we came out into the heat of the bright sunshine to see a vast queue of hopeful people waiting to take our places.

Before returning to Aurora, we had time to move back into the quieter lanes away from St Mark's Square to find more souvenirs, and cool our throats with a wonderful ice-cream.

Deb and I really love Venice.

After an evening sail-away down the canal towards the Adriatic, we relaxed into the comfort and familiarity of Aurora as we began the journey homewards.

The next morning we were on the island of Hvar for the second time, where we simply walked around and explored the shops. From Hvar the ship accelerated down the Adriatic, sped by Sicily and purred across the Mediterranean to the last short stop in Gibraltar. With nothing else to tempt us, we stretched our legs with a stroll around the main street.

Aurora set off again and turned northwards towards home. This had been yet another delightful cruise, and we knew that in just over six months, we would be back on her again for the world cruise.

# Oriana

There was ages left of 2016 until before our World Cruise, and before we knew it, Deb and I were boarding Oriana at the beginning of September, for a quick sail around the coast of Britain.

The first stop of this eight-day cruise was Guernsey. This island is a tender port where cruise ships anchor off the largest town called St Peter Port. It is one of the Channel Islands which are closer to France than England. There are five more recognised islands with Alderney in the north, Guernsey plus the tiny Herm and Sark in the middle, and the largest one Jersey in the south.

*Sark*

On our previous visit we had explored St Peter Port which is the biggest town on Guernsey, but today we had booked a trip to the nearby island of Sark.

With Oriana at anchor, and the sea calm, the tendering process went smoothly. After one of the lifeboats took us ashore to St Peter Port, we walked across the harbour area to a local ferry that would take about ¾ hour to travel across to the tiny island of Sark.

Sark is small. It has an area of little more than two square miles. There are less than 500 people living there, but this number swells with the summer tourism. It has a very slow pace of life, and the locals are happy to meet and greet visitors.

One of the most peculiar things about Sark is that there are no cars.

Being a small island, walking between places is quite easy, but if you are in a hurry the bicycle is the most common form of transport. Horses pull carriages if you want a more relaxing journey, and the only other form of powered transport are tractors. We were actually taken up from the harbour on a tractor pulled passenger trailer, where you sit in two rows looking sideways.

From then on we spent most of the day walking with our guide looking at the culture, and learning about the history of the island and its community.

Late in the afternoon we returned to the harbour and prepared for the ferry ride back to St Peter Port, but as we were a little late, the ferry took us direct to Oriana.

It was a truly special day, and if you visit the Channel Islands, a trip to Sark is recommended.

Sadly for cruise ship passengers, the sea is often rather active around Guernsey, and it is quite regular for the tendering to be impossible. This is all a part of cruising, and safety of passengers is always a priority.

*Scrabster*

From Guernsey we headed north to the port of Scrabster.

"**Where is that**" I hear you say.

Well, it is within a handful of miles from the most northerly point of mainland Scotland, and the nearest town is Thurso.

This was another port where we anchored offshore, and were tendered to the dockside, and it was little more than a dock.

A lot of people chose to stay on the ship all day, but Deb and I opted to catch the shuttle bus into nearby Thurso. This is a small town with a population of just under 8000 people, and we were warned there wasn't a lot to do. Never mind, we enjoyed the walk looking in the shop windows, and had a rather delightful coffee and cake in the café attached to the museum.

*Kirkwall*

Overnight Oriana sailed a little further north to the island group of Orkney and the port of Kirkwall.

We were really packing in new destinations on this cruise, and they were all in the British Isles.

Orkney, or perhaps best called the Orkney Islands, is an archipelago of around 70 islands, but only 20 are inhabited. Our overnight sail was not very far as the port is little more than 10 miles north of the tip of the Scottish mainland. Of the numerous islands, the largest is called '***Mainland***' where we were docked in the largest town of Kirkwall, which is the administrative centre for the island group.

We had a tour today that was mainly about giving us a panoramic tour of the island with its rugged coast, and quite barren countryside. There was however a major stop at a historic site called Skara Brea. Here we looked at a Neolithic settlement dating back to perhaps 3000 BC. The stone buildings were built below ground level to protect against the cold winds, and topped with grass to provide more insulation.

It was quite fascinating listening to the local guide whose soft-spoken Scottish accent sounded almost like poetry, as she recounted the history of the settlement, and how its people lived from day to day. At one point our group of passengers were standing above the stone buildings and we were being blasted by a wind whipping up sand from the nearby beach. Someone asked if this was the normal weather on the island, and the guide replied that it was *"**Only a bit of a blow**"*.

By the time we walked back towards a museum giving more information about the site, we were all rather cold and windswept.

The panoramic coach ride then continued with a further windy walk around another example of the history with an ancient stone circle. For the last hour or so we were allowed to stay in the comfort of the coach as we wound our way around the coast back to Kirkwall. During this part of the tour we drove by a massive area of sheltered water known as Scapa Flow. This was yet more history, but now from the 1st and 2nd World Wars when this was the UK's naval base.

Back on Oriana we warmed up and had some lunch, before returning by shuttle bus into the town centre of Kirkwall for a wander around the shops. The town is quite small, and not geared up for tourism, so it wasn't long before we were on our way back to the ship.

*Stornoway*

While we enjoyed our evening meal, and slept, Oriana sailed south west from Orkney to the Western Isles, where we arrived the next morning in sheltered waters just off the port of Stornoway. This was a tender port, and we had no intention of any organised tours. Instead we took a mid-morning tender to the shore and had a relaxing stroll around the town.

We had a cup of coffee, and then walked up to a castle. Deb and I never found a way in, but it was a pleasant way to stretch our legs.

*Dublin*

Oriana had finished her exploration of the Scottish ports, and our final stop was another visit to the Republic of Ireland at Dublin.

It was a chance to fulfil an outstanding wish from our previous visits. We had a coach tour of the city that looked at a lot of the spectacular sites, and finished with a visit to the Guinness factory to see how the black stuff is made, and then to sample it.

Very enjoyable, but on balance, the creamy stout is not really to my taste.

It was time for the ship to head home again.

With just another day to enjoy this wonderful ship, it was time to reflect on a cruise we never really planned to have. There was no sunshine, and the sea wasn't too friendly, but we enjoyed finding out more about British towns. The island life was at a much slower pace that we normally experienced, and the people were all very friendly.

Deb and I were quite sure we would try a cruise like this again one day, to explore even more of what the UK has to offer.

That was the end of our cruising adventures for 2016, as there was just three months left before we would be setting off on our second World Cruise.

How lucky we are!

## 2017 Searching for New Sunrises

The year 2017 began with another major adventure and our second world cruise.

After we returned home from our first global adventure in 2012, our initial thoughts were to plan for a second world cruise in 2017. The buzz of excitement that was in our heads meant we couldn't wait that long, and we tried to arrange this sequel cruise for 2015. Illness led to that change of plan being delayed for two years, so here we were, just as Deb and I initially wanted.

On the 8th January, we left a snow-covered Herefordshire, in a car full of luggage for the journey to Southampton. The drive is so familiar, and midway through the afternoon we were booking into the Holiday Inn just like we had done so often in the years of our cruising.

In the evening we had fish and chips in the hotel restaurant, and then shared a bottle of wine in our room. I didn't get much sleep in the night, and it was a relief to get up early, look out the window, and see Aurora waiting for us a couple of hundred metres away along the dockside.

Breakfast over, we went for our usual stroll around the city, and then stacked our suitcases back into the car before setting off (very early) for the cruise terminal. This time the car was left with a private company until we would return home in three and a half months' time.

Our level of excitement was the same as five years previously, and the buzz of anticipation was like a drug making us light-headed for the adventure to come.

By the time we came home on 22nd April, the winter had turned to spring, and we were ready to settle down again. There were hundreds of new photographs of different places we had visited, and hundreds of special memories stored away in our brains for ever.

Of course, I kept a blog of our adventure, and it was turned into another book. This time it was called '**Searching for New Sunrises**' and chronicles the places we saw, the fun we shared with four wonderful friends we made on the cruise, and more of the experiences that only long voyages at sea can create.

If you want to know more about what we got up to, or general thoughts about world cruising, I am sure you will enjoy the book.

I won't try and recreate that book here, but as a summary, it was just as special as the first circumnavigation, but this time we went eastwards around the globe. On balance my suggestion would be to travel westwards if you have a choice. The highlights were seeing several new destinations around Australia, New Zealand, and America, and the tours we booked were more about experiencing local cultures rather than bigger, taller, and glitzier spectacles. Perhaps because we knew what a long cruise is like, there wasn't quite the same buzz, and during the last few days Deb and I were ready to go home.

The most rewarding aspect of the cruise was meeting and becoming wonderful friends with our dinner tablemates. Angie, Richard, Rosemary and Robin shared our lives for the 104 days and nights. We drank a lot together; we laughed a lot together and shared some marvellous experiences. The six of us were so close that we planned to meet up again after our return home. We stayed in contact, and even got together again for a weekend in a hotel when our friendship proved as strong as ever. More importantly, while we were on that World Cruise we all agreed to meet up again in 2019 for another major adventure on Aurora.

## Adonia Returns to the Fleet

Early in 2016, Carnival had decided to move a ship called Adonia from the P&O flag to an experimental cruise company called 'Fathom'. It meant that P&O didn't have a small ship in its fleet, and many dedicated cruisers mourned her loss. While on our world cruise it was announced that little Adonia was coming back.

This was obviously quite a sudden decision, as there was no cruise programme in place for the ship. Being at the high tier of the loyalty group, Deb and I were some of the first to hear where Adonia would be sailing to for the first couple of months. She was a ship we had not been on, and we really fancied the idea of seeing what the little vessel was like.

Even more appealing was that the fare prices were ridiculously low to try and fill as many cabins as possible. When we saw the price of a seven-night cruise at the end of July, the temptation was too much. The price was so attractive that we decided to splash out on a suite rather than our usual balcony cabin.

So, on the 28$^{th}$ July we boarded P&O's smallest ship to look at how different it was from our preferred vessels. The cruise was simply sailing south, but rather than crossing the Bay of Biscay, we would be going into the bay and stopping at the French port of Bordeaux. From there the ship would be visiting the Spanish city of Bilbao, before finishing with a day off the coast of Guernsey.

*Adonia*

Built at the 'Chantiers de l'Atlantique' shipyard in the French city of St Nazaire, this ship started life in the Renaissance Cruise Line and named simply 'R Eight'. She was one of several virtually identical ships operated by Renaissance Cruises, and her first season was in 2001.

She had a total of 12 decks with 9 for her less than 800 passengers. They were looked after by about 380 members of crew.

After just two years (2003) her named change to Minerva II for Swan Hellenic cruises. This cruise line was one of the P&O family of companies, and like all the others became a part of the Carnival organisation. Four years later (2007), as with many of the Carnival ships, she changed flag and name again and became the Royal Princess. In 2011 there was another move and this little ship flew the P&O flag and was given the name Adonia. Apart from the brief change with a year in the Fathom group, she was a popular ship in the P&O fleet.

*The Cruise Begins*

Yes, we stayed in the Holiday Inn the night before the cruise, and yes we were boarding the ship very early making the most of our time on-board. First stop was the restaurant where we enjoyed a glass of two of welcome fizz, plus a handful of canapes as we chatted to some other passengers.

Slightly light headed we were quickly given the all clear to go to our cabin, and check out what a suite looked like. It was huge. There was a vast lounge area with a dining table big enough for four people. A big unit was nearby containing a truly large television, with plenty of drawers below it to store cutlery and plates. For relaxation there were a pair of large sofas come armchairs, with side tables for drinks and canapes.

The bedroom area was tucked away in a corner and it was as big as some cabins we had stayed in before. There were four giant wardrobes that would have been wonderful on our world cruises to store all our clothes. Of course this was just a short cruise, so we had room to spread our clothes out, and store suitcases in the cavern left over.

The bathroom was similarly vast with room to swing a large tiger rather than just a cat. This was luxury, with giant sinks, a shower cubicle, and there was even a deep jacuzzi bath to soak in.

Being a suite it also had more than average balcony space. The cabin was on a rear corner of the ship, so had balconies to the side and the back, with loungers plus another large table and dining chairs.

… and then there was the butler.

He quickly made an appearance and offered his service at any time if we needed anything. He showed us the bell to ring if we needed him, and before leaving, he asked what fruit we would like each day. We had plans to use him for an evening meal later in the cruise, but for now we allowed him to go and meet his other passengers.

There was one request on the second day, and that was when Deb asked him how the jacuzzi worked. Suitably demonstrated, we enjoyed this little bit of warm bubbly immersion several times. Deb was on the phone to our daughter, and mentioned about asking the butler to show her how to use the jacuzzi, and there was a momentary silence on the other end. Deb then explained that she and the butler hadn't actually been in the bath during the demonstration.

We were soon unpacking, after refusing the offer from the butler to do it for us. Now it was time to explore the ship. The layout was typical of other cruise ships we had been on, but just on a slightly smaller scale. It didn't take us long to get from one end to the other of the public decks, and there weren't so many flights of stairs to go up and down. We became familiar with the show lounge and bars plus the main dining room and buffet. It all looked good, and we were looking forward to what Adonia had to offer.

It was soon time for Adonia to say cheerio to Southampton, and we made the most of the cabin balcony with a glass of champagne. That was when we discovered that we could hear the sounds of the mooring ropes being pulled in. If you are in a cabin at the rear of a small ship, there is every likelihood that the motors will be heard, and they were quite loud. Fortunately we only experienced this on arrivals and departures, and having left Southampton, we had a couple of days before we would hear it again.

The journey south wasn't the most pleasant, and sailing into the Bay of Biscay was testing my stomach to the limit. Eventually the waves calmed, and I realised we had entered La Garonne River heading towards the city of Bordeaux.

It took a while to sail up the river to the port, and we passed various vineyards and little hamlets before arriving at the city's port early in the afternoon.

*Bordeaux*

Situated in the south west of France, Bordeaux lies on the Garonne River in the Gironde region of the country. It is the sixth most populated city of France with a little over 250,000 people, who are known as *Bordelais* if they are male, and *Bordelaises* if they are female.

The city is all about the wine industry, and tourists come to sample it, while looking at the architecture of the city, and learning about its history. The settlement appears to have been around by 300 BC and known by the Celtic tribes as Burdigala. Like so many other places at the time, the Romans came along, and they spent a few centuries trying to protect it.

Enough of the historical bits and pieces. We were there to take a look at a new destination. As soon as we were set free, we went ashore to explore. Adonia was tied up in the middle of the city, so everything was close by. We wandered for little more than an hour and spent quite a while at a large square where many of the locals were enjoying themselves. The centre of attraction was a water feature with fountains that occasionally sprayed water for children to run in, and for adults (most of them) to avoid. The surface of the area where this water delight was made such that the water left a shallow film that shone in the sunlight. This is known as the *Miroir d'Eau* (Water Mirror).

I think we probably had an ice-cream as we soaked up the atmosphere, but our time was limited with big plans for the evening.

Adonia was staying in port overnight and being tied up with the city backdrop, we decided to have dinner brought to us and served by the butler out on the balcony.

Around us on the waterfront there were many of the ship's passengers, plus hundreds of locals strolling in the evening sunshine, and the air was full of music and laughter.

It was a really special meal, and experience.

The next morning we explored the city a little more. There was a circus very near to where we were docked, and we walked through it as we looked for a little more of the history of the city. There was time for a coffee as well before getting back on Adonia for an afternoon sail-away.

*Bilbao*

Overnight we sailed south to the Spanish city of Bilbao. It is Spain's tenth most populated city with a population of around 350,000. Within the area of Biscay it is the largest city, and I am sure the ship's port presenter gave us lots of information about Bilbao, but it is long forgotten.

We avoided booking any tours, but Deb and I boarded the shuttle bus that took us from the port area to the centre. One of the most obvious tourist attractions in Bilbao is the Guggenheim Museum, and after finding our bearings in the shopping area, we made our way to this amazing building. We didn't go in, but enjoyed ourselves looking at the sculptures around the external area of the museum, and being entertained by street artists. As well as full of tourists, a lot of local families appeared to be spending time there as well.

Some of the passengers who did go inside said that it was magnificent.

We were happy to enjoy the busy atmosphere and have a coffee before making our way back to the shopping area, to catch the shuttle bus back home to Adonia.

This was another port and city to add to the list of places we have visited, and we knew that if we ever came back, we could take a leisurely look around the museum.

That evening we heard the sound of the ropes being pulled back into the ship, and we set off again to sail out of the Bay of Biscay, and head north to our last stop at the island of Guernsey.

This should have been our third visit to the Bailiwick of Guernsey, but sadly the sea was too rough to launch the tender boats. Instead we bobbed around at anchor for a few hours until it was time to begin the final leg of our cruise back to Southampton.

*Final thoughts on Adonia*

We thoroughly loved the atmosphere of little Adonia. Our sail up the river into the city centre of Bordeaux made us realise that small vessels opened up new itineraries that were not reachable even by the next size up of ships in the P&O fleet. We had to look at what other companies had to offer, and certainly the Fred Olsen fleet had small ships, that would be worth considering.

The suite had been a real pleasure to have more space, and the use of a butler was rather special. It was certainly a tick in the box for another aspect of cruising, but we struggled to justify any thoughts of returning to a suite in the future. Apart from the nights, we didn't spend a lot of time in the cabin to make the most of the space we had, and the reality of having a butler was quite confusing. We thoroughly enjoyed having a meal served to us on our balcony while watching the evening life of Bordeaux pass by us, and having canapes left each evening was different, but his constant offers of assistance were quite embarrassing.

On balance the suite was worth trying, but once was probably enough. Unless a similar half price offer comes along again, I don't think we will look beyond a simple outside, or balcony cabin in the future.

*What happened to Adonia?*

That cruise was our only adventure on this ship, because in 2018 P&O said goodbye to Adonia. Hundreds of small ship lovers shed a tear or two at the loss of the atmosphere and intense customer focus possible with such a vessel. She was purchased by another cruise company, called Azamara, and after a major refit she became the Azamara Pursuit. This company liked the size and style of the R Class designed ships, and in 2022 they had three of these virtually identical ships in their higher end market cruise line fleet.

*Oceana*

In the autumn of 2017, another last-minute cruise deal tempted us. It was for just 10 days on Oceana and on the 29th October she sailed south, and dipped her hull in the Mediterranean with visits to Malaga, and Gibraltar. Then turning north towards home she said hello to Lisbon, La Coruna, and Cadiz.

There were no new destinations, but it gave Deb and I some unexpected late year sunshine.

Sadly, I don't remember much about the cruise, but I'm positive that we enjoyed ourselves.

*Back to Fred Olsen*

Before the year ended, we set off for our fourth cruise of 2017. This time we returned to the Fred Olsen Cruise line, and a ship called the Black Watch.

With an original passenger capacity of less than 550, this little ship started life in 1972 as the 'Royal Viking Star'. Nineteen years later she joined the Norwegian Cruise Line (NCL) as the 'Westward', and then in 1994 there was three years with the Royal Cruise Line as the 'Odyssey'. Her final move was in 1996 when she arrived in the Fred Olsen line becoming the very popular 'Black Watch'. By then the various refits had increased the passenger numbers to greater than 800.

This was another chance to sample the Fred Olsen product again, and another small ship.

It left Southampton on 14th December and sailed north to give us a Christmas Markets cruise experience. In the seven days of the cruise we visited three countries with three new ports at Hamburg, Amsterdam, and Antwerp.

In Hamburg we toured around the city with a wonderful guide pointing out the historical aspects of the city, and of course mentioning the Beatles regularly. That was followed by a couple of hours in the vast market to eat Bratwurst and drink Glüwein while we made the most of the colourful stalls and happy atmosphere. There were one or two little souvenirs of course to remind ourselves of the visit.

The next day we were in Amsterdam by late in the afternoon. In the evening we had a canal cruise with a superb guide, to look at the waterside lights, while we sampled local cheeses and consumed far too much wine.

We stayed in port overnight, and in the morning we walked into the city beginning our exploration by spending quite a while looking around the busy train station. Then we moved into the city centre to window shop and absorb some of the atmosphere.

... and found more festive market stalls

Deb and I were quite surprised by the very open selling of cannabis in main street shops, but we kept away from that, in favour of Cumin flavoured Gauda cheese.

Black Watch then travelled on to Antwerp where we had another night in port. The ship was docked in the middle of the city with a fun fair just a few steps away on the dockside. We were 10 minutes-walk from the centre of the city with another Christmas Market to enjoy. We had more continental street food, mulled wine, and wonderful hot chocolate drinks. To make the atmosphere even more magical we wandered away from the market into the side streets, and came across a Christmas Carol concert just outside of the cathedral, with the children of local schools smiling and celebrating the festive season.

The next morning we had time to return to the city before a pre-lunch departure. There was sufficient time to stock up on Belgian chocolate before returning to the ship for the short sail back to Southampton.

Black Watch was another ship that attracted passengers who wanted the small ship atmosphere. The service was amazing with a friendly crew again who always had a smile on their faces, and appeared genuinely happy.

The only personal negative was that the varied menu in the dining room did focus a lot on fish dishes, so my choices were a little limited. The food was still very good, and we had a deal that gave us free alcohol throughout the cruise.

Of course, the entertainment was very much on a smaller scale than P&O. There were good quality cabarets, or performances by the show team each evening in the show lounge, as well as quizzes and games during the daytime. The ship was decorated beautifully for Christmas, but sadly it also meant the ship played continual Christmas background music, which featured Michael Buble versions of festive songs.

... Yuk!!

During the early evening the festive music drove us so crazy, that we looked forward to the resident pianist to come along and play a selection of tunes, and as regular members of his audience we frequently requested non-Christmas tunes.

Black Watch left the fleet during the Covid shut down, and although planned to continue as accommodation by an Indian company for workers, it appears to have been beached and scrapped in 2020.

## 2018 - Four Cruises Again!

Our love of cruising had not subsided. This was a year when we went crazy again and spent our childrens' inheritance on four cruises.

*Cruise 1 - Oriana*

In February we returned to Oriana for 12 nights sailing south to Madeira and three ports in the Canaries. On the way back we had yet another day in Lisbon. There were no new ports, or new cities, and the only tour we booked was a transfer to a large and busy Sunday market in Lanzarote.

This was purely a holiday, and a chance to enjoy the nostalgia of our first ever cruise ship.

*Cruise 2 - Aurora*

Three months later we set off from Southampton again on her sister ship Aurora. She turned left at Gibraltar and we cruised around the western Mediterranean visiting ports in Spain and Italy. Our first stop was new to us, and that was Alicante.

Alicante

This city of around 330,000 people is on the tourist trap eastern coast of Spain. It is less than 100 miles from Cartagena in the south and Valencia to the north. If you sail to the north east for about 200 miles you will arrive at the Balearic Island of Majorca.

Historical records show that the area has been inhabited for 7000 years, but it suffered for centuries of the usual battles between warring tribes, and various Spanish Royal Houses who saw the merits of the coastal port.

The busy port of Alicante is surrounded by various industries, and the city is a major service provider, including being the site for the Headquarters of the European Union Intellectual Rights. But, like so many other Spanish coastal cities, it also depends on tourism.

Being our first visit, Deb and I booked on a tour to get a feel for the city. Our guide took us on a walking tour of the historical Moorish area of the city, plus landmark buildings such as the Town Hall and Cathedral. We also visited the Santa Barbera Castle where we had a taster of Sangria with local nibbles, plus a chance to use the toilets of course.

We enjoyed ourselves, but after just a few hours in this city, I don't think Alicante will ever be on our list of specialist subjects for a quiz.

Repeat visits to other ports

From Alicante Aurora purred northwards overnight to Barcelona. This is one of our regular stops, but we had not been on many organised tours here, so opted to try one that was almost a repeat of a tour we did in 2001. It took us on a walking tour of the Gothic area, and the route allowed us to see various examples of Gaudi architecture. There was then a photo stop at the current city cathedral, before a return visit to the proposed new one called the Sagrada Familia. There is still no hard and fast end date for this amazing building, but even during the time we have been coming here, some of the features we saw being created in 2001 were already having to be repaired.

From the centre of Barcelona we headed up to Mont Juic and a walk around the Spanish Village. This is a series of small areas constructed to be like different regions of Spain, to show the architectural variations and allowing visitors to sample regional food. We had an ice-cream that tasted very similar to ice-cream found in most of the Mediterranean countries ... delicious!

The visit to the Spanish Village had been too short, and we decided that if we ever came back to Barcelona again, we would concentrate on another visit here.

During the night our floating home sailed gently onwards towards our next planned stop at Cannes in France. Unfortunately, our captain announced that we would not be visiting Cannes because Aurora needed to spend more time at a later port, to allow repairs to a propeller shaft.

So, France was forgotten, and our next stop was in Italy at the port of Livorno. We had been here before when we went to Florence, but we booked a tour to go there again, plus a stop on the way at Pisa. Hence, we ticked another box with photographs of the pair of us holding up the wonky Tower of Pisa, as well as enjoying a delightful few hours in Florence.

From Livorno we turned south and arrived at the highlight port of Civitavecchia, to allow hundreds of the passengers a chance to visit Rome. Deb and I have spent quite a time wandering around Rome on our previous visits, so this time we went on a Panoramic coach tour around the nearby countryside. We thoroughly enjoyed the views, had a pleasant snack of local nibbles with wine, and a leisurely stroll in a small village. On balance I think we made the right decision to avoid the hustle and bustle of Rome.

Aurora turned towards home. There were visits to Almeria and Gibraltar to allow us to stretch our legs, but we soon woke up in Southampton for the drive back to Herefordshire.

*Cruise 3 - Azura*

At the end of September, we tried out another new ship to us. This time it was P&O's Azura that is the sister ship of Ventura. The internal layout of Azura and Ventura are physically quite similar, but lounge and restaurants are different.

Since we sailed on Ventura eight years earlier, our cruises had all been on the favoured small vessels of P&O plus even smaller ones with Fred Olsen. This time Deb and I were confronted with a ship that had more than a thousand extra passengers, and a completely different atmosphere. Internally, Azura is beautiful, but it is designed to appeal to party people. The bars were busier with a younger age-group that demanded constant loud music, and an obvious desire to drink more alcohol. Yes, there were quite a lot of older people, but many of them seemed similarly disenchanted, and who occasionally yearned for a quiet spot.

This ship is perfect for the future generation of the majority of cruise ship passengers, but I don't think Deb and I see ourselves as being in that category anymore.

During our holiday we were bombarded with literature, and presentations, about P&O's up and coming new ship. Sadly, it was not a replacement for the aging, Oriana, Aurora, Arcadia, or Oceana, it was an even bigger floating holiday camp that would be called Iona. She would be capable of taking 5200 passengers, feature a vast Atrium which can allow a trapeze act, a giant television screen on the deck, its own gin distillery, and wall to wall partying. Apparently, it will have all the things that passengers have been asking for, but obviously that survey never got to the small ship traditionalists.

Anyway, that Azura 12-night cruise took us to Lisbon, and a number of Spanish ports that we had visited before. It gave us a little autumn sunshine and a chance to make up our minds about ships of this size. By the time we came back, we had confirmed our thoughts that these giant ships are not for us.

*Cruise 4 - Saga*

After sampling what P&O's giant Azura could offer us, Deb and I were most definitely falling out of love with the P&O product, and the huge ships the company appears to be focussing on. We still loved cruising, and we had to make up our minds about other cruise companies.

The next cruise brochure we picked up was for Saga Cruises, and along with discount offers for new passengers, we found a couple of suitable short taster cruises.

One of the reasons for our decision to try out the Saga Cruises product, was that they planned to build brand new small ships in the near future.

The company had been in operation for many years, and limited passengers to those over the age of 50. This meant that the product was most definitely for adults only, and it did lead to many stories of a ship full of pensioners asleep all day, and drinking Ovaltine at night.

When we walked into see our favourite travel agent about an advert we had seen in a newspaper, Saga had two aging ships in their fleet.

There was the Saga Sapphire built in Germany and launched in 1981 as the Europa. As with many cruise ships of that era, she was traded between various smaller cruise lines and had various names, until Saga purchased her in 2012. She was then renamed the Saga Sapphire. The cruise line had several ships over the years with a name of a precious stone.

The Sapphire was small and only carried around 750 passengers which was the typical size for the Saga Cruises product. On her arrival she became the flag ship of the Saga fleet, and had a very loyal following by the passengers.

We saw this ship a couple of times while on our travels, but never boarded her.

Alongside Sapphire, the company also had the Saga Pearl. She was also built in Germany and launched in 1981 beginning life as the Astor. Another cruise ship that swapped companies and names, she came to Saga in 2010 and took on the name of Saga Pearl, or more accurately the Saga Pearl II. In 2012 the company renamed her the Spirit of Adventure, but that was a temporary name, and she reverted to Pearl in 2013.

The Pearl was even smaller than the Sapphire with around 500 passengers.

*Our First Cruise with Saga*

The cruise we were interested in was for a five-night taster on the Saga Pearl. It simply went north to Bremerhaven and Hamburg and we booked one of the cheapest inside cabins. The price was based on a guaranteed grade of cabin, so we didn't even know what we would actually be sleeping in until we arrived at the docks. As well as already being a good deal, our agent managed to get a further discount because it was our first cruise with Saga, and yet another discount for subscribing to their magazine. If it turned out to be a disaster, it wouldn't have been financially painful.

This first adventure with Saga Cruises was very different from what we had experienced before. Their ships were all small, and Pearl sailed with around 500 passengers, and about 250 crew to look after us. The little break was not about the destinations, and wasn't really about the ship, it was an opportunity to try out the Saga product. We had heard that the company was nearing completion of the first of two brand new ships that would be for 1000 passengers, and all cabins had balconies. This sounded very interesting.

Saga charge more than P&O and the other similar cruise companies, so we had to check out what we would be getting for that extra money. There was also the stigma about the company only dealing with older passengers, and stories of Ovaltine, wheelchairs, and hundreds of people asleep all day.

On 4th December we were ready to set off with our bags packed and waiting in the hall of our house in Herefordshire. Within a few minutes of the scheduled time, there was a knock on the door from our transport chauffer. Transport to and from the ship is a part of the inclusive deal, so this was a first for us. Our bright and professional chauffer politely introduced himself and carried our suitcases to the shiny People Carrier waiting outside. We followed and made ourselves comfortable in the leather seats and we set off towards the ship's terminal in Portsmouth.

We shared the transport with another friendly couple and the journey was a pleasant ride. Late in the morning there was a break to stretch our legs and refresh ourselves, but soon we were back on the road. Just before 2:00 we arrived at the terminal, and almost immediately a porter looked at his clipboard and told us what cabin we would be in, before whisking our cases away.

Because it was a small ship, check-in was a simple process with virtually no waiting. After a quick glance around the terminal building that we had never seen before, our number was called, and we boarded a shuttle bus for the short ride to the dockside. There was hardly a chance to draw breath before Deb and I were boarding our floating holiday home, and met by cheerful faces eagerly directing us to the crew member who would be taking us to our cabin.

The experience was already looking very positive.

Our cabin was number 307 on A Deck, and plenty big enough with lots of drawer and wardrobe space. The only weird thing was that the two beds were at right angles to each other, but once we got used to it, there wasn't a problem. Yes, the décor and furniture were dated, the bathroom bits were showing their years of use, but the ship was 28 years old.

After a couple of minutes, a knock on the door heralded our chamber maid introducing herself. She made small talk for a moment and asked if we needed anything special, and what fruit we would like to have. A fruit bowl quickly arrived with what we asked for, and that was kept full daily.

With clothes packed away, it was time to go and explore the Saga Pearl.

Armed with our plan of the ship, we went up one flight of stairs to the main public deck (Promenade) where the Discovery Lounge was at the front. This general-purpose room had entertainment in the evening, talks during the day, and more importantly that day, afternoon tea. There was a good choice of snacks, but we discovered that Saga do not automatically have semi-skimmed milk. We survived the normal milk but hoped that semi-skimmed would be available.

After our little refuelling break, we wandered along the Promenade Deck internal corridor, and just outside of the lounge was Shackleton's Bar that we frequented quite a lot. Beyond that was the library area to one side, plus smaller areas in the middle and one the other side, including future cruises. We regularly sat in the library area to read our books, or just to relax (dozing in my case).

Going a little further towards the back from the library we came to the main dining room that was quite small, but plenty big enough for the number of passengers. Dining was available without booking, and although some people liked the same table each night, we took pot luck, and never regretted it.

Down one flight of stairs to A Deck, and we found the reception desk, and tours office. Another flight of stairs down was B Deck where it was predominantly for cabins, but also had the cinema, plus hairdressers in the middle, and the laundrette towards the front. Finally, down on the C Deck was the salon, treatment rooms, and medical centre.

Going upwards from Promenade Deck was Boat Deck with cabins near the front, but the popular alternate buffet style Veranda restaurant near the rear, that could be opened up onto the stern deck with a swimming pool. Although we used the main dining room in the evenings, the Veranda was our favoured venue for breakfast and lunch. It also had the very popular all-day fruit juices and hot drink machines with jars of delicious cookies.

Up again to Bridge Deck where the superior cabins were, plus the small Sundowner Bar at the back, that opened up onto another area of open deck.

Finally at the top was the Sun Deck with a good deal of space to enjoy the sunshine. It should be remembered that we were on the ship in December, and few people spent much time on any of the ship's chilly outside decks.

We briefly explored as much of the ship as we could, and then after considering our options, we went to Shackleton's and had a couple of glasses of Prosecco. Another aspect of the Saga product was the inclusive alcohol, as long as we didn't try and go for the posh stuff.

Perfect for us!

The rest of our day on Saga Pearl continued with the obligatory Muster Drill before we went for a shower and then to dinner. The food was good, and the table mates were a good laugh, who enjoyed the free wine as much as we did. The meal ended with the optional cheese board, which turned out to be a cheese trolley. There was an amazing choice of different cheeses, that put anything we were offered on P&O to shame.

Feeling very positive about our first experiences of Saga, the evening was rounded off by the entertainment team welcome on board show. It was in the Discovery Lounge where there was a small stage area at the front. The boys and girls sang and danced with enthusiasm, and although not as spectacular as on a large ship, it was professional, and very enjoyable. This lounge was flat and it was difficult for the audience to see what was happening if they were at the back, or to the extreme sides. To overcome this, there were a number of large television screens along the sides that relayed the performance, so that everyone could enjoy the shows and cabarets.

The show troupe also helped out around the ship hosting the programme of daytime activities. They were all far friendlier than some of the aloof entertainers we had encountered on P&O.

By the time we left the show lounge, it was late after a very long day, and it was bedtime.

Over the next five days we made the most of the sea days to find out more about the ship, and saga cruises in general.

We breakfasted in the Veranda each morning, and discovered that Saga provide a mixture of self service and waiter service. At the buffet counter we pointed at what we wanted, and they popped it all on a plate, and a waiter was on hand to carry it to the table if necessary. Hot and cold drinks were brought to the table, and yes, semi-skimmed milk was brought to us each day.

Just as we were wondering where the toast was, it appeared in a basket carried by a friendly waiter. Like all the food we tried on the ship, it was good, and the service was spectacularly efficient and friendly.

We saw one example of very special customer focus in the Veranda. A little lady appeared looking lost and confused. Almost immediately a waiter took her arm, and gently guided her to a table as if she was his grannie. After a brief chat the waiter went away, and soon returned with her breakfast.

Having mentioned the little old lady, I must point out that any concerns about high numbers of old people sleeping in chairs, or crashing their way round the ship in wheelchairs, were quickly dismissed. The passenger age profile may have been a little older, but the majority had a much younger outlook on life, than many I had seen on P&O ships. Yes, a lot of people sat in the library with books, but only a few succumbed to falling asleep and dropping them.

Deb and I enjoyed all the usual activities with champagne receptions, after dinner quizzes, cabarets and glitzy shows. There was an internal swimming pool that Deb tried out, and I used the gym to remind my knee to move a little actively. Deb also went to an exercise class, and was surprised to find it was free. I exercised my vocal chords with the choir, and we gave a performance on the last sea day.

Our first stop was the port of Bremerhaven where we went on a tour to the nearby Bremen. As we waited to go in the

Discovery Lounge, we had a selection of food and drink to choose from as a packed lunch, and it was all free of course. The tour included a panoramic drive, then a trip on a historic tram, before a couple of hours free time at the local Christmas market.

The second port was Hamburg where we originally had a tour booked, but having not slept well, we cancelled it, and had a leisurely walk around the city on our own. It was a chance to explore the historic buildings, and we also found another Christmas market where we sampled the usual festive food and wine.

One of the tours on offer was taking passengers to a ship yard where Saga's brand-new cruise ship was being built. For those who didn't go there, the captain gave us a talk about what was to become the Spirit of Discovery. He described the new concept of Bijou cruising with a ship that only had balcony cabins, which had been designed to reflect all the requests and ideas that Saga passengers had mentioned.

The captain also talked about the Saga cruise product, and described it as offering a complete holiday, compared to some of the competitors who offered a cabin and basics, but charged more for the services and extras that Saga included as a part of the package. His words certainly sounded good to us, and that new ship really did appeal.

We quickly decided we wanted more cruises from Saga, and I visited the Future Cruises desk. This was when we discovered one negative issue about Saga Cruises. When the man asked for my details, it was a shock to discover we didn't exist as customers.

The reason was that we had booked through a travel agent, and she was registered as the customer for this cruise. We thought something was wrong before we even came on the cruise, as we couldn't access our cruise details, or book tours, and even had to wait for the travel agent to pass on the tickets.

It appears this situation was not a one off, and applies to all bookings. If you book via a travel agent, they are the only people that can see, modify, book tours, request information etc.

Saga do not appear to favour their customers booking via an agent. We have learnt our lesson and go direct now, but I often see forum moans about this, so **BE AWARE**, and book online or telephone Saga direct when booking a cruise.

All to soon we were getting up, and having our final breakfast on the ship before beginning our journey home. Although we had begun the cruise in Portsmouth, our return was to Dover, where another polite chauffer took our cases to his car, and we sat back and contemplated the cruise experience while we drove home to Herefordshire.

The ship was old, and possibly just a little too small, but we had really enjoyed the experience. It was a struggle to come up with negative thoughts, and much easier to talk about the positive moments.

Without being silly about it, Saga **do** charge more up front for their cruises compared to Fred Olsen, P&O, or Cunard, but once paid, there is very little else that has to be bought. Transport, insurance, WiFi, and tips are all included. There is no charge for classes, and speciality restaurants are also free for passengers to try out a different style of cuisine.

Once back home we kept an eye on news about the Spirit of Discovery, and looked forward to seeing just how expensive her cruises would be.

Saga Pearl remained with Saga Cruises until 2019, and her farewell voyage was a 54-night cruise around Africa. After the Covid layoff, the ship remained active with the name Pearl until being beached and scrapped in 2022.

Saga Sapphire stayed in service a little longer, but with the arrival of a new ship, and the consequences of Covid, she left the fleet in 2020. She was renamed Blue Sapphire, and continued to cruise, but I have not seen any updates to her current status.

## Our Final Great Seafaring Adventure

While approaching the end of our 2017 World Cruise, Richard and Angie (dinner table mates) had suggested the idea of another long cruise. Richard and Rosemary were the first to say yes to the idea, but Deb and I were reluctant as we had decided against another major expedition. Unfortunately, Richard's pleading proved very hard to ignore, and he was a bit like a little dog snapping at your ankles to get attention.

We eventually agreed to the idea.

The cruise was for just over six weeks, and would be going up the Amazon River, followed by a circuit of the Caribbean Sea taking in several islands, as well as Central American countries. It would be leaving Britain just after the New Year of 2019.

Once the six of us had signed on the dotted line for that cruise, a further seed was sown in our heads. Richard and Angie intended to stay on Aurora when that Amazonian adventure ended, and go north on the next cruise to the Arctic Circle. My heels were being bitten again for several days, and after discussing the cost with the on-board future cruises department, we said yes as well.

So, the six of us would now be leaving Southampton on 3rd January 2019 for a total of 55 nights on Aurora as she sailed south to the equatorial heat of the Amazon, before eventually going to the frozen north of Norway.

Deb and I made it quite clear, that this would be our last Great Cruise Adventure, before we settled down to a quieter lifestyle of retirement.

I am oh so glad we were convinced to go.

I quickly came up with a title for the book that I planned to write for this adventure. It would be called '**From the Furnace to the Freezer**' and having just read it again for the third or fourth time, it really sums up the amazing time we had.

There is no way I am going to include all of the details of the cruise here, but for those tempted to read the book, I will go through some highlight moments.

*The Adventure Begins*

On Wednesday 3rd January 2019, we met up with our four friends in a hotel close to Southampton. This was where we would stay overnight, and leave our cars, before taking taxis to the port the next morning to board Aurora yet again, and escape the British winter.

After an alcohol fuelled evening with Richard, Angie, Robin and Rosemary, we set off on a chilly morning to the terminal in Southampton and were quickly absorbing the atmosphere of Aurora again. Our adventure was a total of 67 nights and began by sailing south towards the heat of the Amazon.

The voyage began with several days sailing south to Tenerife, and then onwards to the Capo Verde Island of St Vincent. It was already getting warm, maybe even hot by the time we got to this Portuguese island about 500 miles west of the African country of Senegal.

It was a chance to stretch our legs before the long crossing of the Atlantic, in the same way as explorers and merchants would have done hundreds of years ago. Only later in the cruise did I realise how this was probably the stopping point for many such vessels as they boarded their cargo of African slaves. As we sailed around the Caribbean, we were reminded almost everywhere of the horrendous trade of those poor souls to feed the greed of European merchants.

On a happier note, the day before we arrived at St Vincent, Deb and I celebrated a renewal of our wedding vows in front of the ship's captain and our very special friends. This was a wonderful way of celebrating nearly 45 amazing years together, made even more special being while cruising. This had become so much a part of our lives, and we were with some of the dearest friends we have ever had.

On a slightly less special note, it was also the day that we were told by the captain that Aurora had a problem with one of her propellers. He didn't sound overly concerned, but the problem would prove to be an issue for most of the cruise.

After an unplanned overnight stay in the port of St Vincent Aurora set off across the Atlantic.

*The Amazon*

A little under a week later, Aurora was leaving the Atlantic Ocean and entering the Amazon River. We were now going to sail quite slowly up this river to our next destination at the Brazilian port of Manaus.

There have been moments on our cruises when my breath has been taken away, and I have stood in awe of what I was seeing. The voyage down the Amazon River was one of those moments. But it wasn't just a 'moment', it was several days.

This river is vast. It is so wide that there were times when we couldn't see land on either side of the ship. When we could see its bank, our view was of the rain forest stretching to the horizon, and only as we neared Manaus did we spot signs of small farms that have been created.

On the river we saw many boats because it is the only way to move around this part of Brazil. Often the boats were just fishing craft, but there were also lots of unstable looking double decker, or even triple decker craft, with open sides to the decks. These were the busses of the river, and they carried locals and tourists from the mouth of the Amazon all the way through Brazil to Peru, a distance of some 4000 miles.

Our journey to Manaus was around 1000 miles from where we turned into the Amazon from the Atlantic Ocean. It took us three days to reach this city, and I never ceased to be amazed at the scene from our balcony.

We docked for an overnight stay in Manaus, and on the first afternoon we simply looked at a nearby market, and in the evening, some passengers went to the theatre. Our only official tour was an amazing trip out on one of those *'unstable looking double decker river boats'*, that took us to a local Indian village deep in the forest. Here we had a chance to wander high up in the trees through the rain forest, before having a motorised canoe trip along the river itself. The wild life of the forest and river was saying hello to us, and there was a magical moment when a sloth was brought to our canoe. Although many of us were a little concerned about the sloth being paraded to tourists, it was a special experience.

After the canoe trip the Aurora passengers had a lunch in the Indian Village of local food and some more European dishes. There was then some free time to look around the Indian's own market selling local clothing, carved wooden objects, even handmade items. There was of course the usual fridge magnets and souvenir collectables that are made in their millions in China. We used quite a bit of our Brazilian currency here to help the local people.

On the trip back to Aurora from the village, we were treated to an amazing visual phenomenon. The Amazon is fed by several rivers along its route to the ocean, but at Manaus the main Amazon waterway is joined by another massive river called the Rio Negro. The water in the Amazon and Rio Negro has a different density and colour at this confluence, and as they come together it takes quite a distance before they mix properly. Before the Rio Negro is absorbed by the main Amazon flow, there are several metres where the different colours remain separate. Along with several other tourist vessels, our boat stayed in that confusing stretch of water to exercise our cameras.

On the return ride to Manaus the wind suddenly got up, and there was a short storm with dramatic thunder and lightning. The wind was so strong that the river became seriously rough, and our boat temporarily rolled and pitched around as if we were in the Bay of Biscay.

Safely back on Aurora, our treasures were stored away, and the first thing we did was to shower to cool and clean up after the intense heat and humidity of our trip out.

Our trip along the Amazon to Manaus had been non-stop, but on the return journey we visited some other riverside cities, making this a superb week that I will never forget.

*The Caribbean Sea*

While on the world cruises, we had visited three Caribbean Islands, and those fleeting glimpses had made me realise how beautiful they are. Now, as we left the Amazon and turned into the Caribbean Sea, we were about to sample several more islands.

The sea was calm, and the sunshine welcomed us.

Beginning our island hop with Barbados, we moved on and spent time at St Lucia, Tobago, Antigua, Tortola, Dominican Republic, Cayman Islands, and Jamaica. We walked, we shopped, visited chocolate farms, sailed on a catamaran, we swam in the warm sea, swam with stingrays, and drank quite a bit of rum punch.

It was wonderful, and we decided we would do our best to come back to explore some more.

We temporarily abandoned the Caribbean islands and had a return visit to Colombia, where the simplicity and gentleness of the island nations was replaced by mainland high rise buildings and commercialism.

*Central America*

Time now for an introduction to Central America with time in Panama, Costa Rica, Honduras, and Belize. There was more time in the sea with kayaking, snorkelling, or just swimming.

In Costa Rica we walked through a forest that was a protected animal sanctuary where we shared our time with snakes, Howler monkeys, sloths, racoons, plus birds galore, and lots of other tourists. Oh, and there was a beautiful beach with soft golden sand.

Honduras was time for a panoramic tour that featured iguanas that walked around with us, happily fed from leafy branches that we held, and Deb even cuddled a baby one. Then there was a visit to a cave followed by a swim and a drink of fresh fruit juice on a sandy beach.

Belize was all about history with a trip to look around the pyramid shaped remains of a Mayan Temple. It rained there for a while, but history trumped the warm shower.

The only downside we were now experiencing, was that most of the ports we visited were also set up to extract vast amounts of money from the thousands of American tourists that holiday in this region. This had also been the case on the western Caribbean islands, some of which were actually owned by the Americans. Thank goodness we had enjoyed the less commercialised islands of the east to begin with.

*Homewards*

Aurora now began the journey back across the Caribbean with stops in Mexico at the slightly less Americanised island of Cozumel, where we got wet in the rain again, as well as swimming in the last of the warm sea.

From there we had stops at the Bahamas and then Bermuda to give us a last bit of sunshine before the long haul back across the Atlantic. As we left the playground of the Caribbean area, the weather broke, and we had near hurricane force wind and rain until we reached the Channel.

*Back in Southampton*

On Wednesday 27th February 2019, we woke up in Southampton. Our voyage across the Atlantic had been a roller coaster of a ride, and it was a lovely feeling to be still again. Normally with a cruise coming to an end, Deb and I would be rushing around to be ready for disembarkation, but not today. While hundreds of the other passengers were getting off, and going home, we were among a small number who were staying on Aurora for the following cruise.

There was a little bit of housekeeping to be done as we were moving from our balcony cabin to a less expensive outside one, and that meant getting our belongings moved, and new keys sorted. Fortunately, the move was very simple as the housekeeping staff moved clothes and suitcases, while we met up with the other four (Angie, Richard, Rosemary and Robin) over a leisurely breakfast.

With breakfast over, we changed our cabin key, and then joined a short queue to get off the ship for an hour or two. In reality this was a part of a carefully choreographed plan where the men grabbed a taxi and took a suitcase of summer clothes back to our cars at the hotel, before returning with another case crammed with cold weather clothing.

Yes, we would now be sailing north to the Arctic circle where shorts and tee shirts were no longer a good idea. Meanwhile the ladies went shopping for bits and pieces that we had run out of, and treats for the journey to come.

With suitcases swapped, and car batteries checked, the men returned to Southampton's shopping centre, and we met up with our wives. Our short break on land ended by catching the ship's crew bus back to Aurora, and then walked through an already busy embarkation lounge where very early new passengers were waiting, while we took a short cut through the crew entrance.

It was late morning by now, and our priority was to get to the new cabin, and pack the vast amounts of clothes into rather less drawer and wardrobe space than we had been used to. With a little bit of effort, and coaxing of drawers, we were ready again for the next part of our adventure.

While queues were growing longer in the embarkation lounge, Deb and I met up with Angie and Richard in the dining room for an early start to the 'Welcome on Board' buffet. The plan had come together, and we were soon onto the second glass of fizz as new passengers struggled in with coats and cases.

This had been our first ever experience of a back-to-back cruise, and it was very special.

---

*Time to Cruise Northwards*

The second half of our adventure was for 12 nights, and Aurora would be visiting four ports in Norway. We would be spending time in Andalsnes, Tromso, Alta, and Stavanger. A lot of people take cruises to Norway, but in the past, these holidays have been more common in the summer. Now a lot of people are going north to see this spectacular and mountainous country in the winter, with the lure of possibly seeing the 'Aurora Borealis', or Northern Lights, a major reason for getting seriously cold.

The North Sea was very friendly with us, and our trip up the east coast of Britain was rather smooth. While over 1000 new passengers were getting used to what Aurora had to offer, our gang of six continued with a way of life we had already experienced for nearly seven weeks. One unfinished bit of business was our attempts at winning a round of the late-night Syndicate Quiz. We were regularly close to winning on the cruise to warmer waters, but never quite victorious. On our second attempt on this cruise, we finally achieved our goal, and won the bottle of cheap house wine.

It was finally a moment of satisfaction that we had proved our combined knowledge was worthy to be victors. The wine was drunk at the quiz on the following night, and we all agreed that it was a wonderful moment, although the wine was absolutely awful.

Andalsnes

Our first stop was at the town of Andalsnes situated at the end of a branch of the mighty Romsdal Fjord. The town is quite small with a population of just under 2500, but it was once a major port for the oil industry. Sadly, as the oil platforms grew in size, the available water space at Andalsnes was outgrown, and all the dreams of wealth disappeared.

The town is now more famous as the centre for Norway's love of climbing, and there is a vast building with a museum of all things climbing, as well as a huge wall as part of the climbing facilities.

The scene that we woke up to was beautiful with a snow-covered town on the edge of a vast bay of clear water, that reflected the giant mountains that surrounded it.

... and yes, it was colder than we had been used to.

Deb and I had a tour booked for after lunch, so once breakfast was over, we simply went for a walk around the town, that was now overshadowed by Aurora at the end of its main street. Just across the dockside from our ship was a train station where Robin and Rosemary were setting off on a scenic ride up the valley of the Romsdal Fjord for a morning tour. Robin was a serious lover of all things connected with railways, and this was one of many train journeys that he took while on our cruises.

Our first impression of the scene before us, was the shock at seeing just how much the mere suggestion of cold was making the British passengers pile on the extra layers of clothing. It was cold, but no colder than a winter's day at home, and certainly didn't justify the puffed-up display of winter clothing that our passengers had purchased before this cruise. It would be getting seriously colder than this in the days to come, and I suspected many people were peaking far too early.

The town of Andalsnes was going about its normal daily routine with local people shopping, and only extending the merest degree of interest in our ship that was blocking their view of the water and mountains. Our first point of call was a small museum set up in an old railway carriage, which even included a tiny church. This didn't thrill me much, so I took the opportunity to take far too many photos of the fantastic views.

We did spend a few minutes in the Mountaineering Centre, but the subject really didn't spark too much interest, and although there was a café where we could have sat for a while, the cost of a drink didn't interest us either.

It was time to explore a few of the tourist shops that have no doubt opened in the last few years to appeal to the numerous cruise ship visits. They were busy of course with our fellow passengers, and most British went away that day with something based on a Troll. Norway has certainly been very successful in using the troll as the basis of most tourist purchases, along with woollen hats and scarves of course.

Yes, we did our bit for the economy and came away with the usual souvenirs featuring the trolls.

There was also a visit to a supermarket to stock up on fizzy drink, and chocolate, but along with our quite inexpensive souvenirs, that was the end of our purchases at this port.

After lunch we joined a coach for a scenic drive up the Romsdalvegen valley which followed the same route as the morning train from the port. The road quickly became flanked by mountains on either side covered with snow. Our guide allowed us off the coach after a few minutes to stare up at the craggy rockfaces. She told us about the history of the Trolls, and even pointed out rocky features that were said to look like a troll's head. I could understand how they might have looked that way if you squinted hard enough, but I struggled to spot the noses and eyes that many others pointed at excitedly.

The guide also talked about a recent stupid pastime of idiotic young people climbing to the top of the snowy peaks, before launching themselves off on a pair of skis to skid and slide back down to ground level. There had been far too many accidents with serious injuries and deaths, and made worse by local rescue teams putting themselves in danger by trying to bring them back down in one piece. The custom had now been outlawed, but I don't suppose that a law would stop all idiots from expressing their perceived immortality.

As we wound our way upwards, we crossed and recrossed the railway line several times, went over bridges and through tunnels. The snow that was quite patchy in the town below, became thicker and thicker on the ground, and the scene was absolutely magical.

We eventually reached our destination at the top end of the valley to a town called Bjorli. This was where we would be enjoying hot chocolate and scones with jam and cream, but first we went to a ski resort to watch the wonderful sight of local people skiing or riding on snow-bikes. It was something I had never seen before, and which I have never been tempted to take part in, but it was spectacular to see the Norwegians enjoying themselves, and showing such skill and expertise.

Anyway, it was time to warm up in the hotel and enjoy our hot drink and cakes. All too soon the light was beginning to fade, and we re-joined our coach for the drive back down to the port.

Almost as soon as we walked back into the warmth of Aurora, the captain shut the doors, dropped the mooring ropes, and with a farewell hoot of the horn set off towards the sea again.

It had been a truly amazing day in scenery I had never experienced before, but we knew there was more to come, and it was promised to be even more spectacular.

Tromso

To be accurate, the official spelling appears to be Tromsø.

Just as with Andalsnes, we heard several different ways of saying the name of Tromso. After listening to several local people talking about their city, I attempted to find the correct mouth shape and tongue position to imitate the sound in my best Pigeon Scandinavian. Like many other passengers I failed, realising this sound does not exist in the English language, and with no way of creating the sound, there is also no way of writing it phonetically. Never mind, they seemed to accept our pronunciation without appearing angry.

Let's begin with a geographical fact to think about. The city of Tromso is within the arctic circle at a latitude of 69° 44' 33". Apart from odd moments looking into a supermarket freezer, it was considerably colder than anywhere else I have ever been to.

It is the 12th largest city in Norway, and has a population approaching 80,000 people. The city lies in an area of multiple islands, and its boundaries spread from one island, across a waterway to the mainland. Tromso has the honour of having the northernmost university, botanical gardens, and planetarium in the world.

When we looked out of our cabin window at around 8:00 in the morning, it was still quite dark, and snowing. The view was of predominantly low buildings, plus a hill with a road that was busy with rush hour traffic. That road was white with snow, but unlike the chaos this weather would have produced in Britain, the traffic appeared to be moving quite normally.

We had a morning tour booked here to go on a coach trip to another island called Sommaroy, that was about 22 miles away to the west of Tromso. The village of Sommaroy has a population of just over 300 people, and its economy relies on fishing, plus tourism to use the currently invisible golden sandy beaches. After being allowed to leave our comfortably warm ship, we shivered our way across the dockside to a warm coach, and a friendly local guide.

After the usual introductions, and an outline of what we would be doing, the coach set off, and was soon going up that snow covered hill we saw from the cabin. Our guide described the city, plus a little about the local area, as well as the island village that we would be going to see. I assume someone asked about the state of the roads, and he said that in Norway the snow is not as slippery compared to what we have in Britain, and all vehicles must have snow tyres on throughout the winter months.

Our journey took us up hills, and then up further into what resembled mountains in my eyes. On the sides of the road there were poles to mark the edge of the tarmac, and they had to be quite tall to be visible in snow drifts before the snow ploughs came along. The snow continued to fall and blow around in the wind throughout most of the journey, and although initially concerned about the snowy roads, I began to accept that this was a normal way of life in this country

In the distance we could see vast flat areas, and the guide pointed out that they were actually frozen lakes.

At the island of Sommaroy, we all put on our extra layers of clothing, and then got off the coach. It was straight into a blizzard making it difficult to see where we were walking, but strangely I was enjoying the chance to battle through whatever the weather could throw at us. Our ten-minute walk took us to a hotel, where we enjoyed hot coffee, plus delicious waffles with jam and cream. There was even a light brown cheese to sample, that was quite sweet, and I initially thought it was fudge.

After refreshments we returned outside, and discovered the blizzard had given up, and the sun was shining. It remained bitterly cold, but at least we could now see the features around us.

Back on the coach our guide talked at length about Norway, and how it is trying to make more use of solar power, combined with battery technology, to avoid the use of fossil fuelled power stations. He also talked for some time about the local indigenous people that are called 'Sami', and told us they do not like to be considered as eskimos.

He then moved on to other facts about his country, and eventually arrived at the subject of whaling. Most of us kept quiet, but questions about the rights and wrongs were raised. He defended the practice, and I think Aurora's passengers quickly ignored what he was saying, and kept our thoughts to ourselves.

When we arrived back at Aurora, we struggled across the slippery dockside and climbed up the icy gangway into the ship. There was then quite a shock as we couldn't find the corridor to our cabin. The ship had been set up for the extreme cold conditions, and corridor doors that had always been open so far, were now closed to avoid the cold spreading throughout the passenger areas. We soon got used to the idea, and began to appreciate just how cold it was, and how cold it was to remain for the next few days and nights.

In the afternoon, Deb and I took a shuttle bus into the city centre for a walk around. After the morning adventure we realised we needed some different clothes. It was all about having good quality scarves and gloves, and these were quite easy to find as Norway offers a lot of shops for good quality warm clothes. We also bought a souvenir or two to remind us of our day in this very special (but very cold) city.

Alta

A lot of the passengers on this winter cruise, had chosen it because there was a very good chance of seeing the Northern Lights. As we sailed northwards from Andalsnes there had been one or two evening 'Bing Bong' Tannoy announcements that the lights had come out to play. These announcements heralded mass exoduses to the outside decks to hopefully catch a glimpse of the shimmering green lights. On one occasion when it was a formal dress code evening, the valiant dinner table six were playing ten pin bowling in the arcade in our finery when the bing bong sounded. The arcade was at the rear of Aurora and very close to an open deck, so we dropped our hand controllers and rushed out into the freezing temperatures. Formal evening wear is not the warmest choice of clothes for such adventures, and it wasn't long before we decided to return indoors and change into more suitable attire to continue our search.

Several passengers had managed to see the lights, but although we managed to see suggestions of activity in the sky, the green hue hadn't been visible.

Never mind, our next port was Alta, and this was where we would get the best chance of seeing the Aurora Borialis.

Other than tiny villages, the city of Alta is the northernmost serious settlement in Europe. It is closer to the north pole than it is to the tip of Scotland. The population is a little over 21,000 making it the 60th biggest in Norway.

When we woke, Aurora was nearing Alta sailing through a beautiful scenery of snow-covered islands that resembled mountains poking out of the sea. The water was calm, and I was told that the air was still, and very cold. I could not confirm this, as I had woken with an infection, and was told to stay indoors by the doctor with a packed lunch of antibiotics.

Around lunchtime our ship was approaching the dockside, and through the cabin window I could see us pass by the end of the runway at the airport. It was snowing of course, and between the quite regular air traffic arrivals or departures, the snow blowers rushed up and down the runway.

Once docked, I was relieved to see our cabin faced the city, as that was just about all I was going to see for the next two days. I was told not to leave the ship, and stay warm.

We had multiple tours booked, but I had my tickets refunded, leaving Deb to go out on her own.

Deb reported on her afternoon trip to the famous Ice Hotel, where as well as the amazing hotel itself, she sampled a vodka and curacao drink from a glass made of ice. By the time she returned to Aurora, she only had time to grab a bite to eat before setting off again to stand in a field and look at the sky to see the Northern Lights.

I quietly drank a glass of wine, read my book, and sulked with an early night cuddling a hot water bottle.

Deb returned after midnight. She was cold and tired, but was thrilled to have seen the lights.

We stayed overnight in Alta, and through the following day Deb stayed with me on Aurora while the majority of passengers set off on tours of the area.

I remained rather ill, and concentrated on eating and drinking to keep my strength up, and hopefully get rid of the lurgy. I never saw the Aurora Borialis, and soon we left Alta and turned south toward home.

## Going Home

There was one final stop at the port of Stavanger by which time I had recovered, and strolled around the dockside area with Deb. We explored a couple of museums and bought some souvenirs.

Back home in Herefordshire I looked back on an amazing adventure down to the Equator, and then up to the Arctic Circle. We had been away for 67 nights, and completely missed the winter in Britain. I looked back on the experience and decided that there had been several very special moments, but there was some unfinished business.

I still wanted to see the Northern Lights, so we would have to go back again.

## Farewell to Oriana

The year 2019 cruising excitement wasn't over yet.

Rumours were spreading around the P&O fanatics, that Oriana was about to be sold to a Chinese company. Those rumours turned out to be true, and as schedules were altered, a chance came along for Deb and I to have one last cruise on the ship that changed how we spent our holidays for the last 20 years.

There were a number of Oriana cruises on offer that declared themselves as farewell opportunities, and the one we chose was a trip featuring various ports in Scotland and Ireland. We had promised ourselves a trip back to Ireland so this was perfect, and it was a very good deal as well.

So, less than three months after coming back from our winter look around the Amazon and Norway, we were back in Southampton again on the 15$^{th}$ June 2019 for a 12-night cruise on Oriana. Having had a lot of cruising time with P&O during the last couple of years, Deb and I had reached the dizzy heights of the top loyalty tier called Ligurian. This meant when we arrived at the Embarkation lounge, we were shown to a special area and served with coffee and cakes.

We had a basic outside cabin that I seem to remember was on Deck 5, and after an early boarding time, plus a few drinks to welcome us back, we unpacked our suitcases before taking a look around the lovely vessel. It didn't take us long to find our way to familiar lounges and memories flooded back of the times we had enjoyed on Oriana. We had seen reports that this

25-year-old ship was looking tatty, but the paintwork looked clean, and the carpets were in quite good condition.

After the Muster drill, I opted for the first shower before dinner. Now there was a problem. The shower had no way of controlling the temperature and it was scalding hot. Having already put some shampoo on my hair, I had to constantly dip my head for a few seconds until it was clear, before making an early exit.

The problem was reported to reception, and within 10 minutes an engineer arrived and confirmed that the controller needed to be changed. Better still, he was back to replace it soon afterwards, but Deb had already been to the Spa for a shower before dinner.

Our dinner was in the Oriental Dining Room and the other diners on the table were chatty and good fun. The first night menu allowed us all to choose something to our tastes.

From dinner we relaxed for a while before going to the theatre to watch the current troupe of girls and boys performing a show called Stage Door. Of course, they were superbly professional as we have come to expect from P&O entertainers.

After the show we spent a few minutes in the Lord's Tavern for a quiz, but we were both tired and ready for our beds with smiles on our faces.

*Ports and tours*

Our first stop on the cruise was the port of Killybegs in the north of the Irish Republic. This fishing port with a population of around 1200 people, relies on fishing, but is also the gateway to the county, and town, of Donegal. Our morning panoramic tour took us for a coffee and cake stop in Donegal and then we took a few minutes on our own to explore its castle.

From Ireland we crossed overnight to the Scottish port of Greenock. We avoided going into Glasgow, but instead took a look at the beautiful countryside around the Clyde. We visited a farm, or country park, where we had a ride on a tractor and trailer, that included a brief stop to get up close to some beautiful long haired highland cattle, including a very young calf. We also had a refreshment break before continuing our look at the countryside.

Oriana then went northwards to Torshavn on the Faroe Islands. We were half way to Iceland by then. Our stop at the island gave us another panoramic tour, to discover just a little of the history of the Faroe Islands.

Heading south again we stopped off at the Shetlands and the town of Lerwick. This was a tender port, and we avoided any of the organised tours, but stretched our legs around the town. This is the location used for much of the Police Detective television drama (Shetland) and a lot of the buildings and locations were familiar.

We rested our legs with coffee in a small café, and struck up a conversation with an American couple visiting the island. There was time to explore a small museum before finding our way back to the quayside. While waiting for a tender ride back to the ship, we smelt the aroma of fish and chips, so munched a snack while watching the busy port area.

The next stop was the Orkneys, and the town of Kirkwall.

In the morning we took the shuttle bus from the port to the quiet town, and simply wandered around the streets and window shopped. After returning to the ship, we prepared ourselves for a visit to a local restaurant for a tasting session of local food, and drinks. This was rather more than a simple tasting, and we all came away well fed, and delightfully tipsy.

That was the end of our exploration of Scottish islands, and our next port was the Irish Capital city of Dublin. This was our third visit to Dublin, and this time we spent a while at the GPO Building to look at some more history of the uprising. The exhibition was very good, and we rounded it off with coffee and cakes, before window shopping in this delightful city.

We had another perk associated with our Ligurian Loyalty status when we sailed away from Dublin. There was a cocktail party in the captain's private lounge just below the Bridge of Oriana. We chatted to several people, and had lots of canapés, as well as drinking considerable amounts of alcohol. We completely missed dinner that night.

Sailing southwards again we had a stop at Cobh on the southern tip of Ireland. This was the final stop made by the Titanic before setting off across the Atlantic, and is quite a poignant place to visit. Deb and I took another look around an exhibition about the history of Irish emigrants, as well as enjoying the museum dedicated to the Titanic.

The final stop on the cruise should have been a tender stop for Guernsey, but when we woke that morning, the sea was unhappy with us, and too rough for the tender to operate safely. It would have been nice to get back to this delightful island, but I am sure we will return there again one day.

*Last thoughts about Oriana*

We were glad to have had a final cruise on Oriana. She is a ship that took our breath away in 2000 for our first adventure, and remained so very special to us on the cruises over the two decades since.

OK, so Oriana lacked the balcony cabins that so many cruisers now desire, but she was one of the last 'traditional' style cruise ships ever built. When Lord Stirling commissioned Oriana and Aurora in early 1980s, he really initiated the explosion of today's cruising popularity in Britain. Until then only a small number of people took a cruise holiday, but as more cabin spaces became available at reasonable prices, a new and expanded group of singles, couples, and families could enjoy a little bit of luxury.

Oriana boasted a sensational theatre, a superb large cabaret lounge with a dance floor, plus a second smaller lounge, and even a cinema, as well as numerous bars. There were also quiet spots to sit and relax, read a book, or simply stare out over the sea. The ship had so many places on the open deck to sit or lie in the sun, or the shade, and the horseshoe shaped decks at the stern were a magnet for couples to simply lean on the rails, hold hands, and stare silently at a sunset.

It set the blueprint for modern ships, but today those vessels are so much larger, with a small army of passengers looking to be amused and pampered. While Deb and I were happy to continue to join in with the traditions, today's passengers are seeking more wall-to-wall excitement. We are among the generation that have seen a way of travel that evolved from the days when the early mail ships began to take passengers. Sadly, year by year there are fewer of us left, as the floating hotels with their towering blocks of identical balcony cabins, cater for multiple thousands of sun seekers and party lovers.

When we got off our first cruise, Deb and I were thrilled with everything we had seen, and done. We were hooked on cruising, and although we enjoy a lot of things that newer ships have to offer, we missed the intimacy that ships of Oriana's size could offer.

A few weeks after our last trip on Oriana, she left the P&O fleet and joined a Chinese company (Astro Ocean) sailing under the name of 'Piano Land'. Although I have not seriously looked for any up-to-date information, I believe she is still in service.

I hope her new passengers enjoy her as much as the thousands of P&O passengers who sailed on Oriana from her launch in 1995.

## Moving House Again

In August 2019, Deb and I said farewell to our house in Herefordshire. We were moving again.

My body was suffering from arthritis, and it was seriously affecting my joy of gardening, and DIY. The new hip was being tested by digging the garden, and the knee was getting worse, but surgeons were adamant that there was nothing that could be done to ease it. Worse than the digging, the twice a year session of cutting the hedges was taking several days to complete, and left me physically wrecked.

I was not going to get any better.

Meanwhile Deb had suffered fractures of bones due to quite innocuous accidents, and was diagnosed with osteoporosis. Just like my arthritis, there was no cure for her condition, and it would quite likely get worse.

We decided it would be best to find a new home where there would be less gardening required, and closer to services we might need as our bodies became less active.

So, along with a lot of thoughts and discussions, we started to look at our options. The result was not something we ever planned to do.

In August of 2019 we set off towards Cornwall, and our new home. It was an apartment in a Retirement Village about midway between St Austell and Truro.

As the days went by, we made friends with many of the other residents, and we became known as the babies of the village. The regular question was why we decided to move there while still so young. Our answer was that we wanted to move to somewhere to secure our future, before our bodies got too bad.

It took quite a while to unpack and fit in our belongings that we had in our three-bedroom house, into the significantly smaller apartment, but eventually the cardboard boxes were all gone, and we could relax.

Of course, the relief from unpacking meant there was time to relax, and think about another cruise.

# Our Last Cruise on Oceana

We really overdosed on cruises in 2019.

As winter seemed to be getting very close, I spotted another opportunity for a bargain cruise. This time it was on Oceana while she was repositioned from her temporary home port in Dubai. It was for 12 nights, and sailing south to the Atlantic islands, plus a couple of ports in Spain.

We didn't know it at the time, but this was to be our final opportunity of sailing on this ship.

On 27th October we woke up in Southampton's Holiday Inn, to begin a very familiar pre-cruise routine with a walk around the West Quay shopping centre after a hearty hotel breakfast. As usual we didn't buy anything special, but there was always time for a decent cup of coffee. Back at the hotel we performed the also very familiar routine of getting our suitcases down to the reception area, paid off our account, and then read our papers while waiting for the taxi to collect us.

At the Mayflower cruise terminal we were soon sitting in the Ligurian waiting area with a coffee and cake while we watched hundreds of other passengers arrive and check in. I have no doubt many of them looked across at us in the roped off priority area and wondered why we deserved better treatment than they were having.

Well, I did that in previous years, but now having spent a small fortune with P&O, I wasn't going to miss out on even the tiniest perk.

**'Bing Bong'**

It was time to gather our hand luggage and make our way onto Oceana. It was possible to hear a small chorus of groans from the other passengers now, as the dozen or so priority group snaked our way around the room and down the slope to the security scanners.

Into the belly of the ship, and we were directed towards the dining room that was serving our top tier canapes and glasses of fizz. It wasn't long before we were chatting to other loyal passengers and comparing how many times, and which ships we had cruised on.

Just like on previous occasions, our determination to avoid too much alcohol failed, and we had to gently stagger to our cabin to unpack suitcases. We had a straight forward outside cabin on deck 5 that was perfectly fine for a late in the year cruise where a balcony would be wasted, and wouldn't cause my stomach too many issues in any bad weather.

The end of the afternoon beckoned, and after the Muster Drill Captain Chris Bourne announced our departure, and we settled in to our cruise.

*Ports of Call*

The ports on this cruise were all very familiar, and after three days sailing south, we spent a day in Lanzarote. From there we crossed overnight to Gran Canaria, and it was Tenerife the following morning. There was then a sea-day before we said hello to Funchal on Madeira. Those southern islands had given us some very pleasant warm sunshine, but it was time now for winter to return.

After another sea-day we were in Cadiz and the temperature was about 10° colder than what we had been spoiled with. The sea was much angrier, and after another bumpy day we arrived at the final port of Vigo.

As far as I remember, we did not go on any excursions at any of the ports, although we did savour coffee and churros wherever we could find them.

On the 10th November we were home again.

Fortunately, it wouldn't be too long before Southampton would beckon us again. Because of my illness in Norway causing me to miss out on any chance of seeing the Northern Lights, we had already booked the identical cruise again for two months' time.

Deb and I would be on Aurora again, in a similar cabin, and going to virtually all the same destinations.

*Goodbye Oceana*

As I suggested at the beginning of this chapter, that trip on Oceana would be our final moments on her.

She became one of the casualties of the Pandemic that was to hit us, and the cruise industry.

In 2020 cruise companies around the world searched for ways of reducing losses, and this meant looking at their fleets and offloading excess vessels. Carnival shed a large number of aging, and smaller ships, and Oceana said farewell in July 2020. She was sold to a Greek company and renamed as 'Queen of the Oceans'.

Sadly, the latest information I could find was that she never went into service, and is currently laid up.

Another small ship had gone from the P&O fleet, and there was no suggestion of a similar replacement.

## 2020 – Boxes Ticked

As we began a new decade, everything seemed fine with our lives and with the world.

… except for that niggling virus affecting the far east.

Deb and I had a couple of holidays to look forward to. In the summer we had a week's hotel break on the Channel Islands with a few days on both Jersey and Guernsey. Before that we had a repeat of the previous year's cruise to Norway, to allow me to complete the unfinished business of seeing the Northern Lights.

On the 27th February 2020, we drove from our new home in Cornwall towards the Holiday Inn in Southampton. The following morning we woke to see Aurora from our bedroom window, knowing that hundreds of happy passengers were just about to disembark after a cruise around the Caribbean.

Breakfast over, we packed away the bits we had used overnight, then strolled across the road to purchase those bits we had forgotten to bring. We were excited by what lay ahead for us, and knew we would enjoy yet another few days and nights on the beautiful Aurora.

Back to the hotel, suitcases were brought into the reception area, and we sat with a cup of coffee to wait for our taxi. Same routine, same hotel, same cruise ship, same taxi firm and same dreams of a wonderful time.

Early at the cruise terminal once more, there was half an hour to wait in the Priority Lounge before boarding, and watching other excited passengers arriving for their twelve days trip to the Arctic Circle.

The cruise went wonderfully. I managed to avoid the various bugs, and successfully saw the Northern Lights while we were in Alta. Deb and I also went to a Sami village and had a ride on a sledge pulled by reindeer. There was only one new port to visit, and that was Alesund where we had a trip out to a museum and park with various historical Norwegian buildings.

As Aurora headed south towards Southampton, we were catching news reports that the Coronavirus, or Covid 19 virus had reached Europe, and there were even a small number of people testing positive in Britain. We thought little about it, but while at our final port of Stavanger, we found out that the city had several cases.

Two days later when we got back home in Cornwall, we discovered that Stavanger had virtually locked down on the day after our visit. Meanwhile in Britain there were queues of shoppers stripping shops of toilet rolls, and food shelves were sparce.

Meanwhile Aurora had set off again to Norway with another ship full of adventurers, but it was a very short cruise, as the Covid Pandemic situation was becoming extremely serious, so Aurora returned to Southampton.

This was happening with all the P&O fleet and the other companies as well.

Within days, cruising was halted throughout the world.

… and of course, our planned visit to the Channel Islands was cancelled as well.

# Covid

After decades of threats from Mad Cow Disease, Swine Fever, and Asian Flu, the world finally succumbed to a virus that affected virtually every country on the globe. The pandemic started in China but to be fair, something was always going to occur eventually.

It took a while to reach Britain, but once here, it spread quickly and badly. Our Health System was rapidly overloaded into submission, and like a lot of so called highly developed countries, we ran out of hospital beds, ran out of protective clothing, and for a while, ran out of ideas.

Even when we beat much of the world in getting vaccines into the system, we faced the battle of rumours doubting the vaccine, and lies about its safety and effectiveness. Soon Britain was one of the worst countries in the world with old and vulnerable people dying on a scale that was astounding.

One of the worst ideas to take pressure off the National Health Service was to send older, and supposedly well patients to private care homes until they could return home. Sadly a few were infected with Covid, and the care homes became the perfect breeding ground for the virus. Here at our Retirement Village we have an associated private care home, and we lost a very high percentage of the residents during the first few months of the Pandemic.

The threat of the virus spreading resulted in the complete village being put into a full-blown lockdown, that was even more strict than the one supposedly covering the rest of Britain. The residents of our retirement village were told to stay in our apartments as much as possible, and when gatherings were eventually allowed, they were very limited. We couldn't even go for a walk outside of our grounds, and although we have some wonderful areas to walk around within the site, it didn't take long to become totally bored, and walking became a chore. Deb and I were virtually alone for most of 2020, and it felt like the world had a cloud sitting on top of us all. For a while it really felt as if there was no way it could get better.

Of course, eventually the viral cloud had a few breaks and we began to return to meeting others, and going out to shops again. But those months of isolation, fear, and boredom had a serious long-term affect.

Thousands of people caught Covid, and thousands died, but almost everyone's lives changed.

A year after some of our elderly residents had been walking and living unaided, the extended period of isolation and reliance on others to help them, changed them physically and mentally. When they came out of their apartment, they struggled to walk, and quickly succumbed to walking sticks and mechanical wheeled aids to move around. Their minds had been starved of the stimuli of meeting other people, and a lot of them struggled to interact again for months.

In my case, I should have been able to use the time to concentrate on writing my books, but my mind seemed to go blank. All that I achieved was to spend the odd hour writing a few less than inspirational words.

Luckily our apartment has a balcony facing south-east that gives us wonderful morning views of the glorious sunrises, and then becomes a spot to sit in the warm sunshine during the mornings. There were lots of sunny days during the worst of the lockdown, and we spent a lot of time out there on our balcony. That balcony is about the same size as those on the ships, and when I closed my eyes and listened to the music, there were moments when I pretended to be at sea again.

The weeks and months of isolation dragged on, and Deb and I began to think that holidays might never happen again, and certainly cruising seemed unlikely to ever return. Cruise ships sheltered around the British coast in quiet bays losing fortunes, and as the first shoots of life were beginning to return to normal, local tourist pleasure boats would go out to allow their passengers a look at the sad vessels as if they were something in a museum.

Fortunately, as time passed the situation did appear to be returning to some sort of normality. Then one day we began to see adverts for cruises again.

Even while Covid was rampant, and ships around the world were empty, the companies were trying to entice passengers to book cruises for an unknown future. The companies were offering very good deals, and of course guaranteeing money back if Covid prevented those cruises going ahead. Everytime we opened a wardrobe, the sight of our holiday clothes shouted to us that they needed to be worn, and so in November 2020, we rang P&O and booked a cruise on Aurora for May 2022. The following day I rang SAGA and booked a river cruise for March 2022.

Deb and I had something to look forward to at last, and the holiday clothes whispered their thanks.

# Spring 2021

Covid was still dominating lives, but our desire to get on a cruise again couldn't keep me away from looking at the adverts. It was a long time to wait until 2022 for the Saga River cruise, and the one on Aurora.

As the weeks passed by, Deb and I began to have second thoughts about those planned cruises.

We finally began to seriously reflect on our recent cruise experiences, and our thoughts were very much focussed on P&O. The product that thrilled us for 20 years had changed, and was no longer giving us the same buzz. The level of care and service was going down, and even the restaurant menus were boring us.

That sample cruise on Saga Pearl in 2018 had ignited a spark of magic again, and we decided that we ought to try out one of their new ships. Holidays on the SAGA Ocean Cruising ships were considerably more expensive, but our first impressions of the product were much more positive than our recent P&O experiences.

We decided it was time to have a cruise on one of the new Saga ships.

I rang Saga, and asked if we could change our booking for the river cruise to a short ocean cruise sailing to southern Ireland. The helpful, and cheerful lady spent quite a while sorting things out, but the outcome was that we were booked on a cruise called 'Celtic Getaway' on one of the new Saga ships.

Meanwhile, the cruise industry was still very much in mothballs, and would remain that way for many months. Although Deb and I now had something to look forward to, the brochures kept coming through the letterbox to tempt us further.

It wasn't long before we suspected that the cruise going to Southern Ireland, might well be cancelled.

It appeared that when cruising restarted, the ships would just set sail for a few days, and not call at any ports. Beyond that the UK industry would be limited to ports around Britain. Our planned cruise would mean going to a different country.

We had another discussion over a glass of wine and the brochures, and it was back on the phone again to Saga. This time I changed the booked Celtic Getaway cruise, to a similar short tester cruise on Spirit of Adventure which was just visiting British ports.

# The Modern Saga Cruises Company

On 1st October 2015, the Meyer Werft shipyard in Papenburg Germany received an order from Saga Cruises to build a brand-new ship. By September 2017, that order had been confirmed to include a second ship, that would be virtually identical to the first. This was the beginning of a new era for the Saga cruise company, and what we hoped would be the answer to our cruising future.

The first ship was launched on 12th May 2019 and named Spirit of Discovery, and a year later the second ship was launched on 24th July and christened the Spirit of Adventure.

The company advertises that the cruise ships offer 'Boutique' cruising experiences, and the holidays are fully inclusive. Saga have positioned their product at the more exclusive end of the market, and hence they are more expensive. It gives an option to people who want to cruise, but without the full-on high-octane experience offered by the majority of cruise companies.

Saga only allow passengers who are older than 50, but travelling companions are permitted if they are 40 plus.

*The Ships*

These ships are sisters, and they look so similar that I would say they were Identical Twin Sisters, looking and feeling absolutely the same. Yes, I am sure there are small external differences with the structures, but I doubt even the most observant would tell them apart. Internally there are some differences, but the general look and feel of the ships are the same.

If you get to know one ship, you will be quickly at home on the other.

They are 236 metres long, with ten passenger decks, and both have a passenger capacity of 999. Perhaps the major change to other ships, is that there are no inside, or simple outside cabins, they all have balconies, and this includes the cabins for single travellers. There are different grades of balcony cabin, starting with the least expensive ones low down at the front, and stern. Then going upwards, and towards the middle, cabins become gradually more expensive, with larger superior ones and eventually suites in the prime spots.

*Quick Tour*

Away from cabins, or perhaps I should now describe them as staterooms, Deck 4 at the bottom isn't a true public deck, but it does have the medical centre.

Moving up we come to Deck 5 which is also called the 'Main' deck.

From the front stairs or lift lobby there is the entrance to the Spa, with its Hydrotherapy pool, Steam room, Saunas, Treatment rooms, and changing areas. Moving towards the stern are two corridors on either side of crew areas, with a shop on one side, and Salon on the other.

Continuing towards the back you come to one of the main communal areas of the ship called the 'Living Room'. The Living Room features a central bar / café surrounded by seating for passengers, to relax with a drink while they chat or read books. Although normally hidden behind panels, this is where the doors are for passengers to enter and leave the ship on shore days.

Further again and there is a shop on one side, and the reception desk plus tours and guest services on the other. Finally, the corridors join again at the stern lift and stair lobby, and entrances to the main dining venue known as The Grand Dining Room.

Taking the lift or stairs up to Deck 6 and you are on Promenade Deck. In true British tradition, there is an external promenade walkway which goes completely around the ship. Inside at the stern end, there are three more restaurants. These are speciality dining rooms, and have different names on the two ships.

On Discovery the central venue is called 'The Club' and is described as a steak house, but the menu offers far more options. The room also offers entertainment during meals or late at night. On the Spirit of Adventure this venue is called 'The Supper Club', offering a wide menu plus entertainment again. Then there are two further restaurants on either side that are themed. On Discovery is 'Coast to Coast' for seafood, and 'East to West' for Asian food. These two venues on

Adventure are called 'Khukuri House' specialising in Nepalese food, and 'Amalfi' for Italian style dishes.

Ignoring food for a while, passengers can go forwards on Deck 6 past the photographer's desk, and come to the 'South Cape Bar' on Discovery, or 'North Cape Bar' on Adventure. These bars are similar to pubs, and a popular place throughout the day and evening.

A few steps further forwards and there is the main entertainment venue called 'The Playhouse' on both ships. These theatres are superb, allowing 400 passengers to sit in comfort to watch shows from the resident theatre troupe, or visiting cabarets. In the daytime it is used for guest speakers or demonstrations, and films on the massive state of the art video screen.

Decks 7 to 11 are all about passenger staterooms, but there is a public area midships on Deck 7 that houses the library, with coffee machines, and lots of seating to relax with a book. This is also where both ships have a card room and craftwork room.

Deck 12 has the Britannia Lounge at the front on both ships, and they are the largest venues on the vessels. The Britannia Lounge has wrap around 270° windows, allowing views out over the sea to watch progress between ports. Passengers can sit in comfort around a small dance floor at the front, or in either of the two quieter side wings at the rear. Of course, there is a bar and the lounge is busy throughout the daytime for a cup of coffee, maybe a beer or a cocktail while relaxing with a book, compete in the regular quizzes, or try out dance classes. In the evening it becomes the alternative entertainment venue with shows, cabaret artists, or simply listening to music.

Walking towards the stern from the Britannia Lounge you come to the open deck with the Lido swimming pool surrounded by plenty of space to relax in the sunshine. There is also a small stage at one end for outdoor entertainment. Behind the pool is another dining venue called 'The Grill'. This is the buffet option for meals throughout the day and evening, and like on most cruise ships, it is a less formal place to eat, if that is what you prefer. At the extreme stern end there is an extension to The Grill with an outside dining area if the weather allows. This area is called 'The Veranda' with cooked to order burgers, hotdogs, or fish and chips. You can even watch them cook your choice before eating it. The Veranda has wonderful views to the ship's wake, and it is a real treat to enjoy the fast food with a glass of beer or wine, with the breeze cooling the sun's heat as you look at the sea.

The Veranda has steps down to the lower decks at the stern, and also up to Deck 13 (Sun Deck) where there is another walkway for a stroll with views down onto the Lido pool. Wherever you go on the open decks, loads of sun beds are prepared early each morning with a towel, allowing you a place to relax in the sun, or the shade. Near the rear end a set of stairs go up further to a sports net for those who are really energetic. At the front of this deck above the Britannia Lounge there are a number of passenger staterooms, as well as the fitness centre and gymnasium to burn off excess calories that all cruisers enjoy to consume.

At the forward end of Deck 13 there are steps up to Deck 14 which is known as the Observation Deck, with the very best views out over the ocean. It is quiet up there, and it has clusters of comfortable furniture to sit and relax on while chatting, or for the most dedicated sun lovers, there are yet more loungers.

# Our 2021 Saga Cruise Experience

During 2021 our lives were virtually put on hold while we waited for some sort of positive news about Covid. Our desire to return to cruising was nothing compared to the hardship and distress that was the headline of every news bulletin, and the main focus of everyone. But the clouds did begin to break, hopes of a future were forming, and lives began ever so slowly, to return to some sort of normality.

Deb and I thought long and hard about going on a cruise. We had a lot of concerns about the ability of the companies to safely have several hundreds of passengers in a ship without mass infections. Regular cruisers will know the speed that colds, sore throats and coughs spread around a ship, and it was obvious that Covid might wreak havoc.

We also had similar long thoughts and discussions about the cruise we were booked on. In essence we wondered if it was worth going on a ship for a week sailing simply around Britain.

The brochures were consulted yet again, and I was back on the phone to Saga.

There was a lot of swapping and changing leading up to the cruise we eventually settled on, but throughout it all the Saga call centre staff had been absolutely marvellous. The impression they portrayed was that they really wanted to help us, rather than trying to make us bend to their wishes. The only issue was that the Covid circumstances meant there appeared to be less operators working, and calls took a little longer to answer than I would have liked.

Of course, that was the situation with virtually all call centres at that time.

Anyway, we finally settled on a holiday. It was on the Spirit of Discovery, and was for five days sailing north to Scotland and Northern Ireland. We were spending a lot of money in order to try out the new ship, and decide if the Saga product truly met our needs.

… and we still had worries about catching Covid.

*The Holiday Begins*

On the 24th September 2021, there was a knock on the front door by our chauffer within five minutes of the expected time. Having introduced himself, he took our suitcases to the car, that was a Mercedes saloon, and settled us in.

Saga Cruises offer free chauffer driven transport to and from the cruise terminal as a part of the package. If the journey is less than 75 miles, it will be just for you, but up to 250 miles it will be a shared service. Over 250 miles the transfer is still available, but there is a charge per extra mile. Of course, this transport is just an option, and free car parking is also available if that is preferred.

Our journey was well in excess of 75 miles, but the Covid protocols meant that Saga were offering the non-shared chauffer service to everyone who were less than 250 miles from the port.

The journey to Southampton was comfortable, and we had toilet breaks and coffee stops as we wanted.

At the port we had a new experience, which was also new to the driver. We had to queue for a Covid test, and then wait for the results before we could proceed to the check-in terminal. We arrived at probably the peak time, and the queue was long. The complete process took some 45 minutes, and while we were aware of the testing requirement, and expecting the delay, our driver got rather frustrated.

We were eventually allowed to go to the embarkation terminal, and it was time to put on our protective masks that would be required at all times while in public on the ship.

At that time the Covid protocols restricted passenger numbers on cruise ships, so check-in and security scans were quite quick. There wasn't even time to sit down in the waiting area before we were walking along the airbridge to the ship.

The next few minutes were a very familiar welcome from smiling crew, plus a line of cabin stewards (also smiling) waiting to show us to our cabin. The walk to the cabin wasn't very long as it was nearby.

Our cabin was the same size as we have been used to with P&O ships, with adequate wardrobe and drawer space. The bathroom was bigger than some we have experienced and the shower had a door, rather than a cold flapping curtain. As with all passenger cabins, we had a balcony and there was sufficient room to stretch out on the loungers – if the opportunity arose.

The next hour or so was spent unpacking, and then we set off to explore the ship. With restaurants found, we searched for suitable looking venues to sample later. We ventured along most decks and soon reached the Grill at the top of the ship.

It was time for a cup of tea. There was a slight disappointment here, with barrels of milk, and no jugs to take it to a table. The tea had to be made, brewed, tea-bag removed and milk added at the quite small drink station. This always produces queues and chaos, but we learnt to adapt to the situation.

Although we were allocated a place in the main dining room for the first night, we had been told to book ourselves evening meals in the three Select Dining rooms as soon as possible. With that organised, Deb and I continued our exploration of the ship. We took a look at the theatre from the back, and from there passed by the entrance to the South Cape bar on the way back to our cabin.

It seemed polite to have a drink as we were passing. The lounge felt right for us, and turned out to be our favoured one for the five days.

*Meals*

Our dinner venue was allocated in the Grand Dining Room, and while the Covid concerns were still quite high, the tables were spaced further apart than normal, and there were more tables laid for two passengers. The evening session on Saga ships is run with a flexible arrangement in the main dining room, meaning that passengers can turn up at any time during the opening hours, and wait for a table to become free. We were able to get a table for two each time we ate in there.

The meal was extremely good, with a menu that kept me happy, and a pleasant selection of wines to accompany the food. Our waiters were superbly attentive and often cracking jokes to amuse us between courses. They also ensured the wine waiter kept our glasses full and it was a challenge to keep the glasses empty, for when we had finished.

Eating and drinking were the only moments while out of our cabin when we could remove our masks, and it gave me serious relief from being restricted. At least the passengers generally stuck to the rules, but many of us occasionally forgot to cover our faces, especially when walking around. Other passengers or crew would politely point out our errors, and we quickly covered up again.

We also opted for breakfast and lunch in the Grand Dining Room. It was less frenetic than in the Grill. These two meals were a mixture of waiter service, plus some 'Choose your own' items from a buffet.

*Daily Life*

During the daytime we took part in the regular quizzes, and spent a lot of time sitting in various spots reading, or perhaps chatting to other passengers over a coffee. There were other activities going on, but this was a moment of rest for us, and we didn't get too involved.

Our evening routine for the week was to sit in a lounge after dinner, and then go to the theatre for the shows. The ship's troupe of singers and dancers were talented, and on evenings when the theatre was used for a guest cabaret act, one or more of the singers might perform in the Britannia Lounge.

If the evening show wasn't to our liking, we would go and sit in the Britannia Lounge and check out the atmosphere there. If that was also uninteresting, we would happily sit in the South Cape bar with a glass of wine, and that regularly led to chatting with other passengers where we discussed the merits of Saga Cruises. Just as during the daytime, Deb and I often simply grabbed a quiet sofa somewhere to read our books.

*Ports*

There were only two ports on the cruise. First there was the Scottish port of Greenock for trips to Glasgow, where we didn't get off as nothing inspired our imagination.

The next day it was Belfast and although free excursions were available, we bought a tour of the coastal area featuring the 'Giant's Causeway'. As we drove away in the coach from the port, I suddenly realised that I hadn't brought any money, or bank cards. The Saga product was such that money wasn't necessary, but I was shocked to have left the ship with no way of paying for anything.

Anyway, the tour was superb. We had a delightful coastal drive, passing through little towns, then absorbing scenic views from the cliffs. Finally we arrived at the Giant's Causeway. There was an exhibition building with the usual toilets, shops and café, but Covid protocols meant we couldn't have a drink, or even visit the souvenir shop.

When we had all used the toilets, we set off down a cliff path to the spectacular Basalt rock formations. I don't understand the science of how nature has created these pillars of honeycomb shaped rocks, but that doesn't matter. It is beautiful, and magical.

We were back on our ship for lunch, and when we left Belfast in the afternoon, it was time for the Spirit of Discovery to turn southwards towards Portsmouth.

After five short nights on this beautiful ship, we had a well organised disembarkation and were soon on our way home to Cornwall in our chauffer driven people carrier. Our cruise had been a lovely experience with good food, reasonable entertainment, and perfect service from the attentive and friendly crew. Somehow Saga's product, the small ship, the smiling crew, and the level of service had rekindled that magical feeling that we felt was beginning to disappear from P&O.

*An eventful journey Home*

Our drive home was not without incident.

Drama Number One

After about an hour of driving, we had to stop because an accident had just occurred ahead of us. Our chauffer was an ex-policeman and he felt it right to go and check if everybody was OK. He was soon back, with news that there were no serious injuries, but the road was temporarily closed until the ambulance and recovery vehicles arrived. Our driver took an alternative route to skirt around the blocked road.

He was getting a little twitchy by now as the country was in chaos with a lack of fuel. He needed to fill up, but so far, our route didn't give him any garages with diesel.

Drama Two

The alternative route chosen involved several sections of rather narrow roads, and some even had grass growing in the middle of them. Deb and I sat back and relaxed, and it was a change for me to be able to look around at the countryside. As we were going up a hill, I was looking ahead and to my horror I saw a car in front of the van we were following crash into the side of a lorry coming in the other direction. I saw debris from the car flying into the air and coming our way, and the debris included the front wing of the car. Fortunately, it landed without hitting us, and slid under the van.

This looked a little more serious and our driver stopped and set off to check the scene again. We were stationary for perhaps 15 minutes before our chauffer returned to announce no serious injuries again, but the road would be blocked for some time.

There was a lane that we could take to use yet another route, so off we went again. I was getting fed up of roads with grassy patches by now, and the lanes were getting more and more narrow.

Drama Three

We were constantly stopping and reversing to allow cars to pass from the other direction, and it was obvious our driver was well skilled ...

... well almost.

He was getting frustrated about the delay to our journey, and a lack of fuel garages. On one stretch of lane, he stopped over and over again, but finally he forgot to look behind before reversing. He drove into a car following us.

It was not at high speed, and nobody had any physical issues, but it really annoyed our driver that he had made such an error.

There was another delay while damage was inspected, and insurance details swapped.

We set off again, and I was rather relieved. I have a superstition that things happen in threes. This was our third incident, and we had got away with nothing worse than a delay or two.

Very soon afterwards we got back on the initial planned route, and the driver finally found some diesel. Soon afterwards we had a quick stop at Exeter Services and then relaxed in the comfortable seats for the last 80 or so miles towards home. By mid-afternoon we were back at our apartment, and cases brought in by our apologetic driver.

The journey had been far longer (in time) than we anticipated, and Deb and I were tired. It wasn't long before we were sitting down with a cup of tea, and even the journey couldn't spoil what had been a wonderful few days away.

# A Cruise for 2022

Moving forward several months from that short cruise on the Spirit of Discovery, the early months of 2022 still had the dark shadow of Covid hanging over Britain, and the rest of the world. Things were however improving, and the British Cruise companies were at long last venturing towards different countries.

Deb and I wanted another holiday, and of course it was going to be a cruise. But we were also questioning what we really wanted for the future.

The P&O product was losing its appeal. We were truly uncomfortable with the idea of large ships, and also disillusioned by our perceived drop in standards. There were also continuous charges being applied on board the ship for things that we used to be getting for free.

I bought shares in Carnival Cruises several years ago. Those shares had given us multiple dividends per year, and this was accompanied by quite generous 'on board credit' perks each time we had a cruise. Covid had reduced the value of the shares quite dramatically, but it didn't bother us as we had received far more from the shares than their original value.

The decision was made to sell the shares.

**Was this possibly the moment we were saying goodbye to P&O?**

As our thoughts continued to be focussed on what and when our next holiday would be, another factor was added to the mix. My arthritis was getting worse, and my knee became more and more painful making long periods of walking impossible.

I had an appointment to see an Orthopaedic consultant in February 2022. He wasn't overly concerned about my knee, but after various questions, plus a little bit of leg waggling, the outcome was that my name was put on a list for a hip replacement. He hoped it wouldn't be long before the operation, but I would certainly have to wait a few months.

This focussed our minds a little more, and a decision was made to organise a cruise for as soon as possible.

It would have been nice to get a cruise with some guaranteed sunshine, but there weren't many options. One major complication was because Saga were using multiple ports to start and end cruises. The totally free chauffer service only applied to a journey of 250 miles each way, and that meant we needed a cruise that began and ended in either Southampton or Portsmouth. Sadly, the most interesting cruises were when the Saga ships had switched their home port to Dover, and that would mean paying for the transport for the considerable increase in mileage

We had to find a cruise earlier than desirable, and eventually from our list of suitable cruises, we decided on a return to the

Spirit of Discovery for a 15-night holiday to Portugal, Spain, and France setting off from Southampton on the 31st March.

Because we already knew the standard of the cabins, we simply booked what was described as an unassigned cabin number, meaning we wouldn't know where we would be sleeping until close to the departure date. This type of booking meant a reduction in the price.

With the holiday booked, we settled down to wait. As the end of March approached, Deb and I were very careful to avoid exposing ourselves to Covid. In the final couple of weeks, we hardly left our village site, took regular Lateral Flow Tests, and didn't mix with others too closely.

## Flavours of the Mediterranean

It was time for another cruise.

On the 31$^{st}$ March 2002, we were up, breakfasted, washed, and our cases were quickly closed and moved near to the front door. This was part of a well-rehearsed routine at the beginning of a holiday. We had let our neighbours and the reception staff know that we would be away for 15 nights, and the apartment was put into slumber mode while we were away.

There were just a few minutes wait beyond the agreed time before the chauffer rang the doorbell, and our latest adventure was about to begin.

Our drive to Southampton would take about four hours including a break at Exeter Services to stretch our legs, use the toilets, and grab a snack. The car was comfortable and the driver chatted to us as the miles passed.

When we arrived in Southampton, there was a pleasant surprise to find the Covid testing procedure had been well practiced, and within 30 minutes we were cleared and away to the departure terminal. Check-in was quick, but boarding was delayed, so we had to sit in the vast lounge until the Spirit of Discovery, and her crew, were ready to greet us. Because of the unexpected delay, we were offered free glasses of fizz plus a selection of finger buffet food to keep us content.

Although we were never informed officially, I assume the delay was to ensure deep cleaning had been completed around the ship before we boarded. Covid problems were reducing, but it was still a threat in the confined environment of a cruise ship.

It wasn't long before we heard the first of the instructions for people to begin boarding, so we drank the remaining glass of fizz, and waited until our coloured card numbers were called. Then it was the walk along the air-bridge and the welcome on board calls from the smiling gangway crew, and the waiting line of cabin stewards to escort us to our cabin. We convinced the steward to take us up the stairs rather than using the crowded lifts, but my knee soon screamed that it was probably not a good idea to climb four flights of stairs to B Deck where our cabin (B003) was near the front on Port side.

Our luggage was waiting for us, but we decided to go and find a cup of tea in the Grill buffet one deck above us. We took the long way back to our cabin with a quick exploration of the ship, but then settled down to filling the wardrobe and drawers.

There was plenty of time for a glass of wine before having a shower and changing for dinner. We were in the main dining room that night, and asked for a table for two rather than sharing. The room had been laid out with as many small tables as possible to make it more comfortable, and we never had to share on any night.

Our group of waiters were happy and efficient as they served us delicious food and a side dish of humour throughout the meal.

… plus of course the never emptying glass of wine.

*First day on-board*

Our week's cruise on the Spirit of Discovery earlier in the year meant that we knew a lot about the public lounges and bars. This allowed Deb and I to relax much quicker into our on-board routine as we knew where things happened, and where it was quieter when we needed it.

We regularly sat in the 'Living Room' for a daytime hot drink, and usually someone else would join us for a chat. These moments were a chance to remove our face masks that had to be worn when moving around the ship. When eating or drinking it meant conversations were enhanced by being able to see mouths and expressions that were normally hidden.

Of course we also investigated more of the ship than we managed to do on the previous short adventure. While exploring corridors, we found a door with no obvious sign to say what was beyond it, and after quietly opening it, we found it was the way into the library area. There were no books on the shelves because of the Covid protocol, but there were plenty of comfortable chairs or settees to sink into and read our own books.

This area isn't just a library. In the centre is a more condensed grouping of seats with a self-service coffee machine. This machine gave delicious hot drinks including some of the best hot chocolate we have found anywhere. If by any chance our stomachs demanded a snack, there were jars of cookies as well.

The library is created around the central ship's staircase, and to one side is a room that is slightly separated from the rest, and that is the craft area. Although separate, it has no wall to one side, and other passengers can look at what is going on. The craft work and art was always delightful, and no doubt tempted others to join in.

A less open room is also in this complex, and that is for the serious card players. There's no chance of peeking at what goes on in there.

While we were sitting there on the first morning, there was a loud '**Bing Bong**' on the public address system. An officer from the watch crew gave a simple announcement ...

... **"Code Quebec, Code Quebec"**

Seconds later the captain took over the microphone to make sense for those who were new to this warning code.

Although the passengers who had arrived on-board had all passed the Covid Lateral Flow Test, there were a number of the crew that were already infected, and it was being spread around with their colleagues. This Code was to alert the ship that new cases had been discovered, and the affected crew were being move to an isolation area.

All passengers were instructed to return to their cabins while the poorly people were being moved around the ship, and all activities and bars were temporarily closed.

Yes there were a few grumbles, but the passengers obeyed the instruction reasonably happily, and the ship was handed over to the medical and evacuation teams.

Discovery was not sailing at its full passenger capacity while Covid was still a serious hazard, and a number of cabins near the stern were turned into an isolation area. One block was restricted for isolation of crew, and meant that the unlucky crew members catching Covid found themselves in a passenger cabin with a balcony.

The shut down lasted for about 45 minutes, and soon the captain came on the PA again to give us details of what had been happening, and thanked us for our cooperation.

What we didn't know at that time, was that the Code Quebec alerts were about to become quite routine for several days.

Although passengers were negative on Lateral Flow Tests, we all took the full-blown PCR test before boarding as well. These were checked in Southampton after the ship sailed, and the results would become available during this first afternoon.

We shrugged off the Code Quebec interruption to our cruise and had lunch up in the Grill, and we realised it was a very popular venue. Although we found a table quite easily, trips to and from the buffet involved some serious care to avoid bumping into other passengers. Worse still the mask wearing regime was regularly forgotten and the crew were constantly pointing out naked chins.

There was a reasonable choice of food, and it was all perfectly fine, and the pleasure of being offered a glass of wine certainly softened the slight uncomfortable feeling in the crowded restaurant.

We made a decision that the main dining room would be our lunch venue from then on.

The ship's newspaper had warned all passengers that after lunch there would be another Lateral Flow Test. We had to all go to the Britannia Lounge for the test, and each cabin had an allotted time to join the queue. To be honest this was very well organised, and the process only took a few minutes. Once the test had been taken, we returned to our cabins until receiving a phone call with the result. I think in less than 30 minutes we had been tested and declared negative, meaning we could carry on normally around the ship.

The weather wasn't brilliant, and the outside decks were very unpopular, so any thoughts of Deb having a swim in the outside pool were off the agenda. The lure of water was too much for her, and she went to the Spa to have a soak in the hydrotherapy pool there. When she came back the pool was described as being really good, and I should come with her next time.

One of the things we did immediately after boarding, was to book dinner in the three specialised dining rooms. On our previous cruise we were thrilled with the food and service in these venues, and this evening we were looking forward to eating in the 'East to West' Asian restaurant.

Late in the afternoon while relaxing with a cup of coffee in the Living Room, we were just thinking about going to get a shower before dinner, when there was a 'Bing Bong' on the PA and another **"Code Quebec"** alert.

We didn't even wait for the captain to make his announcement, and made our way back to the cabin to isolate until those with the lurgy were moved.

Our first thoughts were that the post lunch test must have found a few passengers testing positive, or more poorly crew were identified. Those initial thoughts were soon proved wrong by the captain.

Although the afternoon lateral flow test might have found a few, the majority of new cases had been identified by the PCR tests taken before departure.

So, we already knew that there was Covid spreading around the crew, but now there were passengers infected, who might have already spread it around.

The Code Quebec announcement and subsequent message from the captain, suggested our period of isolation in the cabins wouldn't be very long. Deb and I had our showers, and got ready to go to dinner, but it was an hour later that the all-clear Bing Bong announcement was made.

It seemed a few of the passengers were not overly cooperative about moving cabins.

Anyway, by now it was long past our dining time, so we dashed up to the restaurant. In the corridor outside of the venue we found another couple talking to the front of house manager. Inside there we could see a panic of waiters getting things ready, and a longer queue was forming behind us. The slightly flustered manager assured us it wouldn't be too long a delay.

True to his word, we were shown to our table little more than ten minutes afterwards, and the meal was delicious, and the service superb.

We left the restaurant fully content, and were already looking forward to eating in the other two speciality venues.

It wasn't quite time to go to the Playhouse Theatre, so as we wasted time, we dropped in at the South Cape bar for a post dinner glass of wine. In the theatre we found a perfect spot in the centre to watch the show, and where I could stretch out my legs. That was where we aimed for each time we went to a show. It was strange seeing the audience spread out with one seat spacing between them, and everyone wearing face masks.

As we entered everyone also had to give their cabin numbers that were recorded for track and trace precautions.

What a strange world we were now living in.

An hour or so later we were on our way back to the cabin after a most enjoyable evening. The wind wasn't causing Discovery to be uncomfortable, but there was enough movement to remind me that we were at sea. I had become quite used to this over twenty-two years of cruising.

*The Daily Routine*

Over the next few days we settled into a routine.

Breakfast was taken in the main dining room with its mixture of self service and table service. It was so much more relaxing than the buffet. This was also our preferred venue for lunch, although sometimes when we just needed a snack, we used the buffet.

Between meals we occasionally took a walk around the Promenade Deck, or took our books up to the Britannia Lounge. As well as using it as a place to read, we took part in quizzes that were run there mid-morning, post lunch, and post dinner.

We regularly had a morning coffee in the Living Room. This lounge was busy throughout each day and evening, and quite often friends gathered to chat. At times during the day a pianist might appear, or sometimes a harpist would bring a bit of music to entertain people. Quite often it was really busy, and then Deb and I would go and get a hot chocolate (and cookie) in the library.

In the afternoon Deb often took advantage of the hydrotherapy pool, and one day she convinced me to go with her. It has soothing warm water to soak in, but at several points around the pool, there are powerful jets of water that can be trained on our bodies to massage the muscles. On the side of the pool there were several lounging points to lay back and relax in the warmth.

Late each afternoon we would prepare ourselves for dinner by taking a shower and changing clothes. We were nearly always ready far too early, so we wasted a few minutes with a glass of fizz in the South Cape bar while we watched the world walk by us.

The dining experience was usually very good, but on the first formal night we were in the main dining room, and unfortunately things went wrong. We had a table for two, close by several other couples, and the initial menu selection, starters and wine appeared promptly. Then for some reason the waiters seemed to forget us. They continued to service the tables around us with their main courses, and then desserts, but we were ignored. In the end we called over the section waiter and asked what was happening. There was a series of discussions between the waiters resulting in major apologies. The main course quickly arrived (with more apologies) but while the other tables drank their coffee, and stared at us, we lost our appetites, stood up, and walked out.

It was only that one evening when it went wrong. By the next evening we had received a phone call from the manager who sorted out a nightly table for two, in a different area of the restaurant. From then on, the service was prompt and friendly, and we had no further complaints.

We went to the theatre most evenings, where we enjoyed the shows and cabarets. We did try out the Britannia Lounge one evening for a show, but it was very busy, and noisy. Our preference was the theatre, and then a less frenetic time in the South Cape bar or the Living Room.

But there was also one other thing that became a part of all the passengers' routine.

Each afternoon, between 3:30 to 4:00, there was a Code Quebec announcement.

*Code Quebec*

To begin with, the '**Bing Bongs'** and **"Code Quebec"** announcements were greeted with audible gasps of frustration around the ship. The captain would then summon all his patience and make the daily apology, and we were sent for a period of temporary isolation. As the days passed, a growing number of passengers were being diagnosed with Covid and moved to the isolation area of the ship. After a while we began to organise our afternoon so that we were ready for the Bing Bong, and for several days the captain would announce an even higher number of passengers with the virus.

*Isolation Wing*

Saga Cruises did all they could to get their ships back into business. They knew there were risks from Covid cases, and sailed with way below maximum passenger capacity. The ships also had a section of cabins left empty at the stern. From the last watertight door towards the stern, the cabins on several decks became the Covid Isolation Zone.

The watertight doors had signs to inform passengers should not pass through them. The unfortunate people banished to these cabins were not allowed out of their cabins. All food was ordered and brought to a table outside the passengers' door by room service dressed in full safety kit.

When the recommended period of isolation was completed, the guests were asked how they felt, and if they were OK a final test was made before they returned to their original cabins, and re-joined their fellow passengers.

Of course, the crew were just as susceptible to catching the virus, and they were told to report any illness as quickly as possible. If the tests showed they had Covid they were taken out of their shared cabins and isolated in the same way as the passengers. I'm sure they hated not being able to work, but having a cabin to themselves must have been quite a treat.

*Other precautions around the ship*

Facemasks were mandatory as passengers moved around the ship, and they had to remain on when in the theatre. The only time anyone could take masks off in public, was when eating or drinking. A very small number of people rebelled, and they were quickly reminded of the rules by the attentive crew. I saw the theatre ushers coming to people during the shows when they had dropped their masks in the darkness.

We all accidently forgot the mask rules at times, and this was usually when leaving a bar, or standing to get another course of food from the buffet. Once politely advised, we apologised and quickly covered up again.

Unlike some of the passengers, the crew were very aware of the need for masks, and seeing anything other than a pair of eyes became quite normal.

When passengers went on tours, masks were required on the coaches. In reality most of the passengers were quite happy to wear their masks in the confinement of a coach.

The cleaning regime around the ship was good before Covid smacked us all on the chin, but now it was noticeably increased. There was hardly a moment through the cruise when you didn't see someone with a bucket and cloth wiping down every visible surfaces.

Passengers were audibly and physically herded towards sinks at the entry of restaurants.

Announcements and instruction in the daily paper reminded us all of the need to thoroughly wash our hands before eating, and after going to the toilet.

The traditional cocktail parties, or meeting the officers, was not possible. To be honest even seeing anyone from the bridge crew was very rare.

For the first few days, all the passengers were regularly being called to go for Lateral Flow tests. The medical team, and other trained swabbers, went through a well-rehearsed process of quickly and efficiently poking our noses. The sample cotton buds were then put into regimental rows of plastic tubes until the result was available.

By the time we left the room and returned to our cabin, there was just a short wait before the phone would ring and let us know we could go out to play again.

… sadly, that wasn't the case for everyone.

*Things Got Worse*

As we sailed down the west coast of Spain on day two of the cruise, a major impact of the Covid attack on the ship was announced.

We were due to visit Lisbon the following day, but the numbers of Covid positive passengers (and crew) meant that the Portuguese authorities were threatening to refuse permission to allow the ship to make landfall. This information was announced to us by the captain late in the afternoon of day 2. He then continued by saying that to avoid any potential issues, he was cancelling our stop at Lisbon.

As an alternative to the planned Lisbon stop, the captain announced that we would be making an unscheduled stop at the Spanish port of Malaga on day 4.

We already knew the Covid protocol for port visits meant that passengers could only go ashore if they were booked on an official tour. The Tours Team now went into overdrive and were hastily organising tours in Malaga, but with such short notice, they were restricted to panoramic coach rides with minimal stops.

There were some grumbles around the ship, but the decisions being made were all based on keeping us as free of Covid as possible.

What we didn't know at that moment, was that the situation was about to get even worse.

*Back to our cruise*

The Spirit of Discovery had a reasonably comfortable crossing of the Bay of Biscay, and by the afternoon of Day 3 we were south of Portugal and heading towards the Mediterranean Sea. The weather now took a turn for the worse, and the ship was less than steady, with a warning from the captain that it was going to be like this for a day or two more.

The atmosphere around the ship was still quite positive even with the change of plans, but rumours were rife suggesting the Spanish might ban us from their ports as well.

Late in the afternoon Deb and I were relaxing in the cabin, and I was watching the navigation channel on the television. I suddenly noticed that we had changed course, and rather than heading southwards, we were heading to the north.

This continued, and I suggested to Deb that perhaps the captain had made a decision to go back home instead of risking a rejection from the Spanish ports. Nothing was announced for some time, but after the usual Code Quebec he came on the public address system to tell us that we were heading towards the Portuguese port of Faro, to meet a helicopter for a medical evacuation. It was obvious that we would think it was to take off a Covid victim, but the announcement made it quite clear that this was **NOT** Covid related.

The evacuation was a very rapid process, and although we heard the helicopter, we never actually saw what happened.

Life continued as normal, if perhaps a little less comfortably with quite a serious amount of movement from the stormy conditions.

Overnight our ship wobbled and lurched into the Mediterranean and although we were suffering Storm Force winds, it wasn't overly uncomfortable.

*Malaga*

Discovery arrived in Malaga as planned, and those passengers booked on tours were allowed to get off. Like many other passengers, we hadn't booked a tour, and had to spend the day aboard the ship. It suited Deb and I as we were keeping away from crowded and cramped coaches until we got to the new ports later in the cruise.

When we left Malaga in the evening, the captain warned us of yet worse weather conditions as we sailed overnight towards the port of Cartagena.

His warning was correct, and the winds actually got up to Hurricane force, giving us a very bumpy ride. We had dinner in the Main Dining Room with a table for two that was close to a window, so we could watch the waves crashing against us. My stomach was fine with the conditions, and we made the most of the evening entertainment, but when we went to bed, I found it difficult to stay still and was continually rolling around.

This was not the sort of weather we had been used to in the Mediterranean.

*Cartagena ... or maybe not*

After a very uncomfortable night, we woke with expectations of being docked in the Spanish city of Cartagena.

I stared out of the window, and we were still at sea, and that is where we remained for the day.

The captain let us know the situation, and as well as a delay due to the bad weather conditions, the Spanish authorities had decided we had too many Covid patients on board, and we could not dock. This didn't bode very well, as we had three more Spanish ports on the itinerary.

At least the weather had improved so there was some sunshine and warmth. Our day reverted to a normal sea day routine of quizzes, coffee, chatting to other slightly frustrated passengers, and the daily Code Quebec of course. We came on this holiday to find out more about the Saga cruising product, but we were aware that Covid might produce a few problems.

In the evening we had our dinner in the speciality fish restaurant called Coast to Coast. I am not a fan of fish, unless covered in batter, but the restaurant manager had arranged for me to have a meal from the main dining room menu, and allow Deb to enjoy her choice of sea food. It was a lovely evening, the food was good, and the service amazing.

We just wanted a chance now to have dinner in the third speciality restaurant (The Club) but it had been closed since we boarded the ship. With several crew members suffering from Covid, the remaining waiters were concentrating on the main dining room, and The Club was just being used as an overflow venue to allow greater spacing between passenger tables.

*Valencia?*

After passing by Cartagena, we sailed around the coastline of Spain, with the next scheduled destination being Valencia on day 6 of our cruise.

The Spanish continued to show their dissatisfaction at our Covid numbers, but we were allowed to dock in Valencia. We had a tour booked for here, and were looking forward to getting off the ship. Sadly, although able to look out over the city in the sunshine, the authorities refused to let anyone off the ship.

Our captain was working hard behind the scenes with telephone calls to Saga head office, and various port agents. He was looking for a port that would allow us to dock, and more importantly, allow the passengers to get off. His daily update was more positive about the next day in Barcelona.

*Barcelona*

It was the 7$^{th}$ day of our cruise. The overnight voyage north from Valencia had been smooth, and passengers woke wondering if we would be allowed to dock in Barcelona, and perhaps even get off the ship.

We had been on the Spirit of Discovery now for a week, and had not stood on terra firma since leaving Southampton.

Well, as we looked out on the world, it was obvious we were coming into the beautiful Spanish port of Barcelona.

By this stage of the cruise, Deb and I had decided to use the Main Dining Room for breakfast and lunches rather than the crowded buffet. Sitting at our window table we watched arrival activities, but without a tour booked, we knew we wouldn't be getting off the ship, but at least we had a hope that things might be getting back to normal.

It was time for the captain to update plans for the day.

The authorities had agreed to let some passengers, and crew, to leave the ship, but ...

... they would only be those with Covid, and only to allow them to be repatriated.

Our very frustrated captain continued by saying that as soon as the sick people had left, we would be setting sail again, but he didn't know where to. Discussions and negotiations were still going on to find a port willing to accept us.

After breakfast there was the Code Quebec announcement, and all the healthy passengers were locked away in their cabins while the disembarkation was in progress.

We watched from our balcony as thirty or forty couples of passengers, and several tens of crew left the ship with their suitcases. Those still suffering badly were taken to hospitals, while those less poorly were isolated in hotels until they could fly home. A small number of passengers who were healthy, but totally fed up with the cruise, were also getting off for immediate flights back to Britain.

Little more than a few minutes after the portside activity was completed, Discovery was freed from the shore, and we set off out from Barcelona, but the next destination was unknown. There were lots of rumours, but the most common one, was that we would be turning back towards Britain.

Soon the ship returned to sea day activities, and announcements were made of changes to the programme with guest speakers, craft sessions, and games to take part in.

We were half way through our cruise now, and it was sadly turning out to be a bit of a Magical Mystery Tour.

*Week 2*

While we sailed away from Barcelona, I spent the day with a few concerns. I had a sore throat, and a niggling cough. Around this time on a cruise, I often get what is referred to as the *'Cabin Cough'*, and this was what I thought to be the case, but I was aware that the symptoms also suggested I might have caught Covid.

Just after lunch, I had one more coughing fit, and I phoned the Medical Centre. Within a few minutes they came to the cabin in full hazard kit and took a swab. About 20 minutes later they came back to say that the Lateral Flow test was negative, but they wanted to take another swab for a PCR test.

After another few minutes wait, they telephoned to say it was positive. We were told to stay in the cabin and wait to be sent to the isolation area.

*Life with Covid*

It was all a bit of a shock to begin with. We had survived the worst of the Pandemic, but now I had succumbed. Deb proved to be clear of the bug, and was even offered the chance to stay in the original cabin on her own while I was isolated.

Fortunately for me, she refused the offer, and remained with me.

We didn't move on the day I was pronounced unclean, but had meals brought to our cabin by the room service team. Luckily, we had a balcony and could get fresh air, but we quickly realised that on other ships, isolation might mean no windows, and only air-conditioned air.

The next morning, we woke to find ourselves at sea, and the captain announced we were on the way to Palma on the Spanish island of Majorca. Agreement had been reached for the ship to dock, and for passengers to go on tours. It was also hot and sunny for the first time on the cruise. Even though isolated we had the bonus of a balcony to at least be able to enjoy the weather.

Just after lunch we were told to expect a move of cabin to the isolation wing, and to pack our suitcases of everything but the clothes in the wardrobe. They would be moved on a transportable hanger, and the luggage would be taken on a trolley.

The next thing we heard was "**Code Quebec**", and soon we were escorted by a group of bio-hazard suited crew, along the eerily quiet corridor towards the stern of the ship, then down the crew staircase to our new cabin. It was identical to what we had been in, and within 10 minutes, clothes were put away, and we settled in.

Several other couples had moved at the same time as us, and as we leant on the balcony rail, we said hello to the other newly 'unclean' passengers.

We didn't know it at the time, but this was where we remained until disembarkation day.

Everyone did their best to make the time as comfortable as possible. We were regularly rung by the hotel team asking if we needed, or wanted, anything. Even the hotel manager (Werner) called us daily to see if everything was OK. Room service called to ask for our meal choices, and they always arrived promptly at the requested time. We had as much wine to drink as we wanted, and the room service team seem to take offence if we didn't order at least one bottle per meal.

At one point Deb asked if there were any jigsaws available, and 30 minutes later, a brand new one arrived. There was one slight problem, as the jigsaw was too large for the small table in the cabin. Deb jokingly mentioned the amazing jigsaw story on Facebook, with the comment about not having anywhere to make it. The next morning there was a knock on the door, and a sheet of wood arrived to be used for the jigsaw. We realised that the ship's hotel staff constantly monitored the popular Saga users Facebook sites, and after seeing Deb's comment reacted immediately.

We could watch any talks and entertainment in the theatre on the television, and there was a vast choice of films on the system. From that point onwards, the sun seemed to be out every day, so we made the most of the balcony.

There were no complaints about the way Saga looked after us, but however well we were treated, the lack of freedom to wander around the ship, chat to other passengers, take part in quizzes and watch shows live meant our cruise was no longer the holiday we anticipated.

*The Final Days of our Cruise*

There were still several days remaining on our holiday, but it would be spent in the isolation cabin. Those days coincided with a significant improvement in the weather, and while Deb and I were restricted to the balcony for the fresh air and warm sunshine, the other passengers were able to lie by the pool.

Our days began with the room service breakfast that was literally anything we wanted, and rarely was there more than a few minutes after we had eaten, before the team were asking what we wanted for lunch. After eating breakfast and having a wash, we settled down to catching up with our online newspaper about what was happening in the world, plus testing our brains with the online puzzles. If we had sunshine on the balcony we could then enjoy that while reading a book, or in my case doze in the warmth. There was a daily phone call from the medical team to establish how we were, and if we needed anything from them, such as paracetamol, or cough medicine. Another daily call was from the hotel management team to check how we were, and if they could get us anything.

Nothing was a problem with virtually immediate deliveries of milk, tea bags, and even fizzy drinks and chocolate, and all without charges. We also had to request a couple of cabin tidy up sessions with a change of sheets. This involved hiding out on the balcony while a team of cleaners and stewards in safety kit blitzed our room.

We made the most of sunny days, but if our side of the ship was in the shade, we relaxed on the bed or the sofa with our books, or watched a film on the television. The boredom was made worse by hearing the public address system tempting non isolated passengers a chance to go to talks from visiting speakers, or afternoon champagne tea and cakes, as well as sail-away parties as they departed from the ports. There were far more things going on than we had experienced during the early days. While we could watch anything happening in the theatre on the television, any visiting speakers or cabarets in the Britannia Lounge were not shown.

The routine quickly became very boring.

The day after our isolation began, the Spirit of Discovery had an unscheduled stop in the port of Palma with numerous tours for the passengers. From the island of Majorca, the ship began the journey home and had another surprise stop at the small Spanish port of Motril. We had a view down onto the quayside here and the local band came out to march up and down while playing a welcoming tune or two.

Although we sadly couldn't get off and enjoy this port, it was quite special for a completely different reason.

When we booked our very first cruise, we bought some promotional videos, and on one of them was a sequence where the captain was speaking to a passenger, and he mentioned that the next stop would be at Motril. In the following two decades we never actually visited the port, but now here we were, but not able to see what it offered.

From Motril Discovery sailed on and predictably missed the last scheduled stop at Gibraltar. Instead, we stopped at Cadiz, where passengers set off on their tours, while we simply looked at the very familiar sight of this beautiful city from our balcony. The ship had a long stay here, and in the evening the new captain of Discovery arrived to begin his period of duty a few days later. He had to go immediately into isolation for a mandatory quarantine period before taking command in Portsmouth after our return.

As we sailed up the coast of Spain there was another helicopter evacuation, in the same position as when we sailed south a fortnight earlier. By now I was declared clear of Covid, and offered a chance to go back to the original cabin, but Deb was now shown to be positive, and I stayed with her for the final days.

My dose of Covid wasn't serious. It started with the cough plus a sore throat. Then my limbs became heavy and ached, followed by the cough turning to sneezing, and my nose was constantly running. This was annoying but not disastrous. After a few days I suddenly realised I had lost my sense of smell and taste, and that was quite frustrating. When Deb began the illness, it followed my initial symptoms quite closely, but she avoided the aching limbs and her taste and smell was not affected.

We were both very thankful for having the various jabs over the months, and although we had eventually caught the virus, it was nothing like as severe as many thousands had suffered.

On our arrival back in Britain at Portsmouth, we had to stay in the cabin while all the happy and healthy passengers disembarked. Finally, an hour and a half later, a sad little snaking queue of isolated couples trooped off past crew members in their hazard suits. Our shuttle bus to the terminal was reserved for the 'unclean' but we didn't notice many precautions once in the terminal building, and our driver was not aware of our illness.

I hope he never caught it from us.

We had been on the ship for 15 nights and our feet never touched land. During that cruise, the only ports that were as scheduled, was our departure from Southampton, and the short stop in Barcelona to offload the first group of Covid passengers. Even our return port changed from Dover to Portsmouth. Fortunately, we at least enjoyed a few days at the beginning of our ill-fated holiday to explore and enjoy the Spirit of Discovery, before that very disappointing period of isolation.

Deb and I could have decided never to go on a Saga ship again, but the service we had been given before isolation had been superb, and while shut away, the crew made it as comfortable as was possible. The ship is beautiful, the venues are varied and comfortable, and the crew had been magnificent.

We would happily cruise again on Saga ships, but perhaps when the Covid threat has reduced a little more.

As a postscript to our 'Cruise to Nowhere', all the passengers on the cruise were generously compensated, and like us, probably very keen to book another cruise with Saga.

*Home Again*

The journey home was long, but passed without incident. Back in Cornwall we set about unpacking, and made do with food from the freezer rather than going shopping. We had managed to get some milk when we stopped on the journey, and there was no need for anything else until the following day.

Over the next few days, our tale was repeated over and over as we met up with our friends. They were upset and astounded to hear about our mystery holiday to nowhere.

## Medical Matters

Before going on our cruise, I was already aware that I was going to have my left hip replaced. The holiday had been intended to be a last chance before the surgery, but the cruise didn't really provide real satisfaction.

Things began to happen quite quickly when a cancellation meant I had an almost last-minute offer of an operation in the middle of May. Unfortunately, my medical record showed several incidents of chest pain and visits to A&E, so I needed to see an anaesthetist as a part of the pre-op checks.

The appointment for the pre-op was too late for that cancellation date, but the anaesthetist checked me out and was reasonably happy for me to go ahead with the next available date. To be careful, he wrote a letter to the Cardiac team who had performed an Angiogram on me in the previous year, just to confirm their views about me having surgery.

I heard no more for several weeks, and eventually my frustration led to me ringing the hip surgeon's secretary for more news. She was the ultimate customer focussed secretary, and explained that the previous person had changed roles, and my name had slipped from the list. Two days later she called me back with a date for my operation. It was to be at the end of October 2022.

I was naturally quite worried when the morning of the operation came and I arrived at the hospital at 7:00 in the morning, but I had high hopes that the day would eventually reduce my pain.

Sadly, it seems 2022 was a bad year for me.

I was second on the surgeon's list that morning, and having starved for 12 hours, I sat in my elegant surgical gown waiting for the first patient to receive his new hip. The suggestion was that I would be in theatre before lunch, but at 2:30 in the afternoon a doctor came in to say that there had been a serious problem with the gentleman's operation, and there was no time for mine to go ahead that day. I dressed and went home with a promise of an early call back for my surgery.

That efficient secretary was on the case, and I was rescheduled for the following week.

Then I had a phone call from the anaesthetist who would be looking after me in theatre, and he was concerned that the letter his colleague had written to my cardiac doctor had never been responded to, and he decided I needed to be checked properly before he would let me have surgery.

Fortunately, he pulled some strings and got me a date for two CT scans of my heart using a radioactive dye to check my heart functions at rest, and under stress.

Those two CT scans were completed by the end of November, and the outcome had to be assessed by the cardiac team as a high priority.

My friendly efficient secretary said my name would be kept at the top of the surgical list awaiting the cardiac team response.

Finally, in January 2023, I saw the Cardiac team doctor. He would not agree to me having surgery until I had another angiogram to compare with the one in October 2020. That new angiogram was on the 26$^{th}$ January, and the outcome was that I was deemed fit to have surgery.

After a considerable wait from the first offer for an operation in October 2022, my operation was eventually rescheduled for the 24$^{th}$ May 2023. Even getting this date had meant pestering my surgeon's secretary almost weekly.

This new hip date was pencilled on the calendar, and knowing that I wouldn't be allowed to go on a cruise for many weeks afterwards, we decided to try and fit in another cruise before my surgery.

We rang the Saga customer line.

Firstly, I cancelled two cruises we had planned for summer and autumn 2023, and then rebooked for the 27th April for a 15-night cruise on the Spirit of Adventure.

## Pre-Hip Cruise

Several of our friends thought we were mad to consider another cruise after the previous Covid affected one.

We didn't listen to them.

On the morning of 27th April 2023, I answered the door to our Saga chauffer and within five minutes we were on our way towards Portsmouth. Our transport was a large people carrier and we were due to be sharing it, but whatever reason, the other passengers had cancelled their trip at the last moment, and we had six seats to ourselves.

We chatted to the driver and the miles passed by without incident, and I spent quite a while dozing. There was a break at Exeter for coffee and toilet relief, and then well before 3:00 we were pulling into the harbour area in Portsmouth. Our driver was aware of the procedure and talked us through the luggage offload, before saying cheerio at the embarkation terminal building.

There was only a short queue, and Deb and I quickly snaked our way to the check in desk. Details inspected, and photos taken, there was hardly a chance to draw breath before we were off towards the security scanners, and then outside to a waiting shuttle bus towards the ship.

*Welcome to the Spirit of Adventure*

Quickly on board the ship, and as expected from looking at the brochures, this ship may have had a different décor from her sister Discovery, but corridors, stairs, lifts, and lounges were all very familiar.

Once scanned onto the ship, the next smiling steward in line was tasked to take us to our cabin.

*For anyone wanting to know all the details, our cabin was E533. This E deck standard cabin was on Port side and situated just a little towards the stern from the rear staircase.*

Then, just like on so many previous cruises, we took a quick look around the cabin, stared briefly at the waiting suitcases, and then left them until we had been for a drink and snack in the buffet.

On the way back to the cabin, we confirmed just how similar the ship was to Discovery, except for furnishing and pictures. After considering a quick welcome on-board drink in the North Cape bar, we decided the suitcases were more important while we had clear heads.

We had already looked at the programme and knew we had to be back in the cabin for the Emergency Muster Drill.

The drill was slightly different than some we had experienced. It started with an announcement from the Bridge for all passengers to return to their cabins, and then to watch the Emergency Video on the television. Next the Emergency signal was sounded, and shortly afterwards Captain Kim Tanner came on the public address system to give the very familiar information, about what to do in emergency situations.

So far this was all happening while we were in the comfort of our cabin.

Then there were commands for everyone to go to their Muster Stations, but rather than a chaotic crush with all the passengers moving together, the announcements asked for us on a deck-by-deck basis. Once we had got to the Muster Station door, our cards were scanned, and we were then told to leave by a different door, and go back to the cabin.

This was all very civilised.

Normal activities were quickly resumed, and it was time for a shower, and a change of clothes before settling down towards dinner time.

... but first we went to the North Cape bar for that first drink on board the Spirit of Adventure.

*Settling In*

After a delicious meal with superb friendly and efficient service, it was soon time to find a seat in the theatre for the first show of the cruise, and that was a classical guitarist who mixed his repertoire with folk tunes. We weren't thrilled by his act and decided not to go and watch him again. Despite the show, the afternoon and evening had been a lovely experience, and like the crew, we were smiling again to be back on a cruise ship.

By the time we made our way back to the cabin for an early night, we had become familiar with the ship's layout. At the beginning of any cruise, and especially on a new ship, there are moments when we (*sorry I*) turn the wrong way in a corridor, or forget what deck we were heading for, but there was almost an immediate familiarity on here. Firstly of course there were several less decks to choose from, and if you do turn and walk in the wrong direction it quickly becomes apparent.

Saga have been very clever having two physically identical vessels, so once comfortable with one ship, the other takes little more than a few minutes to trigger the memory again.

… well, it did for me, for most of the time.

*The Cruise Itinerary*

The 15-night cruise was described as being '*Islands of the Mediterranean*', and after the first stop in glorious Cadiz, it did indeed island hop. Our ports of call took us to Menorca (Mahon), Corsica (Ajaccio), then two different ports on Sardinia (Olbia then Cagliari). Our ship then turned for home with a final stop at Lisbon, and then disembarkation in Dover.

The sea was generally calm throughout the cruise, and we were very lucky with the weather, with warm sunshine almost every day.

Of course, one of the major happy moments on this cruise, was that we actually docked at all of the planned ports, and we were allowed to get off the ship.

Deb and I were happy to simply take a walk and sample the coffee at some ports, but we did go on two of the free panoramic tours and thoroughly enjoyed what we experienced.

*Meals*

Our dinner on the first night was in the Main Dining Room, and the little information card said we had fixed dining at 6:30, plus a table number.

The majority of passengers had to arrive at the dining room and were then allocated a different table each evening, but due to the bad experience at dinner for one night on the previous cruise, we now had this fixed dining arrangement with the same table for two each time.

We were not aware of this special arrangement until that first meal, but it was a real treat. We ate in the dining room most evenings, and got to know our waiters, and especially the wine waiter, very well. There was also the return of smiling crew, as they no longer had to wear masks.

Although Covid was still a concern, it was no longer completely ruling our lives.

Of course, we also tried out the speciality dining options during the cruise. The Supper Club and Amalfi were absolutely splendid, with wonderful choices and excellent service. While the Khukuri House was equally wonderful in terms of service and quality of food, the actual meals were not inspirational to our tastes.

We nearly always had our breakfast in the Main Dining Room, and often returned there for lunch. On some of the beautiful sunny days, we also made the most of the Veranda Grill with fish and chips, burgers, and hot dogs. We only used the Buffet on a couple of occasions for lunch, but it was not our first choice.

*Daytime Activities*

Deb and I are always up for a quiz, and during the cruise we took up the challenge regularly. The entertainment team took it in turns to run themed or general trivia quizzes each morning, afternoon and evening. They were held in the Britannia Lounge and there was nearly always a serious number of passengers joining in. We usually did quite well, but never managed to win.

Elsewhere around the ship there were craft classes morning and afternoon, and I believe there were people playing Bridge in the card room, but the door was always firmly closed. There was a very chatty and popular dance instruction couple, and they had a good following. With my hip in its final few weeks, I couldn't take part, but hopefully on the next cruise I will be able to take Deb for a spin or two around the dance floor.

In the theatre there was a full programme of talks. They included the usual port talks, but visiting speakers had something different to think about as well. Deb and I attended a number of these, and unlike many talks in dark theatres over the years, I managed to stay awake, and quite alert.

Saga look after single travellers very well, and they had daily opportunities to meet up and chat over a cup of coffee while one of the ship's team hosted the session, and encouraged everyone to join in.

Rather less popular, because the majority hadn't found it, there was the indoor hydrotherapy pool. This was in the Spa complex at the front of Main Deck, and was like a giant jacuzzi with attitude. The water was hot, and I mean hot, with places to sit and simply enjoy the water, but in some spots jets of water pummelled your body. In other places around the pool there were even more powerful blasts of water that meant having to hold the rails to stop being sent across the pool.

Of course, one of the most popular activities was finding somewhere to sit in the Living Room and enjoy a cup of coffee, plus a cake maybe. Chats with strangers was quite common, but people watching, was always a pleasant option.

Outside there were the usual deck games for those passengers wanting a bit of physical competition, but when the weather felt good enough to actually go out on the decks, we were more interested in worshipping the sunshine. Each day passengers spent hours simply watching the everchanging colour and movement of the sea. They also guarded against any playful wildlife that might get close to the ship, and shouts of "**Dolphins!**" would wake dozing sunbathers to rush and catch a glimpse of these enchanting mammals.

The swimming pool was rarely busy, but the more serious swimmers often spent time early in the morning to make their bodies work, in hopes of burning off excess calories consumed. Except when the weather was bad, or if we were going ashore, Deb used the pool, and even I went in a couple of times.

*Evening Entertainment*

On our twenty years with P&O, the passenger numbers meant two sittings for dinner, and hence the entertainment was repeated each evening.

Although not a major problem, Deb and I are struggling coming to terms with Saga ships with half the passenger numbers. Dinner is a single rolling session and that means evening entertainment begins later than we are used to. My stomach dictates that we have an earlier meal each evening, leaving quite a gap before the single nightly shows begin in the Theatre and Britannia Lounge.

We were treated to a very good mixture of entertainment during the cruise, and each artist or act appeared in both venues on different nights. Of course, there was the resident Theatre Show Troupe who were superb, and the six dancers and four singer/dancers gave eight shows in total.

The visiting cabaret acts were:

- The guitarist already mentioned
- A couple who performed acrobatic dance on trapeze and ropes
- The Beatles Experience tribute act
- A Classical violinist
- Classical quartet
- A superb magician
- Female Vocalist
- Female trio who sang classical songs mixed with pop
- Of course, there was also the Crew Show

Virtually all of these acts performed shows in the theatre, and they had an alternative show in the Britannia Lounge on a different night. Although the resident Show Troupe performed most of their shows in the theatre, three of them were given in the Britannia Lounge. The singers all had solo shows that were performed in the Britannia Lounge as well.

Acts are never to everybody's taste, and we certainly chose not to see all the acts, but they were all very good, and I don't remember hearing negative comments from passengers about them.

I will give a special mention of the resident show vocalists. On each sea day they hosted a passenger choir session, and the time flew by with their professionalism and humour. We learnt to sing a number of sea shanties, and near the end of the cruise we performed to the other passengers on the stage of the theatre. The passenger choir show is quite a common thing, but there was a twist to this one.

As well as the singing, there was a short exhibition on the stage from the members of the Line Dancing sessions. These sessions had been hosted by the show dancers on sea days.

Finally, the ever-popular ukulele class, with their guest instructors, also took to the stage and gave a short performance of what they had learnt during the cruise.

It was really good fun for all of us, and yes, the audience applauded, and went wild in appreciation of our efforts, but also to the group instructors.

*The Crew*

It was a pleasure to experience service with a smile.

Everyone from the passenger facing waiters, waitresses, receptionists, tour sales team, down to the guys putting towels on the loungers, or the sailors drying the decks with a mop and his mate touching up the white paintwork with his tiny brush, they all smiled. They all said hello when you passed them in a corridor, on the stairs, or out on the deck. It really was as if they **wanted** to please us.

As I said earlier, it was a pleasure to see their faces without masks, and it was great to be able to talk with them and see their facial responses.

… and yes, the waitresses wore shoes that fitted

The entertainment team always tried to interact with us. After completely bamboozling us with their quizzes, they tried to speak to as many of us as they could, rather than escape to their private space. The dance instructors spoke to everyone, even if they had not been to their classes, they just wanted to be sociable.

Even the majority of the cabaret artists found time to stop and chat if someone said hello to them.

The only people we didn't speak to often, in fact rarely saw, was the bridge team of officers. Yes, they came to the cocktail parties, but any other appearances by them was unusual and very brief. This may be a leftover from the Covid protocols, or perhaps Saga rules, but it was noticeably different to our experiences on P&O.

... but of course, we haven't been on those ships for nearly three years now.

*Time to come home*

All too soon we were getting ready to come home. We had enjoyed the ship, soaked up its luxury, been entertained daily, and had wonderful food. The crew had been amazing, the service was superb, and any small problems or confusions we had were quickly sorted. The ports on the itinerary were all visited as scheduled, and we had made the most of our time at them.

Even the weather had been good to us, and the nightmare of our previous cruise was forgotten.

**This had been a proper holiday.**

Docked in Dover on 7th May, we were up early to allow a reasonably leisurely breakfast, and were waiting in the Supper Club to be called for disembarkation by just after 8:00. Our estimated escape time was 8:25, and it was within a handful of minutes of that time when we were bid farewell.

This was not the most cruise friendly port, but Deb and I weren't concerned too much as we made our way to the luggage retrieval barn. It took a little while longer than expected to locate all our cases, but soon we had them perched precariously on the trolley, and away we went to queue for our driver.

He wasn't there.

The controller of drivers shouted and shouted for him, but without success.

We were sent, with our overbalancing by now mountain of cases, to the *'We don't have a driver'* waiting area. With an apology we were told to sit for a moment while a *'find the naughty driver'* lady went away with her clipboard.

Still no driver.

Then in the distance I heard someone calling our names, and the *'find the naughty driver"* lady investigated. She came back and said the driver had been sent to the *'find the naughty passengers'* area where they were trying to track us down.

It turned out that the driver had found his first passenger, and was settling her into the car just at the moment we arrived at the front of the queue, and when he returned, we had already been sent away to the *'We don't have a driver'* compound.

Never mind, we were soon settled into the car, and the journey home to Cornwall began.

It was a long journey and took more than eight hours, even with a driver who was very keen to complete it as soon as possible. To be honest he was trying too hard, and by the time we got into Cornwall in the middle of the afternoon, he was driving far too fast.

I closed my eyes and let him get on with it.

Home at last, and I decided I didn't want to book any cruises starting or ending in Dover.

Over the next few days while we changed back to normality, we met up and chatted to our friends, and praised Saga as much as we could.

We were back in love with cruising.

Now, where can we go next?


… the hip replacement went ahead as scheduled, and I am recovering well.

*Final thoughts after*

*Twenty-Three years of Cruising*

# Cruising Twenty-Three Years on

Time has flown - well actually floated - since that day we stood in the observation gallery of the Mayflower embarkation lounge, and looked up in awe at the sight of Oriana towering above us. There were no thoughts in our plans at that time of ever repeating the adventure, but life has a way of surprising us.

So far in this book, I have wandered through twenty years of cruising, and recounted some of the amazing moments of sailing around the world on the beautiful white ships of P&O. But, during the last few chapters I have sprinkled a few cruises on ships flying a different flag as we looked for an alternative to P&O.

It's time now to round off my reflections on cruising.

I will give you an idea of the modern cruising experience, and tell you my thoughts on how some things have changed.

Beware:

*Most of our knowledge is based on times riding the waves with P&O, they will remain the main source of my memories.*

*The Modern Cruise Ship*

A very obvious difference is the size of the ships. Like them or loathe them, the majority of modern cruise ships are gigantic.

When we first encountered Oriana, she weighed in at a mere 68,000 tonnes and stretched 260 metres from pointy end to her stern. This beautiful ship had a maximum passenger capacity of around 1800 people, with 800 crew to look after them.

Launched in 1995, she was one of the biggest cruise ships in the world. But by the time she left the P&O fleet in 2019, she was nothing more than a small or medium sized vessel.

Currently, the biggest ships in the P&O fleet are Iona and Arvia. They each have a passenger capacity of 5200, with 1800 crew, and are 340 metres long.

As a comparison, Cunard are just about to launch a new ship called Queen Anne, which is quite small at 322 metres carrying around 3000 passengers.

Saga's Spirit of Discovery, and Spirit of Adventure are 236 metres long, with a maximum passenger capacity of 999 looked after by 523 crew members.

Going to the other extreme, in 2023, the largest cruise ship around the world, at around 235,000 tonnes, is Royal Caribbean's 'Wonder of the Seas'. She is 362 metres long, and can squeeze in around 7000 passengers on their holidays, cared for by some 2200 crew.

Apart from having a tonnage of almost four times that of Oriana, this ship is the length of an Olympic Sprint Lane longer.

As well as being longer, these ships are wider and taller, and can carry the total populations of villages or even small towns, so do bigger and bigger ships provide benefits for the cruise companies and their passengers?

Efficiency

Firstly, they are far more efficient.

Hull shapes and construction techniques have improved dramatically over two decades, but a more significant improvement in efficiency is down to the motors and fuel used.

The very latest ships have done away with diesel and are using a much cleaner fuel called Liquified Natural Gas or LNG. There was initially a slight complication with LNG as the infrastructure at ports had to be upgraded to have the ability to store the gas, plus actually getting it into the ship's tanks. So as these new ships first came into service, the lack of ports where the ships could refuel, meant that some regular cruise destinations were not accessible. Fortunately for the industry, many more ports quickly began offering LNG fuelling, so the popular cruise ship destinations have returned.

The LNG makes the ships cheaper to power as they sail between ports, and of course the ships carry far greater passenger numbers. Maritime mechanical and electrical technology has improved in leaps and bounds, and while there will be more engineering crew looking after one of these modern giant ships, it is less than the crew numbers required to maintain two (or more) smaller ships carrying the equivalent passenger numbers.

While on the subject of crew reduction, I must also mention the number of officers working on the bridge. According to the details in the P&O ship's newsletters, there are fewer of them, compared to when we began cruising. I remember when there were far more 2nd and 3rd officers than are listed now.

Our experience with P&O shows that cruise ships further reduce fuel costs by sailing at lower speeds. On our first few cruises, the ships would be rushing from port to port. As an example, on that memorable first cruise, we reached Lisbon by lunchtime of day two, while now the ships might have only just completed the transit of the Bay of Biscay, so half a day behind.

Port charges are huge, so the cruises generally have fewer ports of call, and quite often, the duration of a stay in port is shorter.

The resulting extra sea-days also mean passengers can be coaxed into spending more of their money on board the ship, rather than spending it ashore. The bars remain busy, and the spa sessions or beauty treatments bring in more revenue.

Higher Passenger Numbers

One negative aspect of giant ships, is that the increased number of passengers, all want to be looked after, and entertained. The majority of these people expect, or to treat themselves, to a week or fortnight of fun, and that 'fun' usually involves a lot of alcohol and a party atmosphere. If you are someone who sometimes wants to escape the partying and find somewhere to relax quietly with a book, it is almost impossible.

Another negative is that big ships struggle to dock in the smaller ports. There are many beautiful smaller ports in countries around the Mediterranean, Norwegian Fjords, or the Baltic, but even if docking is possible, disgorging (sorry disembarking) thousands of passengers who all want to get off the ship at once, is difficult and chaotic. When anchoring offshore is the solution, it can be even worse tendering passengers to land. With the latest 5000+ passenger cruise ships, it has to be remembered that there must be sufficient life boats remaining on the ship to evacuate those left in an emergency, so only a small number of tenders can be used.

Finally, a drawback of big cruise ships, is that while the port and local people want the money the ship and passengers provide, it can sometimes mean there are more passengers than local residents. This will sometimes lead to negative attitudes towards the innocent holidaymakers invading their villages or towns, and this could be several times a month, or even each week in the height of cruise seasons.

Fortunately, P&O have so far kept two smaller ships to suit passengers who are more interested in some peace and quiet, and which can visit the smaller ports and islands. Sadly, those two ships are getting older, and purchasing new small cruise ships doesn't seem to be a priority of the Carnival parent company.

# The Modern Cruise Experience

The travel sections of the weekend newspapers demonstrate just how popular cruising has become. When once there were pages and pages about land based or fly away package holidays, now the emphasis has changed with huge sections of adverts for cruises.

There are choices of long ones, short breaks, exotic adventures to the other side of the world, river cruising, or simply sailing around the British Isles. There is a vast choice of ship, with most offering holidays targeted at families, but some companies are attracting the older passengers preferring a slightly slower style of adventure. Many are Fly Cruises to avoid days at sea before arriving at warm sunny locations, but a lot of the home market passengers prefer the idea of a cruise starting and ending at a British Port.

So, what is it like in the 21st Century for the thousands of passengers that choose a cruise?

*The Magic of Embarkation*

I will begin with embarkation when new passengers get their first sight of the ship.

Many decades ago, when passengers boarded a ship, it was a special moment, and the dockside buzzed with activities and people. There was a razzamatazz atmosphere with a band playing while passengers arrived with their friends and relations. Everyone was crowded on the dockside, while around them the dockside workers were still noisily loading the essentials for the journey ahead. Then the buzz of the scene quietened as the chaos subsided, and it was time to set sail. First applause would celebrate the gangway being removed, and that would soon follow with the roar of the ship's horn bringing cheers from passengers looking over the deck rails, and the dockside onlookers waved, and shouted farewells.

In the years to come, that razzamatazz has turned into a well organised quieter, and less frantic process. The ship can offload its previous passengers, load supplies and welcome another batch of holidaymakers in the space of seven hours. There is still a band perhaps, but the chaos of the dockside has gone.

For the passengers, the spectacle and magic of embarking on a ship is more like booking into a hotel, but without having to carry your cases.

*The Current British Cruise Industry*

One of the questions that ran through my head as we were booking our first maritime holiday, was wondering if Deb and I were the right sort of people to be going on a cruise.

Well, after twenty-three years, I can confirm we **were** the right sort of people.

However, the industry has evolved, and the changes have made me ask that question again.

The answer is still a resounding yes, but there are now different styles of cruising for different groups of people, and they are not all suitable for everyone.

In 2000, Deb and I were some of the first of a new generation to sample and fall in love with cruising. There were more ships available to the British market, offering a level of service and luxury that had previously been restricted to a small section of people, with money and time to enjoy a quite niche style of holiday. These ships meant greater passenger capacity, and at a price that allowed a new group of people a chance to sample something different from the fortnight package holiday to the sunshine of Spain.

At that time there were a handful of British based cruise ships allowing perhaps 10,000 people to take a cruise. Those independent cruise companies included Cunard, Fred Olsen, P&O, Thomson, and Saga, who were just dipping their toes into the market. Moving forward to the present, and the British fleets are offering more than 40,000 passenger places, but only Fred Olsen and Saga have remained independent. In addition to the more traditional British based ships, almost all the US and European cruise lines regularly sail to and from Britain offering even greater capacity.

Year by year the ships are becoming unbelievably bigger, and they offer a package that is more than simply a cruise. Although the companies didn't like it, several years ago the monster ships were being called floating Holiday Camps, but it has gone beyond that comparison, and are more like floating holiday resorts. As well as comfortable accommodation and superb food, the traditional entertainment has been enhanced, offering passengers fun fairs, climbing walls, leisure pools with flumes, giant outdoor television screens, dawn to dark (and beyond) alcohol and never-ending music throughout the ship.

This style of cruise ship is a magnet for modern young people and families.

But the problem is people like us, who prefer something a little less holiday camp, and a little more country house.

Fortunately, there have always been smaller companies with low passenger number capacity, catering for the more discerning customer who want a slower pace of holiday. They are now being given a label of Bijou Cruising, and some of these companies are investing in new ships to meet the growing market. Their new ships are smaller and mainly designed for adults, offering places to sit and relax in peace and quiet, yet still provide traditional organised activities, and still feature daily entertainment in theatres or show lounges.

These Bijou cruising companies have ships that offer a little more luxury, a higher standard of food, and certainly a more personal level of service. On the down side, smaller ships are more expensive to operate because there are fewer passengers paying for that extra level of personal luxury. Hence the cost of such cruises have a markedly higher price tag.

Saga is one of the companies offering Bijou Cruising, and many people who have fallen out of love with the big ship product, have tried the Saga alternative way of cruising, and some of those people are falling back in love with cruising again.

*British Based Cruise Lines*

I have included the following information as a spot check of British Cruise Lines as of August 2023.

**P&O (Carnival Owned)** has seven ships with a capacity of 24,193 passengers.

**Cunard (Carnival Owned)** will be launching their new ship (Queen Anne) in 2024 bringing their fleet up to four ships. This will increase their capacity 9829 passengers.

**Fred Olsen (Self Managed)** has three ships with a capacity of 4109 passengers.

**Saga Cruises (Self Managed)** has two ships with a capacity of 1998 passengers.

**Marella Cruises** is the new identity of what was previously called Thompson Cruises, and sits in the same family as ships flying the Tui flag. Although the company appears to still brand itself as being British, I couldn't find any of the ships regularly sailing to and from British ports.

They have five ships offering fly cruises for the British market, that have a capacity of 9316 passengers.

**Princess Cruises (Carnival Owned)** is very much an American cruise line now, but still has a place in many British cruisers' hearts.

During 2023 they had two ships that regularly sailed in and out of Southampton, with a capacity of 7220 passengers.

**Cruise and Maritime Voyages** (CMV) was one of the casualties of the Covid enforced cruise ship layoff. They had really only been in existence for a short time, and could not survive without income. I have no idea what happened to their ships, but some were very likely scrapped.

**Ambassador Cruises (Independent)** is a new company on the British market that seemed to grow from the ashes of CMV. They are currently still trying to make their mark on the cruise market, and presently have two ships with a capacity of 2600 passengers.

If the capacity of the ships sailing out of British ports in 2023 were added together, there was a potential for almost 40,000 passengers being at sea for 365 days a year.

Of course, as well as Princess Cruises, there are several other cruise lines regularly sailing in and out of British ports that are popular with the British market, but I know very little about them. Most are from mainland European and American giant companies, such as Royal Caribbean, MSC, Celebrity, Mein Schiff and Norwegian Cruise Line (NCL). The British also enjoy some of the less talked about companies including, Viking

Cruises, Hurtigruten, Virgin, Seabourn, Regent Seven Seas, Azamar, and Oceania.

I am quite sure there are several other companies attracting British customers that I have never considered.

# Welcome to your cruise

So, you have decided to have your very first cruise.

The next few pages will walk you through what you might see and experience, as well as giving you a few ideas that might be useful to consider.

Don't panic if things I say are not giving a good impression, as one of the best ways to approach a cruise for the first time, is not to come with pre-conceptions.

Just let the world of cruising absorb you.

*The Hotel Side of a Cruise Ship*

The cruise is booked and paid for, you have arrived at the terminal, and are now entering the ship, so what can you expect for the next fortnight?

The modern cruise ships provide an enormous hotel complex for the passengers, and the majority of crew aboard the ship are actually working in that hotel. A small army is constantly preparing food, while another army is cleaning toilets, carpets, furniture, or polishing the miles of handrails and keeping mirrors, and hundreds of shiny objects clear of dust and finger prints. From a passenger perspective, while the cooks, and cleaners are virtually invisible, other crew members play a more passenger facing role, and they are the cabin stewards, and waiters.

*Your Stateroom*

Officially your bedroom on the ship is referred to as a stateroom, but no matter how hard the cruise companies try and change attitudes, most passengers will continue to call them their cabin.

No matter what style, size, or price of accommodation you have booked, I think the majority will be very satisfied with a modern cabin. Compared to a multitude of land-based hotels that I stayed in for many years while working, a cruise ship cabin is generally larger, brighter, and better equipped, and they all have air conditioning

The soundproofing between cabins is good, and with the walls being metal, they handily allow fridge magnets to be displayed as you move from port to port. More importantly, many hundreds of cruise passengers have discovered small and powerful magnetic hooks that stick firmly to the wall, and take the weight of quite significant items of clothing. I use one to take a shirt and jacket comfortably, and Deb's dresses can also be displayed before going out on formal nights. Unfortunately, if I try and hang my DJ, trousers, and dress shirt from one hook, they amusingly gently slide down the wall. No problem, I just use two magnetic hooks.

The beds, are King size or Queen size, with good quality thick mattresses, a choice of pillows, and different tog duvets. These beds split into two to allow a twin bed configuration. If you have personal preferences, ask your steward if anything can be changed. In our experience they will nearly always find a solution to keep passengers happy.

The designers attempt to squeeze in as much wardrobe space as is possible, but the more cruises you do, the more clothing you will probably take with you. Usually, you will find a safe in the wardrobe, where you can store away money, credit cards, passports, and jewellery. Cash on a ship is rarely needed, as the keycard you are issued with as you board also acts as a payment system, and in most cases, an alternative to carrying your passport ashore.

Cabins have fridges. They are small, but from our experience, they are big enough to store some water to keep it cool, a bottle of fizz, and a big bar or two of chocolate. Although the ship's air conditioning is quite effective, you should always have cold water, or similar, to stop your mouth and throat drying out. If you need ice, the bars around the ship will gladly give you a glass full.

There is a writing desk with drawers that gives more storage for smaller items of clothing and the ever-important electronic devices. Most of the British based cruise lines have UK power sockets, but there are not many of them in a cabin. The companies don't like passengers using extension leads or multi-sockets. A recent enhancement in the cabins is the arrival of USB charging sockets near the writing desk, or close to the beds.

For relaxation there will be a large screen television that nowadays is interactive showing daily programmes, your account, as well as multiple channels. There will be easy chairs, or a sofa to sit on, plus a table and chairs if you fancy eating from the room service menu.

The cabins are always en-suite, which usually has a separate shower, although sometimes there is a small bath with a shower over it. These bathrooms are generally large enough to swing the proverbial cat, and on some ships can be quite large and luxurious.

Nowadays modern cruise ships are built with balconies for the vast majority of cabins. Some are rather small, and maybe hardly bigger than a Juliette balcony, but most have a space large enough and comfortable enough to stretch out on the loungers provided. It is a joy to sometimes hide away in your little private space to escape the 'full on' atmosphere of the ship

The rooms are kept clean daily, beds are made, and stocks of tea, coffee, and milk replenished. This is all down to highly efficient domestic systems and your own all-important steward.

Cabin Stewards

The cabin stewards are vital to a cruise as they quietly improve and sometimes even enhance the customer experience. They clean and tidy up the cabins in the morning while the passengers are out at breakfast, or maybe while you are lazing in the sunshine. Until quite recently, they would return in the evening while you were at dinner, to turn down the bed clothes and perhaps leave a chocolate on the pillow. I gather from some reports on the internet, that P&O are stopping the evening steward visit.

Deb and I are early risers compared to many, and in the pre-Carnival years we rarely left the cabin for breakfast without catching sight of our steward. He, or she, would be waiting for passengers to leave so that they could clean up the cabin and make it ready for our daily needs. Except on rare occasions, our cabin was spick and span by the time we came back from breakfast. In those early years, the stewards were responsible for maybe a dozen cabins, and worked quickly, but always very carefully. They also had time to get to know us all, and occasionally chat with us to see how we were, and what our plans were for the day.

Sadly, in the constant push to save costs and boost profit, P&O and probably other companies have taken a look at the role of these hard-working men and women.

Over the last 10 or so years, one of P&O's cost-cutting solutions was to reduce the number of stewards. This resulted in their workload increasing, with more cabins to be serviced. Initially it was just a small cut in the steward numbers and we hardly noticed the difference, although we were aware that our cabin wasn't always completed by the time we came back from breakfast.

If nobody noticed the cuts, or nobody complained, those cuts could continue with another reduction in numbers of stewards.

Currently the experienced stewards have a seriously bigger number of cabins to service, and may be dashing around 15 to 20 cabins. We have found our cabin untouched until late in the morning, and rarely see the steward after the initial welcome on-board introduction.

It doesn't take a mathematician to work out the resulting savings by reducing cabin steward numbers.

The money savings unfortunately create some less obvious drawbacks.

There is hardly any spare time for the stewards to get to know the occupants of the cabins, and remember the way some passengers want their cabin to be left.

It is rare to even say hello to them, let alone discussing plans, or perhaps getting to know more about their family.

… and possibly the change of steward to cabin ratio, has meant that the service, perhaps, is less stringent than it used to be.

Of course, if you are a more recent convert to a cruising holiday, you will probably be quite pleased with the cabin cleaning, and assume the situation is as it always was. It is only the pre-Carnival passengers that have noticed the reduction in numbers and the changes it has made.

Now for three treats that few modern cruise passengers experience anymore:

- For the first few years, our day would start each morning with a tap on the door by our steward at the agreed time bringing us tea or coffee with biscuits. Now this can only be ordered from room service.
- Each night we would get a different chocolate on our pillow with a picture of the ship, or maybe a heart shaped one on special evenings. Nowadays the chocolates are a standard thin and tasteless square. We used to look forward to them each night, but now the thrill has gone. It won't be long before the pillow chocolates will be declared as unwanted on customer feedback forms, and P&O can stop supplying them, meaning perhaps a penny saved each night for those thousands of passengers. If they cost a penny each, across the fleet P&O would save in excess of £80,000 a year.
- There were also very special moments when on birthdays, the freshly laundered bath towels would be artistically arranged by the steward to look like an animal, or perhaps as a heart to celebrate an anniversary. That custom is no longer very common, and has almost disappeared. Thinking back to the world cruises there were hardly more than a handful of nights when we came back to towel art in our cabin after an evening of entertainment, but the rare swans, and other delightful creations always brought a smile.

*Eating*

Comfortable in your cabin, and having wandered around the ship to get your bearings, one of the next most important things to do, is to sort out where and when to eat.

Main Dining Room

Most passengers have a preference for what, where, and when they like to have their meals. Dinner is the most important meal of the day, and the majority, from my experience, prefer the '**Main Dining Room**' where they can share a table with other passengers while making friends and chatting between courses. Others prefer a table to sit as a couple and get on with their food while avoiding too many discussions.

Most cruise ships traditionally offered the choice of a set time for dinner to begin. On the larger ships this means having two sittings with the first quite early, and then another sitting a couple of hours later. Many passengers have a preference to whether they eat early or late, and this can often be for medical reasons when people cannot eat after a certain time.

As the years have gone by, the Main Dining Room evening meal routine has changed. P&O now refer to the traditional set early or late dining session as '**Club Dining**'. A less time restricted option has been introduced when a dining room operates with what P&O call '**Freedom Dining**'. This is where passengers choose when they want to eat, and the dining room is open all evening with a rolling service, allowing passengers to turn up at the time they prefer. I have no doubt that clever use of statistical customer feedback gathering, means ships will probably turn to Freedom Dining as the only option, but hopefully that is a little way off yet.

A lot of the British cruise lines still have a formal dress code on certain evenings around the ship, and this is most strictly adhered to for dinner in the main dining room. Although pre-warned in the brochure, a lot of passengers prefer not to abide by the dress code. Many of these people give in to tradition and dress accordingly for the short duration of their dinner, before perhaps reverting back to informality. But a small number stubbornly refuse to abide by the dress code, and have to eat elsewhere on the few formal evenings on their cruise.

To avoid the formal dress code, the rebels will go and eat in the buffet, where they join a significant number of passengers who prefer this more casual and relaxed style of eating every night. Here they can dress how they wish, and choose the food from the counter at a time of their choice.

Just to annoy the **'rebels'** further, many of the regular buffet diners still abide by the formal dress code like the majority of the ship's passengers.

If you are someone that would prefer not to dress up on the two or three formal nights on a fortnight's cruise, please don't take your annoyance out on the majority who enjoy these evenings.

*… or perhaps consider the option of booking a cruise with the numerous companies that have a more relaxed attitude to dress code.*

All cruise ships offer room service for those moments when passengers just want to relax in their cabins and avoid other people, or do not want to dress formally. Of course, some passengers spend a lot more of their time in their cabins and prefer to have room service on a regular basis. The room service menus normally have a number of items that tickle the taste senses, and on some ships (or for the more exclusive passengers) the menu allows diners to choose from the main dining room options as well. The cost of room service also varies, and while free on some ships, it is becoming more common for a small charge to be applied. Over the years, that charging has become more obvious to increase revenue.

## The Buffet

Breakfast is also available in the main dining room, but a high percentage of the passengers tend to go to the Buffet for a grab and go style of meal. The buffet opens early, and stays available for several hours so it suits those who rise early, as well as those who avoid getting out of bed until much later. They can choose what, and how much, is piled onto their plates, and it is no surprise that those plates are really piled very high sometimes.

Lunch is again a popular meal for the passengers to go to the buffet, but the main dining room is also available for those people wanting a less frantic meal. Deb and I were certainly buffet fans for breakfast and lunch, but as the years of queuing and searching for empty seats has become annoying, we are turning towards the main dining room, especially at breakfast. We don't eat a big meal at breakfast and lunch, and there is always something small and tasty on the main dining room breakfast and lunch menus, plus a far more relaxed atmosphere.

Throughout the daytime hours, the modern ships usually have different outlets serving burgers or hotdogs, and maybe a pizza, and these are always busy on a sunny day when the snacks can be eaten on loungers around the pool.

Speciality Restaurants

Returning to evening dining options, the ships also offer speciality restaurants. Although the main dining room and buffet menus are adequate and tasty, a cruise ship usually tempts passengers with smaller and more intimate restaurants where they can enjoy a special meal, with a higher standard of service. These speciality restaurants are often themed with Asian, Mediterranean, or American Diner food, and another might concentrate on seafood dishes. We came across these restaurants early in our cruising adventures, and they were a thrill to have even more superior service, and food that had an extra level of flavour and presentation.

... and yes, they were mostly free!

P&O's next step was to have restaurants specialising in a menu from a top-level land-based chef. We were lucky enough to have several evenings in the Gary Rhodes restaurant on Arcadia, and more recently the ships have had menus inspired by Marco Pierre White. That was when the Speciality restaurant surcharges really began, and they have increased by leaps and bounds over the last decade.

For the Asian food fans, the '**Sindhu**' restaurants with menus from Atul Kochhar also had dedicated venues on the ships. Around the same time a wine expert called Ollie Smith suggested what should be in the P&O wine cellars, and it wasn't long before he expanded his profile from simply wine matters, to another speciality restaurant called the '**Glasshouse**'. This offered various meals, and instead of a single cover charge, the different courses were priced separately.

Another popular restaurant is the '**Beach House**' that appeared quite near the end of our P&O cruising adventures. It didn't have a Celebrity Chef associated with it, and served what could be described as American Diner meals.

The latest giant vessels have venues with even more choice of international style cuisine, in spectacular restaurants that often feature entertainment with the meals. Of course cover charges are increasing, and approaching close to what would be paid to eat out in city centres.

The changing P&O passenger profile is being thrilled by the range of food available, but these restaurants don't suit everyone, and although we are quite happy with some of the choices of cuisine available, the increase in speciality restaurants can produce negative results.

When Aurora was launched in 2000 it had a venue called Café Bordeaux. For early risers and Suite passengers, it offered a quieter waiter service breakfast where the food was cooked to order. When the breakfast session was completed, the venue turned into a bistro style café, and passengers could turn up whenever they wanted for daytime snacks or slightly more substantial meals. In the evening it became a far more exclusive restaurant, and passengers had to book in advance to eat from a very special menu. When that finished it changed again and became a place to get hot chocolate and simple snacks until late.

It was busy, and often very busy throughout the day and evening, and like many seasoned Aurora passengers, we loved Café Bordeaux.

Then as the need for extra venues to accommodate speciality restaurants arose, Café Bordeaux was converted into The Glass House.

Instead of being a popular and very busy place to eat throughout the day, it became a semi-deserted venue. On the large ships with their families and the new generation of cruisers, the speciality restaurants, including the Glasshouse, are packed with happy passengers. But, with Aurora being adult only, the passenger profile was older, and many of them tended to be longer in the tooth traditional cruisers. They were not struck on the Glass House, and many conversations featured comments about bringing back Café Bordeaux.

Deb and I used the speciality restaurants to suit our tastes, but year by year we were very aware of the increasing cover charges.

## Has the eating experience changed?

I hear a few of you ask why so many passengers pay to eat in the speciality restaurants. Well, that takes me to my disappointment aimed at P&O with the standard of the menus, the actual food, and the level of service in the main dining rooms.

Don't get me wrong, the vast majority of the modern passengers are thrilled by the quality of food and service when eating in the main dining room, or the buffet, but some of us have noticed changes that have not been for the best.

OK, it was never Michelin Star food, and not true 'Silver Service', but 20 years ago the dining experience was of a standard that made an hour and a half in the restaurant a wonderful moment. The food and service was historically tailored to satisfy the needs of loyal passengers with more bulging wallets, who might perhaps have sampled top quality restaurants on a regular basis. So, when a new generation of passengers could afford cruising on these amazing ships, we were thrilled by dinner, in fantastic venues with menus featuring food from all over the world, with vast numbers of cutlery items to choose from, and waiters that seemed to appear from nowhere if you wanted something.

Almost immediately after being guided into our seats, and having a linen napkin flicked across our laps, water was brought to the table and glasses filled. After gathering our breath, the menu would arrive describing five or six courses with options to delight the most awkward of passengers. Then for a few minutes you could chatter with your table mates, but soon the chosen dishes were brought artistically to the table, placed before you, and the plate turned to have the Wedgewood emblem at precisely 12:00. Then another waiter would offer vegetables and sauces served directly to your plate. Water glasses were refilled the moment they appeared to be half empty, and the waiters checked that everything was to the individual's satisfaction. Needless to say, the rest of the meal had the same wonderful service, and delicious food.

Although working to time restraints to enable a second service, dinner never felt rushed.

Even the menus were special. Each day the cover was a historical picture of a different P&O ship, and inside were recommendations for each course, and choice of wine. Each course had several different choices, some with unfamiliar names that the waiter quickly described if he saw a confused face.

*By the way, there **was** a complete lack of ladies in the serving process, which has now begun to be addressed for the better.*

Back to the menus, and there were far more courses than we could manage - although we often tried - but we always finished with chocolates, and a piece of fruit.

Deb and I were gobsmacked with the evening eating fantasy, and although we used the buffet for breakfast and lunch, we rarely had a meal in the main dining room that wasn't absolutely sensational.

As Carnival began to steer the way P&O progressed, there was initially no visible difference, but it wasn't long before we began to notice changes.

Main courses arrived plated, complete with the chefs' portion of vegetables and sauces, so the number of waiters required was reduced, and that number quietly shrank further as the years passed. It meant that waiters were responsible for more tables, which slowed down the service, and took away some of the interaction between waiter and passenger. The overworked men and women continue to do their best to learn what each person prefers, and make changes to the plates before they are brought to the table, but there was an obvious reduction in the level of service from our early years.

One outcome of the changes was that the resulting slower and less intimate service, reduced satisfaction levels with the meals. This led to more passengers trying out the Specialised Restaurants, and succumbing to the surcharges.

The main dining room food has also been simplified. There are less dishes with magical names, and the choices reduced to little more than a red meat, white meat, fish and vegetarian option. The vegetables appear to be from a simpler list, with a variation of potato, accompanied by roughly chopped chunks of root vegetables, plus an abundance of green beans.

On Formal nights, P&O often enhance the dining experience with a menu featuring special choices, and one regular such speciality is *'Beef Wellington'*. To be honest it is usually a very tasty piece of beef, which of course is covered with pastry. I often have it, but refuse to believe it is close to a real *'Beef Wellington'*. My issue is that the pastry is always soggy, so I just enjoy the beef.

This may not be just a P&O problem, as I have never tasted proper pastry on any cruise ship, and of course, we have not been on a P&O ship for over two years, and things may have changed.

As a general view, I believe the quality and range of food, and the standard of service has changed from something approaching that of a 5-star restaurant, to a little better than average night out quality. Don't get me wrong, it is still good, but don't allow anyone convince you that it is the same as 20 years ago.

Thousands of passengers continue to find the eating experience wonderful, and rave about it on Facebook pages and customer feedback surveys. The cruise companies have obviously got it right for the target passenger base it wants to attract, but perhaps a small percentage of their loyal customers are looking elsewhere.

*The Bars and Drinking*

Many passengers enjoy a glass or two of wine with their dinner, and around the ships there are numerous bars to tempt you. There is rarely a lounge or room where there isn't a bar in the corner, and even if you do discover one, cocktail waiters will probably appear on a regular basis.

There are different styles of lounges, with some designed to look and feel like a traditional pub, while others might resemble a Sport's Bar or perhaps a city nightclub. Some lounges are quiet and feel like being in a private club with comfy seating, while others are busier with close together tables and chairs.

When the sun is shining, or on a warm summer's evening, there are bars outside on the deck overlooking the wake of the ship. Or you can sit out on the promenade deck watching the sun go down, and waiters will always bring you a glass of wine while the moon casts dreams across the sea.

The prices are the same wherever you are, but beware that some cruise lines add a service charge to each drink.

Of course, drinking isn't all about alcohol. The bars around the ship are always happy to bring you a soft drink, as well as coffee or tea. There is usually a dedicated coffee bar offering a Highstreet Chain Barista blend of milk, coffee and chocolate. Of course, you pay for these drinks.

There is one positive addition when using the P&O coffee bars. If you purchase a drink, you can have a free slice of delicious cake. I personally find the cake to be better than the standardised coffee.

... and if you are not a lover of High Street chain coffee, there is always the free stuff in the buffet, and usually there is a cake or something nearby.

Cocktail Waiters

Up until 2000, my less than adventurous holidays never included cocktail waiters. That amazing adventure on Oriana was the first time somebody wanted to save me getting up from my seat and ordering a drink from the bar. It was a shock to begin with, but as Deb and I settled down to life on a cruise, we happily accepted the attention of friendly waiters. They got to know us, remembered our names and addressed us as "**Sir George**" or "**Madam Debra**", and even asked if we wanted the usual. When the bars were quiet, we chatted to them, and became temporary friends. But, although we rarely had an empty glass in front of us, the waiters did not pester us to order more drinks unless we made eye contact with them.

Each bar or lounge had adequate waiters in attendance throughout the day and evening, and while they had a few relaxation moments when all their customers were served, their urgency increased as drinkers filled more seats, but they rarely left passengers waiting very long for drinks. This was the situation for many years, but a moment came when the quieter bars and lounges, seemed to be less attended, and waiting times increased.

As profit margins on the basic cruise prices were cut, the cocktail waiters were obviously tasked to sell more drinks to increase revenue, and almost certainly, their bonus payments depended on those sales.

Before dinner a lot of passengers enjoyed a cocktail or pint of beer, and there was always an abundance of waiters to service them. As their happy and hungry customers set off for the dining rooms, there would be a massive clear up, and then the bulk of the waiters disappeared to serve elsewhere.

After dinner, Deb and I would often go to a bar before the rush arrived, and there was always a waiter available.

But then the atmosphere seemed to change, and there were times when the attention waiters were giving us was a little excessive. If we didn't order a drink, they seemed seriously annoyed. It got so bad, that as we entered the bar, the gang of eager waiters would approach and follow us towards the seats, and they even tried to coax us to follow them to what they suggested was the best place to be.

At this moment in our cruising history, we also saw another major difference.

Up until the Carnival revolution really took hold, the sight of someone with a drink in the theatre could be counted on a single hand, and there was rarely a waiter in attendance. Now a swarm of cocktail waiters gather in the theatre as soon as the doors are opened, trying to get orders from all the passengers. They continue until the moment the curtain is due to go up, and for the first few minutes of a show, waiters can still be handing over the last few drinks in the dark, and getting his (or her) receipt signed.

During the sunny warm days, the open decks are constantly busy with waiters trying to sell drinks to the passengers relaxing in the sunshine. Anyone who appears awake is asked on a regular basis if they want a drink, and if you are asleep, or perhaps pretending to be, they offer their service loudly enough to rouse passengers from their slumber.

I understand they are doing their jobs, but it is difficult not to get annoyed with them.

I don't think I have been the only passenger to complain about the very '*hard sell*' techniques that were being employed.

*Entertainment*

A very important part of any cruise is the entertainment. Some passengers might prefer to avoid much that is on offer, but the majority scan the daily ship's newspaper to see what tickles their fancy.

It's time to raise the curtain on my experiences of the entertainment that thrilled us, or perhaps made us cringe over the last 20 years.

As with all of my recollections, please accept them as **MY** personal thoughts, and will not be the same as hundreds of other cruise ship fans. Life has changed in those 20 years, and so have the passengers who fill the ships. If you perhaps have radically different views, that is because we *are* all different.

## The Venues

All cruise lines are very careful to provide sufficient venues to offer choices of daytime, and evening entertainment, with sufficient capacity to seat the passengers in comfort. My memories of evening entertainment on P&O ships have always been very positive.

Deb and I never totally believe the glitzy pictures and overhyped descriptive adverts, and those first brochures in 2000 were similarly doubted, but wow!

As we took our initial walk around Oriana, one of the first things we found was the theatre, and even empty, it was truly amazing. It was capable of sitting 800 passengers comfortably, with just a small number of blocking problems. The seats even had cool air vents.

The stage was big both side to side and front to back, with amazing backdrops to match the variety of shows on offer.

The sound and lighting system was equally impressive, and as the years have gone by, I always look in awe of the lighting systems on the different ships that can create such magical spectacles on the stage.

All the major cruise lines have superb theatres, and the only limiting factor of the vast ships is the width available of the hull. The stages come with moving sections or revolving areas, hatches for appearances or disappearances, computerised backdrops, and even trapeze systems.

The seating spreads over multiple decks with their own entry and exits to ease the audience movement.

There are shows every evening, and usually multiple performances to allow everyone a chance to see it.

In the daytime the stage might have a guest speaker talking to hundreds of passengers about their celebrity lifestyle, or sporting prowess, and so many other subjects. Alternatively, it could be a classical concert, or perhaps a play, and they regularly use the theatre as a cinema with a huge screen.

With passenger numbers of multiple thousands, a single theatre is not big enough to cater for everyone, so the ships always have alternative entertainment lounges. With the theatre typically at the front of the ship, there will also be a major show lounge at the stern. They may not sit as many people as the theatre, but usually cater for many hundreds of passengers with variety shows or cabaret acts each evening.

Like the theatre, these show lounges also have talks or demonstrations during the daytime, or dance classes perhaps.

Depending on the size of the ship, and the number of passengers, there might be numerous other lounges of different sizes. There might be bands playing different genre of music, or gameshows, karaoke or late-night disco dancing.

Certainly, if you walk around a cruise ship in the evening, it is like visiting a street in the entertainment district of a quite substantial town.

Almost all tastes are catered for, but our experience is that they have forgotten that sometimes people want a quiet space to chat with friends without any music.

## The Theatre Show Troupe

I think virtually every cruise ship has a resident show team of singers and dancers. On P&O, these troupes became known as the '**Headliners**', and on the ships that we sampled, the troupe was usually made up of three male and two female singers, plus two male and perhaps six girl dancers.

They were always good, and often superb.

Before they stand behind the stage curtain for their first show, the young men and women would have already spent weeks on shore being moulded into a tight group of performers. Like all budding stars of the stage, they'd first have to pass an audition to win a contract, and then endure weeks of long days rehearsing. As the rehearsal process began, some of the youngsters would already have experience of similar work, but many with little or no experience, would have their raw talent cultivated. I'm sure along the way, many struggled and left, but eventually there is a group of fully professional performers with wonderful singing, amazing dance routines, and blossoming stage presence.

During those weeks of training, they would rehearse half a dozen or more 45-minute shows in a warehouse, and be fitted for a vast wardrobe of different costumes for each show.

Finally, the day comes when they board the cruise ship.

The boys and girls would already have at least one show ready to go live with on the stage, as their opening performance could be on the first or second night. From then on there would be constant rehearsals to get all the shows ready, and the difficult conversion of performances practiced on a flat and steady floor into one that was now on a stage, which would soon be rocking and rolling during the first storm they encountered. These practice sessions can only happen when the theatre isn't in use, and that means early mornings or late nights while passengers sleep or laze in the sunshine, unaware of the tired voices, aching legs and continual shouts of "**From the beginning again!**".

Of course, they additionally need extra mandatory instructions and training on how to be a member of a ship's crew. They would learn the basics of life at sea, how to behave according to ship rules, and know what to do in an emergency.

It's time for their first show, and with jangling nerves they hear the opening music, and watch the curtain rise. Just forty-five minutes later, with adrenalin charged sweaty bodies and smelly costumes, they bow and wave at the audience who are cheering their performance.

On P&O ships the now experienced team has to be ready for the repeat performance in little more than an hour's time. But even when they finally leave the stage for the night, there is little time to congratulate themselves and celebrate, as perhaps less than 24 hours later they would be back behind that curtain waiting for the next show to begin.

There will now be five or six months of performing on their floating home with a range of revue style shows of different genres, or different ages of music. Some shows concentrate on a single composer, perhaps a Broadway show producer, or maybe songs from a single band such as Abba or Queen. The theatre or show lounge will have superb scenery to suit the show themes, and the cast have amazing costumes that again reflect and enhance a show. Each of the different 45-minute shows are very expensive to create and choreograph, as they have to entertain a critical audience, who will quickly find fault and not go back to other shows during a cruise. New shows are added to the list each year, and will have to be learnt while passengers are unaware of just how much time the boys and girls spend rehearsing.

After several months performing perhaps four or five shows a week, their contracts end, and they return to shore in the hopes of being offered a new one. The lucky ones then begin another period of rehearsing with some new shows, and are soon back on a ship again to entertain thousands of holiday-makers. The unlucky ones join the masses of similar young performers looking for jobs, and perhaps join the cast on board a different cruise line, or maybe a West End show.

Over the years we've seen most of the different P&O shows several times over, and we avoid watching those that are less special to us, but many were so good that we always made a point of going to see them again. No matter what ship Deb and I are on, an important part of the day is looking at the ship's daily newspaper to see what the evening entertainment is from the theatre troupe, and look forward to any new show, or maybe decide to miss the more familiar ones.

Primarily the Headliners perform on stage in the theatre, but sometimes their show is more exciting to be in the Show Lounge where their singing and dance routines are performed on the dance floor, right in amongst the audience. For those shows we often try and get a good place to sit near the action, with dancers and singers just inches away from us.

On the evenings when the Headliners are performing in the lounge, a visiting cabaret takes over the theatre stage, then that cabaret takes the floor in the lounge when the troupe are back in the theatre. The show team occasionally have a night off, meaning visiting performers star in the theatre and the lounge, so there is always plenty to keep us happily entertained.

... well, most nights anyway

There have been some additional roles for P&O Show Troupes in the last few years.

Firstly, as the theatre curtain goes down at the end of a performance, the show troupe used to switch off and rest, but not anymore. While the announcer is on stage describing what else is happening around the ship, or what the programme contains for the following day, the singers and dancers are grabbing a cold drink, quickly towelling off the worst of the sweat for a final task. They have to rush through the emergency stage area exit, and go along the outside deck to the lobby area at the entrance to the theatre. Standing in their costumes they say goodnight and thank the audience for coming to their show, responding to any passenger comments, and smile even though their bodies are probably aching to sit down and get their feet up.

In the past, the girls and boys tended to keep away from the passengers, but this simple, yet tiring gesture, makes the audience feel they are almost friends, and completes their evening entertainment experience.

Secondly, the Headliners are now being used during the daytime by interacting with the passengers.

For many years I have enjoyed being a part of the passenger choir, when one of the entertainment team organised the group of amateur singers. This was sometimes less than ideal for the choir who were always being presented with the same simple songs, with little or no harmony parts for the different voices. The entertainment team member sometimes did little more than give out song sheets, tell the pianist when to start, and wave school day imitations of a conductor.

On our World Cruise there was a change, when the show vocalists organised the choir practices. We learnt about the voice warm ups that they do, and then we did it with them. Some of the songs were the same, but a lot of new ones were also introduced to challenge us. The choir was split into the four main voices (Soprano, Alto, Tenor, and Bass) and there were different parts to sing during the songs. The professional singers actually sang the different parts before we tried to follow them, and eventually some very enjoyable sound was created.

It meant our little group of amateur holiday singers were singing alongside professionals and creating a real choir. It was also a great chance to get to know the singers, and ask questions about their experiences.

The dancers didn't get away with a rest either. They turned up at the ever-popular line dancing, and introduced tunes from their shows as music for the dances. It also meant performing some of the same dance routines as they used on stage. Other dancers became leaders of the Salsa sessions, and even tap dancing. The professional dancers passed on new dance steps, and created a new level of footwork skills.

I'm not sure how the Headliners felt about these new duties, but like true professionals, they never appeared anything other than happy to assist us.

Of course, I doubt the Headliners volunteered to perform these extra duties. Almost certainly it was a way of reducing the need for one of the entertainment team to take on the roles, and allow them to work elsewhere.

## Visiting Cabarets

Cabaret artists perform on the ships to provide something a little different. The majority of them are singers, either solo, duets or other small groups. Some of these groups play instruments as well, and might be tribute acts for a more famous band, although once in a while a band arrives with a more unique act. There are also a reasonable number of comedians on the cruise circuit, and less common are a few speciality acts offering ventriloquism, juggling, or magic.

Our experience with P&O was that cabaret artists would embark at a port, perform a couple of different acts (twice a night), and then leave at the next port. This is different on the longer cruises when the cabaret acts might have to stay on the ship for extended periods because of the number of consecutive sea days to cross the oceans.

A high percentage of the visiting cabaret acts on P&O were solo singers. Some might have been members of a 60's or 70's pop group that are now disbanded. They are always terrific singers, and can remind us of the music that we grew up with. Others have 45-minute tribute acts to a particular singer, and they can be extremely good, but if you didn't like the original artist, there is no appeal. Without trying to be sexist in any way, the list of popular cruise ship singers does seem to be mainly female, and the majority feel it necessary to pretend to be divas.

Occasionally we have been surprised by a duo or small group of singers, and it is such a change. The repertoire no longer concentrates on a particular singer, or genre, so there is a variety of songs where some might not appeal to us, but others will.

Even more fun is an act that has multiple musicians. Unlike a classical ensemble, these groups of men and women often have unusual instruments, with a mix of violins and guitars, maybe with a French Horn thrown in the mix. The mixture of tunes played usually include a variety of modern and old music, and can sometimes confuse the mind, but enhance the experience.

One very memorable group was called '**Ukebox**'. We saw them on two cruises, and they consisted of five young men all playing Ukuleles of different shapes and sizes. Their music was varied, including heavy metal with just Ukeleles, and that was extraordinary. This was definitely not a George Formby tribute, and I only hope they appear again on a cruise ship, or somewhere near us.

Another style of visiting cabaret is the tribute act bringing back to life pop bands such as the Beatles, Madness, Dire Straits, or Four Seasons. They have to be good to even be considered for a chance to play on a cruise ship, and in most cases, they are magnificent, taking care to mimic the originals in every way possible, and even left-handed Paul McCartney look alikes.

... but once again, only enjoyable if you liked the originals.

Although rare, there are also the speciality acts such as jugglers, ventriloquists, and magicians, but also a lot of comedians. On those evenings when these niche cabaret artists have the theatre stage to perform to packed houses, it can be a sensational experience with laughter, applause and even occasional standing ovations.

I always look forward to a good comedian, and most of them are really very entertaining. Sadly, some have been entertaining audiences for several decades, and our laughter muscles often struggle with the very familiar jokes. Fortunately, even those who have been drawing a state pension for many years, still manage to brighten up our evening with their jokes reminding us of our younger years.

There does come a time however, when that same joke, told by seemingly every comedian, becomes just too painful to be appreciated.

In the last decade there has also been an abundance of singers, and other acts, who have failed to win television talent show programmes. The clue here is that they hadn't won any competitions, so are perhaps less than brilliant. While some have turned out to be really good, many failed to impress us any more than they impressed the talent show judges.

Other Contracted Entertainers

As well as the show team, and visiting cabaret acts, a lot of entertainment in the bars or lounges comes from singers, or classical musicians, who have short or perhaps longer contracts aboard the ships.

The classical musicians might be a soloist, duo, or even a small ensemble of different instruments. They are usually very talented and mostly perform in the smaller venues during the afternoon or early evening, but sometimes they take to the theatre stage with a major performance to give a larger audience a chance to sample their skills. Generally, they receive masses of praise from the passengers who might be true lovers of classical music, but others perhaps new to this type of music, appreciate what they have heard, and often want to hear more.

There is another very important group of people who are the main band. On our early adventures, there was an orchestra on the ships that played music for the shows, or provided backing for cabaret acts. One ship actually had an orchestra pit at the front of the stage. It had a lid that allowed the stage area to be bigger while the musicians were below, and it was even part of the entertainment to hear them warming up.

A later ship had an orchestra area at the back of the stage that could be hidden with a backdrop curtain.

When not needed in the theatre, these musicians would entertain in the show lounge, and demonstrate their skills.

Nowadays, there are no huge ship orchestras on P&O vessels, and virtually all the shows, and all the cabaret music is pre-recorded and played from the control booth, along with the unbelievably complicated stage lighting system.

There are still bands however, that might be simple three piece or maybe more. They have to play music of various genre and could be asked to play outside around the pool after lunch, with songs to remind the sun lovers of their younger days. Later they will probably be in the show lounge with strict tempo music for the dancers, or maybe quietly playing background music up in the Crow's Nest during a cocktail party.

They are usually very good musicians, and when they've been working together long enough, can become quite special. Thinking back several years, my memory is of bands that were really good, and professionally able to change their acts to suit the audience. They interacted with the passengers, and had stories or jokes to tell between songs to keep us involved. I will never forget listening to '**Natural High**' on Oriana, and '**Caravan**' on Aurora who never tried to be, or thought themselves to be cabaret artists, but were perfect for all times and moods of the day.

Several years ago, I began to notice that the ship's resident bands were no longer very special. They were often made up of agency musicians brought together to form a four-piece band fronted by a female singer. Yes, they played the right music, and played it well, but because they were strangers to each other, there was no smoothness or sparkle with their performance. They sat playing their instruments, and hardly spoke to each other during their sets. When asked to leave their prepared short list of songs, to maybe play a ballroom dance tune, their limited list of music usually produced the same tune each time, and occasionally they had nothing to offer.

Then come the duos who work mainly in the bar, or smaller lounges. They are usually a couple who have worked together for some time, and hence quite good. Typically, one will be playing a keyboard and the other singing, but sometimes they are a trio with a drummer or guitarist to make the music sound fuller. Being well established as a musical team, the banter between songs is often well rehearsed, and keeps the audience listening to them.

A sad example of entertainment that recently began to appear is solo singers, who might possibly play a guitar, but primarily rely on a machine providing backing tracks. Again, they are sometimes good musicians and singers, but more often they little more than ambitious Karaoke artists, and certainly not always the best.

During our latter years with P&O, there were more and more of these Karaoke style musicians being used for evening entertainment in the lounges.

### Guest Speakers

This is an area of cruise ship entertainment that has improved during our 20 years. A lot of cruise passengers enjoy listening to a good guest speaker, and they can be the highlight of the morning and afternoon for many.

On our early cruises there were daily talks about the ports we were going to, and perhaps more of a tour selling exercise than general information to excite unprepared passengers. I like to think the current port lecturers are better at talking about important and interesting facts about a destination, although they are obviously trying to sell tours as well.

Away from these talks, there were just two or three guest speakers on our earlier cruises, but as the years have passed, more and more people have joined the cruise ship talk circuit.

Most talks fill the theatre, and there have been some really special speakers - some famous, and some not so well known - who have given interesting, funny, or often downright amazing talks. They included sporting stars, television and radio personalities, news presenters, or retired police detectives, authors, and chefs. Almost everyone has something special in their life to talk about, but these guest speakers not only have a story to tell, but are also very good at standing in front of an audience and making those stories interesting.

There are too many people to mention, but here are some of the men and women that have left a mark on my memory.

Sporting wise I begin with Alan Mullery and Norman Hunter who were on our first cruise, and as well as talking about their lives, they organised football coaching sessions in Oriana's netted court for the children, and some of their parents. They both played for England in the 1960s and while many of the children may not have known who they were, the parents certainly did.

Another cruise, and another footballer was Neil (Razor) Ruddock. He played for several top teams such as Spurs, and Liverpool, as well as one match for England in 1994. The talks about his career were amusing, and featured many examples of his sometimes-over-enthusiastic defending skills. He also became well known in the bars around the ship for his love of alcohol.

Moving to a different sport, there was athlete Derek Redmond. Once British 400 metres sprint record holder, he also won European (1986) and World (1991) gold medals in the relay. His most well know moment was at the 1992 Olympics when he had an injury half way through the 400 metres semi-final. In agony, he limped towards the end of the race with tears streaming down his face. In front of the world television cameras, his father jumped over the barrier and supported him to the finishing line. Of course, he was disqualified, but his place in history was secured.

One of my favourite guest speakers was jockey Bob Champion, who survived testicular cancer, and returned to horse racing to win the Grand National on Aldaniti in 1981. His amazing story from near death to the Grand National was made into a film, and he was awarded an MBE.

Someone else who gave a wonderful series of sporting talks and has had a film made about his career, is Eddy (the Eagle) Edwards. He is apparently still the best ever British Ski Jumper, but better known as the idiot who almost killed himself at the 1988 Winter Olympics, when he landed a 71-metre jump before slithering to an undignified halt in last place. His jump was around 50 metres shorter than the winner.

Pierre de Coubertin, the father of the Modern Olympics said **"The most important thing in the Olympic Games is not winning but taking part**."

Some of the many other personalities who entertained us were from the world of television.

There were two stars from 'Only Fools and Horses'. John Challis (Boycie) and Sue Holderness (Marlene) were regular guests on the P&O fleet and always amused us.

John Lyons - Detective Sergeant George Toolan in 'A Taste of Frost' who stayed around for most of a World Cruise, and as well as giving talks, he quizzed with us most days.

Michael Buerk a BBC Television news reader and journalist, had people standing in the aisles of the theatre when he gave his talks.

On another cruise there was the white suited Martin Bell television journalist and MP. More exciting to listen to was ex MP Edwina Currie. She gave a couple of very amusing talks with some candid stories of her career and bits of scandal as well.

One very outstanding guest speaker was Wayne Sleep – Ballet Dancer and more. He thrilled the theatre with his life history talks and video clips. He was truly a celebrity, and even with replacement joints, he still showed us his skills, including dancing, jumping, and then landing in the splits position, on the stage.

Not everyone was quite so visually well known.

There were authors who weren't necessarily trying to increase their sales, but their talks definitely did. The notable one I remember is Gervase Phinn who started my love of his books about schools and teaching in the Yorkshire Dales. I have bought several of his books because of his appearance.

Then there were numerous retired policemen with some amusing, and some gruesome stories of their career or intriguing murder cases. Others talked about their speciality subjects such as Concorde, diving on wrecks, sailing around the world alone. There were at least two television antique program personalities, and Martin Roberts from Homes under the Hammer.

I'm sorry that I can't remember or name everyone that gave talks on the ships, but trust me, there is a wonderful variety of guest speakers that turn up on the cruise ships.

The Ship's Resident Entertainment Team

More important than the visiting cabaret acts or the guest speakers, are the ship's own entertainment team. The Cruise Manager (or Director) leads a small team of enthusiastic men and women, and some of them appear to have only just left school. Unlike some of the crew, these team members smile all day, and greet each passenger as if they were old friends.

They appear mid-morning and forget their tiredness to cheerfully look after activities all around the ship. First perhaps outside on the deck as referees for quoits or shuffleboard, then quickly hosting a quiz, before supervising a craft class, or looking after morning coffee for the single travellers.

Their afternoons are maybe slightly less busy, but one or more of them will appear at all of the organised activities with smiles and advice.

In the evening they suffer the arguments at further quizzes, introduce acts in the theatre and show lounge, perhaps laugh for an hour through a karaoke session or game show, and are always ready to help passengers who look lost or upset. It is a long day for them, and it will be the early hours of the following morning before the last of them head to their beds.

This team provides a confidence and calmness to make the cruise enjoyable for the majority of passengers, but really make their money if problems arise when the weather is bad, or a port has been missed.

Twenty years on, the P&O entertainment teams continue in the same smiling, confident and helpful way. The only difference is that cost cutting has meant there are less of them. The numbers have only been reduced by one or maybe two on the ships we sailed on, but they continue to look after the same numbers of passengers, competitions and events. They look more tired, the smile occasionally drops when a moaning passenger is arguing about the same minor issue, and perhaps they manage to disappear more regularly to have a short break from the role.

The Cruise Manager used to be the primary person in our early days, but now he (or she) spends more and more time in an office organising programmes, fielding complaints from passengers, completing forms and liaising with the shore management. On several cruises we realised they were almost invisible except appearing in the theatre to introduce a high-profile cabaret act.

Sadly, as far as the company is concerned, the hard-working Entertainment Team might be doing a good job, but they don't provide any extra income. Perhaps the modern cruise passenger is less interested in how these men and women enhance their holiday, and won't make a complaint, but us who are longer in the tooth, still have our memory, and ensure the company knows we have noticed the slimming down of the entertainment team numbers.

Daytime Activities

Much of the entertainment I have spoken about so far is focussed on keeping the passengers happy in the theatre and show lounges, but there is plenty of other things going on as well.

Once again much of my experience is based on P&O ships, but Saga and Fred Olsen have similar activities.

Outside on the decks

In the morning, and again in the afternoon, there are organised competitions between the passengers for the traditional cruise games of Quoits, and Shuffleboard. Based on games played for centuries, both Quoits and Shuffleboard have a playing area marked out on the decks.

Players can play the game as individuals, but usually one of the entertainment team acts as the referee, taking names, sorting out who plays who, and generally keeping the peace while getting to know the passengers.

When playing Quoits, an area of the deck has a large circle painted on the decking, with smaller circles inside it to resemble an archery target. The inner circle has a higher scoring value than the outer ones. Between the circular target and the starting line, there are two lines that identify a zone where the quoit must land once thrown.

Players then take turns to throw small circular quoits, that are traditionally made of rope. The quoit must initially land in the marked zone, and then slide into the circular target. The other players then take their turn to get into a higher scoring part of the target, and might possibly push the opponents quoit away.

Obviously, the winning passenger, or team, is the one with the highest score. Sometimes there are small prizes, or points that can eventually be *'cashed in'* to receive a prize. Or, as is often the case on Saga, the winners have the bragging rights.

Shuffle board is a little bit along the lines of shove halfpenny.

Players have sticks with a pushing end, that is used to propel a small circular lump of wood (like an ice-hockey puck) across the deck from a starting point towards a target. The target is a series of lines painted on the deck with the gaps between the lines showing their scoring points. The furthest away is the highest value.

As with quoits, the referee picks teams and they compete against each other to find the winner.

The puck is pushed from the starting point (behind a line) and it slides noisily across the deck and should stop within the target area. It gets the score between the two lines where it stops. The opposition then push their puck to get a higher score, or push the first puck out of the scoring zone.

Both Quoits and Shuffle board are very popular, and the games usually become 30 minutes or so of laughter and banter.

Most ships have small netted tents for practicing golf driving, but it is becoming quite common now to have an electronic golf simulator where passengers can practice, or to hold competitions. I have personally never tried these out, as my golfing prowess does not stretch beyond pathetic attempts on a putting green.

On all the cruise ships we have been on, there has also been a larger net where passengers can play various games such as tennis, basketball, football, or even a ship-based cricket match. Before my hip let me down, I regularly played cricket as we sailed across the oceans, and thoroughly loved this version of one of my favourite sports.

Of course, sunbathing is the most popular outdoor summer pastime on cruise ships, but if that becomes boring, or it is too cold, one of the most popular traditional British pastimes is walking around the promenade deck. The magic of walking along one side of the ship in the shade, and then returning on the other side in sunshine can be quite special, and all the way around you can look out across the sea and try and spot dolphins.

## Indoor Activities

From mid-morning to late afternoon, a cruise ship usually has something to offer. There might be a video to watch, a talk about an upcoming port, or one of those guest speakers telling his or her life story, or simply educating and amusing an audience with a topic.

On most days there will be a classical concert to bring a little musical joy to the discerning ear, or a taster for others.

If you are feeling active there will almost certainly be dance sessions when you can learn how to Tap Dance, or try out Line Dancing or even Salsa. A lot of cruises will feature more formal dance lessons where novices can learn the first few steps of a waltz, quickstep or cha cha, while others simply improve their basic skills.

A popular twice daily game of Bridge usually attracts a large following, while many take the opportunity to attend an art class, or a craft workshop.

A well-attended offering is the passenger choir giving trained or untrained voices a chance to be expressed, and a popular new workshop gives passengers a chance to learn how to play the ukulele.

For those who just want to spend a quiet hour with a book, most ships will have places to sit in comfort without music, and where people naturally keep their voices low. This may not always be the case with the newer 24 hour a day nightclub atmosphere, where music seems to be mandatory everywhere, and sitting quietly is deterred.

# Prices of a Cruise

There is no way I could finish this book without saying a little bit about the current costs of a cruise.

Strangely, in a world where we are accustomed to prices continually increasing, cruise companies are bucking the trend.

To put that comment into perspective, I need to go back to 2000 and our first cruise.

Sitting at that Lunn Poly's travel agent's desk, we were totally naïve about booking a cruise. The agent showed us the brochure, and we assumed the prices we saw were what everybody paid. After much deliberation and a lot of advice from the agent, we booked an outside cabin on a reasonable deck, which was not at the extremes of forward or stern. Although the exact figures have long been forgotten, I am quite positive that the total price for us was over £4000 and nearer to £4500.

The cruise lasted 17 nights so with a simple bit of mathematics, that equates to somewhere in the region of £120 each per night.

Twenty plus years later, the inflation rate in the UK has meant that things are over 100% more expensive, but looking at a price of a cruise, it feels as if the industry seems to have forgotten inflation.

The prices of cruises have remained almost static for two decades. Although improvement in engine and control unit technology is a major reason, the biggest efficiency has become possible by having vast numbers of passengers on the giant ships, leading to cheaper fares.

While I was writing this chapter in October 2023, I scanned around the cruise company web sites and looked at some examples prices of cruises for 2024. These cruises were not special offers, and did not include the price of any optional extras, but be aware that all companies use 'Fluid Pricing' to match demand, and price changes can occur on a daily or even hourly basis.

**P&O's Aurora for a 16-night cruise at a similar time to our 2000 cruise:**

Inside cabin £1329 each or £83 per night

Outside cabin £1649 each or £103 per night

Balcony £2499 each or £156 per night


**P&O's Arvia for 14 nights Mediterranean cruise in June 2024:**

Inside £999 per person or £71 per night

Outside £1349 or £96 per night

Balcony £1569 or £112 per night

**Cunard's new ship Queen Anne for 16-night Mediterranean cruise June 2024:**

Inside £1419 or £89 per night

Outside £2479 or £155 per night

Balcony £2749 or £172 per night

**Fred Olsen's Borealis 14 nights to the Baltic in June 2024:**

Inside £2229 or £159 per night

Outside £3099 or £221 per night

Balcony £3639 or £259 per night

It is obvious that the costs of cruises have not increased with inflation, in fact P&O are cheaper. It was interesting to see that Fred Olsen has moved from being one of the cheapest British based cruise lines to be more expensive than P&O and Cunard.

One optional extra that I can show you, is the drink packages from these different companies. If you purchase the packages, they cover most alcoholic and soft drinks around the ship.

The drinks package with P&O is around £50 per person per night

Cunard charge about £73 per person per night for a similar package

Fred Olsen charge about £25 per person per night

## Saga Cruises

As well as showing prices from P&O, Cunard and Fred Olsen, on the same day I noted the pricing details for a cruise from Saga.

**Saga's Spirit of Discovery 13 nights to Iceland June 2024:**

Basic Standard Balcony Cabin £4994 or £384 per night

The Saga price is much higher than the others, so I think the time has come to talk a little more about Saga cruises, to explain why we have booked with them, rather than returning to P&O.

Once Deb and I had seemingly been everywhere in Europe with P&O, and were thrilled by our longer voyages, we thought it was time to experiment with other cruise lines. We tried Fred Olsen twice, and quite enjoyed their small ship experience, plus the far more customer focussed attitude of the crew.

So, having been happy with Fred Olsen, it seemed natural to try out Saga as well, especially as we knew they were building two new small ships that were designed for the older passenger.

**Warning:**

*Try to book Saga cruises direct with Saga.*

*If you use a travel agent, **they** will become the customer as far as Saga are concerned, and any direct communications between Saga and yourselves will be very limited.*

*If you are panicking about the usual travel agent discount, fear not. Saga's policy over discounting is quite strict, and I doubt a travel agent gets much to share with you.*

*The Saga website is quite simple if you are reasonably computer savvy, and if not, the phone line consultants are very helpful and will talk you through the options for the best cabin.*

*As elsewhere, single travellers will pay the usual extra.*

*I include this little warning because we were not initially aware of Saga's unusual attitude with travel agents.*

Naïve about any booking issues, our initial five-day taster cruise on the tiny Saga Pearl was organised with our regular travel agent. The discount we received from the agent was minimal, but we did receive a very good price for being new customers with Saga, made even better because we took the Saga magazine each month.

This was a last-minute cruise deal, and following on from my warning, we quickly discovered an ongoing problem. We had several questions to ask about the cruise, and when we spoke to the Saga help desk, they advised us that the travel agent was the customer, so **they** needed to make the inquiry. Every question was put to our agent, who then spoke with the same Saga help desk, and the answer relayed back to us. Even the tickets and luggage labels, and details about our transport came to us via the agent.

Our travel agent (Judith) had become a good friend, and given generous discounts for many years on cruise deals, but her comment when the Saga cruise had been booked, was not to use her again for that company.

*Incidentally, we visited Hereford recently and dropped into the travel agents, and had a catchup chat with Judith. She is still doing the same job, although the company has changed from Thomas Cook to Hays.*

Anyway, the resulting five-day cruise was a delight, and although we knew longer adventures would be far more expensive than similar P&O cruises, the Saga product has so much more to offer.

- All cabins on their new ships have balconies
- Free transport to and from the docks.
- Free travel insurance unless you have something serious to declare.
- Free drinks, both soft and alcoholic.
- Free Wi-Fi that can be used on multiple bits of equipment, and it seems quite good compared to other ships.
- Free use of indoor spa pool plus steam rooms and sauna.
- Some free excursions to give basic panoramic tours of the ports and surrounding countryside. Other tours are available for specific locations or experiences, and they are the same price as other cruise lines.

… and rather importantly, free smiles from the crew.

OK, if you look at the deals in the newspapers, you will instantly see that Saga are one of the most expensive British based cruise lines. But if you add the costs of those extras listed above to your favoured cruise company's prices, the difference may not be quite so dramatic. Saga will still be more expensive, but how can you put a price on the better level of service.

... and those smiles.

Deb and I thought long and hard after that taster cruise, and decided that P&O were still quite special to us, but rather than continuing to have one or two cruises with P&O each year, perhaps having a Saga cruise, but less often, would give us a lot of pleasure.

We eventually sailed on both of their new ships, and yes, we had a disaster with our Covid cruise, but even then, the crew did everything to make the experience as painless as possible.

At the moment we look towards Saga as a preference, but I still keep an eye on P&O bargains, and especially for longer duration cruises.

# Last Thoughts

I will ask another question:

**"Is cruising right for everyone?"**

Probably not.

Firstly, just as I have a morbid fear of flying, there are those that are similarly afraid of ships and boats.

There are also thousands of people all over the world who get a great deal of pleasure just relaxing on a beach for a week or a fortnight. Some would rather have their holiday in a single country to explore a place and its culture in depth, while others just want to get away from the rat race, and escape to be with nature by camping on a secluded cliff or out on a moor.

But I think for the vast majority of people who feel they want an alternative to a package holiday, then cruising could be the answer. If the idea of visiting different places, sampling different cultures without multiple packing and unpacking sessions, or want to give their family a full-on fun holiday, then cruising is worth a try.

Old *'fuddy duddys'* like myself continue to compare the large cruise ships as being more like holiday camps, but in reality, they are totally different and offer so much more.

... and anyway, a lot of people quite like the holiday camp experience.

Today's cruise market has ships that match most peoples' desires. There are big glitzy party style vessels that head to the sunshine, and smaller ones that explore different ports where you can relax and get away from the 100 mile and hour life we live.

I wish Deb and I had found cruising much earlier, and had the chance to introduce our children to it, so they could perhaps understand why we love it so much.

Twenty years ago, cruising was expensive, but the current situation is that a family can have a near luxury cruise at little more than an all-inclusive package holiday.

If you decide cruising might be a good idea, you need to first ask yourself and your family a few questions:

- Decide what sort of holiday you want to have
- Compare what is on offer from the different companies for the most ideal solution
- Ask your local travel agent, or cruise company agent, lots of questions
- Calculate how much extra you might have to spend on-board the ship
- Perhaps take a serious look at plusses and minuses on social media

Focussing back on P&O for a moment, I believe they have got the right product to suit the people they target as passengers, and at an amazing price. The giant ships with superb cabins, ample delicious food, and almost every kind of entertainment possible, provide the perfect solution for so many people.

It has been quite a surprise that the two smaller and aging P&O ships have remained in the fleet. Aurora and Arcadia are now highlighted as being adult only ships, and attract those of us who still want some of the more traditional aspects of cruising. Sadly, the time will come when they have to go, and I haven't heard any whispers that Carnival has anything to replace them.

Every year there are passengers who tire of the current big ship razzamatazz, and wonder if there is something a little slower and quieter on offer. This can be seen with the number of P&O passengers that now talk about their happy experiences with Saga cruises. It won't affect the P&O product, as new passengers will replace us and take a step into the world of cruising.

*Single Travellers*

Unfortunately, there is one group of people that find cruising the perfect holiday, but they are treated oh so badly.

They are the single traveller.

Cruise lines advertise that they have cabins for the single traveller, and yes, they are virtually the same standard as a cabin for a couple, but the pricing policy is ridiculous.

The price is almost the same as for two people.

Companies insist that providing single cabins is physically complicated, but this is only because they don't ask, or want, the ship designers to come up with a solution.

The companies say that they keep fares low, and assume all passengers will spend 'x' percent more on extras while on their cruise, and hence a cabin with a single passenger will not generate as much income from those extras. The accountants have failed to notice that many passengers spend nothing on extras and simply enjoy the cheap fares with free food and free entertainment. Even Saga (and other more exclusive cruise lines) with their fully inclusive price, still penalise the single traveller by near double fares, and being fully inclusive, there are virtually no extras to purchase.

What the companies have failed to appreciate is that many of those single travellers have already spent a fortune on cruises over several decades, but now no longer have a partner. It is yet another example of not valuing loyalty.

It is time cruise companies change their thinking, and make designers create proper single cabins, sold for true single occupancy, with little or no price penalty.

*Our Immediate and Future Plans*

Deb and I have gone for something new at the end of 2023.

We are booked on a Christmas and New Year cruise with Saga. The pair of us have never been away from family at Christmas before, and we hope to enjoy the experience.

Further into the future we have no ocean cruises booked, but we hope to book something for 2025 in the next few weeks. We also have our Golden Wedding Anniversary in that year, so that might throw up something different to do.

We continue to consider the idea of a River Cruise to broaden our experiences of cruising. So, for 2024 we have booked a six-night cruise on a River Severn boat with English Holiday Cruises. It has 11 cabins, and offers a short fully inclusive holiday.

With nothing else planned, we can be flexible and maybe even look at P&O bargains for a bit of sunshine during the summer.

One other place I would like to go to is the East coast of Northern America. Suitable Saga cruises are outside of our budget, but P&O might be an option if a suitable adventure across the Atlantic Ocean pops up.

That is enough of my thoughts about 23 years of excitement, as Deb and I explored the world on cruise ships. There have been one or two unhappy moments, but they are vastly outnumbered by marvellous experiences of new places, different cultures, history, architecture, with fun, laughter, and sometimes absolute amazement at what we saw and done.

Our adventures have taken us across the three major oceans, visiting 58 countries and stopping at 140 cities, of which 25 were capitals.

We enjoyed nearly 650 nights at sea, sampling three different cruise lines on 13 different ships, and travelling well in excess of 200,000 nautical miles around the world.

It has truly been a dream.

I want to thank all the people who became temporary friends on our holidays, plus those whose friendship became rather more special.

Thanks must also go to all the wonderful and professional people in the land-based offices that organised the bookings, plus the crews on the cruise ships who kept us safe, and looked after us so well for almost a quarter of a century.

This book was always planned to complete the '*A Cornishman Goes Cruising*' series, so now I can switch my attention to several other projects in the bulging '***to do***' folder.

# Other books in 'The Cornishman Goes Cruising' series

A Cornishman Goes Cruising

A Cornishman Cruises to Venice

A Cornishman Cruises the Western Mediterranean

Around the World without Wings

Searching for New Sunrises

From the Furnace to the Freezer

Printed in Great Britain
by Amazon